Devotions & Prayers for a Resilient Heart

Print ISBN 978-1-63609-569-1

Published by Barbour Publishing, Inc., 1810 Barbour Drive, Uhrichsville, Ohio 44683, www.barbourbooks.com.

Our mission is to inspire the world with the life-changing message of the Bible.

Printed in China.

LINDA HANG
VALORIE QUESENBERRY

Devotions & Prayers for a Resilient Heart

6 MONTHS OF ENCOURAGEMENT & INSPIRATION

BARBOUR
PUBLISHING

Introduction

*I love you, G*OD*—you make me strong. G*OD *is bedrock under my feet, the castle in which I live, my rescuing knight. My God—the high crag where I run for dear life, hiding behind the boulders, safe in the granite hideout.*

PSALM 18:1–2 MSG

Are you. . .
> *Strong?*
> *Flexible?*
> *Tough?*
> *Capable?*

Each devotion and prayer in this inspiring book will remind you of all the reasons it's possible (and *important!*) to be a strong and capable woman of God. With the strength-giver Himself by your side, you can live each day as it comes—ready for the unexpected.

Turn the page and begin paving the path to resilient living!

Just a Preview

Beloved, we are God's children now, and what we will be has not yet appeared; but we know that when he appears we shall be like him, because we shall see him as he is.

1 JOHN 3:2

She looked at the packet of seeds in her hand. On the outside was a picture of beautiful flowers; on the inside was a sprinkling of tiny brown pellets. She went to work—breaking up the soil, planting the seeds, watering the earth. When she was done, she sat back on her heels and smiled. In her mind she saw the flowers as they would one day be.

The Christian life is a little like those seeds. Once we believe in Jesus, God adopts us into His family. We are children of God, heirs with Christ (Romans 8:17), but we're not exactly like God's perfect Son yet. God still has some work to do as He grows us into the likeness of Jesus. Through the process, though, we have the hope of glorified lives in heaven. Think on these words from the apostle Paul:

> *The body is sown in corruption, it is raised in incorruption. It is sown in dishonor, it is raised in glory. It is sown in weakness, it is raised in power. It is sown a natural body, it is raised a spiritual body. There is a natural body, and there is a spiritual body. And so it is written, "The first man Adam became a living being." The last Adam became a life-giving spirit.*

However, the spiritual is not first, but the natural, and afterward the spiritual. The first man was of the earth, made of dust; the second Man is the Lord from heaven. As was the man of dust, so also are those who are made of dust; and as is the heavenly Man, so also are those who are heavenly. And as we have borne the image of the man of dust, we shall also bear the image of the heavenly Man. (1 Corinthians 15:42–49 NKJV)

What is our role as we await His appearing and the moment we will be like Him? "Since we have these promises, beloved, let us cleanse ourselves from every defilement of body and spirit, bringing holiness to completion in the fear of God" (2 Corinthians 7:1). God has begun something beautiful in us, and He will finish it one day. *Guaranteed.* In the meantime, the promise fills us with so much anticipation that we can't wait for heaven to be like Him. So we start now.

FATHER, TO BE LIKE YOUR SON—I CAN ONLY
IMAGINE WHAT THAT WILL BE LIKE! HELP ME TO BE
MORE AND MORE LIKE HIM EVEN NOW. AMEN.

Lead Your Life

Only let each person lead the life that the Lord has
assigned to him, and to which God has called him.

1 CORINTHIANS 7:17

Social media. Do you love it? Do you hate it? With it, we can keep tabs on family members and friends; we can laugh, cheer, and share with others. On the flip side, it can also become a black hole of comparison. We know "all about" a college friend's engagement. We see hundreds of congrats and well wishes when another friend has twins. We get a play-by-play of a neighbor's remodel. We hear about job promotions, vacations, Zumba classes, parties (that we may or may not have been invited to). . . While each of these things is good, if we're honest, can't social media sometimes be a drag, especially when we find our lives looking slightly dull next to all the shiny in someone else's life? If we aren't careful, we can start to yearn for blessings that aren't ours to enjoy, to desire a life that isn't ours to walk.

Each time you use social media, remember Paul's words in his letter to the Corinthian church. Paul advised believers to be content in whatever state they were in—whether married, unmarried, circumcised, uncircumcised, slave, or free. Like a horse wearing blinders, the Corinthians were to "lead the life" God had for them, without being distracted looking to the left or the right at what others were doing or being swayed to think they were inadequate in their current state.

God crafts and blesses the best life for every one of His children. Yet in His amazing, boundless love and wisdom, He blesses and leads each of His children in a unique way. He cares about you individually. He has a plan for your life distinctly. You are not one in a numberless crowd. You are [fill in your name]. And as long as you still breathe in and out, He's not finished guiding you down your life's path. He's not finished blessing you as only He knows how.

Don't let social media drag you down! The next time envy or discontentment pops up, when the devil whispers that God isn't present in your life the way He is in everybody else's, cry out to God for blinders to see the road He's placed you on. Like a horse confidently *clip-clopping* along the road, have faith in your heavenly Father's ability to call you to the perfect path, to bless you in exactly the right way.

FATHER, YOU KNOW THE BEGINNING AND THE END. I REST IN YOU AND YOUR PLANS FOR ME, BELIEVING YOU'LL SEE THEM THROUGH. AMEN.

Sacred, Surprising Sacrifice

Greater love hath no man than this, that a
man lay down his life for his friends.

JOHN 15:13 KJV

John 15:13 is often quoted in battlefield stories—a soldier sacrifices his life to save his buddies. It's a verse that speaks to something deep within us, that part of our hearts that resonates with loyalty and love.

One of the ways we might see this verse played out today is in the relationship of pets to their owners. Animals develop lasting bonds of affection for their owners and sometimes display that in amazing ways. A dog may attack a person mistreating its master or even jump into harm's way to save the human it loves.

The classic story *Where the Red Fern Grows* brings us to tears with its recounting of a pair of coonhounds whose hunting days are ended when Old Dan is fatally injured protecting his boy from a mountain lion. The children's tale *Old Yeller* recounts how a mongrel dog earns the love of a family and then is infected with rabies while trying to protect boys in danger. These narratives remind us of the power of sacrificial love and of how a surprising act of devotion moves us to our very core.

Of course, Jesus is the very best image of sacrificial love. He had to *give up* His life. It couldn't be *taken*. In John 10:18 (NKJV), Christ said, "No one takes [my life] from Me, but I lay it down of Myself. I have power to lay it down, and I have power to take it again. This command I have received from My Father."

The whole excruciating ordeal of the scourging, carrying of the cross, the crown of thorns, the nails, and the hours of agony was something Jesus chose to go through. He willingly laid down His life for us.

You might not have the opportunity to physically die for a friend today, but you might have the option to die in some other way. When we refuse to stick up for our rights, we are dying a small death. When we let others choose, we are dying a small death. When we swallow a retort or sarcasm, we are dying a small death. We can show love by following our Lord's example and denying self.

JESUS, THANK YOU FOR LAYING DOWN YOUR LIFE FOR ME. TODAY I ASK YOU TO EMPOWER ME TO DENY MYSELF AND LOVE OTHERS SACRIFICIALLY. AMEN.

The Road Ahead

But, as it is written, "What no eye has seen,
nor ear heard, nor the heart of man imagined,
what God has prepared for those who love him."

1 CORINTHIANS 2:9

If you've ever stood at a figurative crossroads in your life, you probably know what it's like to need wisdom. Which direction? Which choice? The "roads" stretch out in front of you, wide open, but you're unsure which to take. They both continue beyond sight, but you can't begin to see which one is best. The not knowing paralyzes you, preventing you from moving at all. *What if I make the wrong decision, go the wrong way?* you ask.

When we feel stalled, God is still moving. And He's preparing the directions if only we'll ask and allow the Holy Spirit to answer. In fact, what He has for us is beyond anything we've seen, heard, or imagined.

Sounds amazing! But waiting on His direction is not so easy, is it? It can be pretty difficult.

The problem is focusing on God when this life demands our attention. (It's always around us, bumping into us, after all.) The problem is trusting God when we've been told to rely on ourselves. (We're self-made women—hear us roar!) The problem is waiting on God when we desperately want a solution *now*. (Instant download, please.) The problem is believing in something we have not seen, heard, or imagined.

The good news is this: Our God is absolutely able and more than willing to help us with these problems. He has not left us to struggle on our own; He has equipped us with the Holy Spirit. "Now we have received not the spirit of the world, but the Spirit who is from God, that we might understand the things freely given us by God" (1 Corinthians 2:12). If you are His child, God's Spirit is alive within you, working to illuminate His Word, shedding light on the way ahead.

Keeping an open mind to all God has in store isn't always easy; it takes faith. But each moment you choose to exercise faith strengthens your faith. Like muscle memory, our eyes become sharpened to see His hand at work, our ears become attuned to hear His voice, our hearts become conditioned to hope in Him. At that crossroads, take comfort in the words of Isaiah: "And your ears shall hear a word behind you, saying, 'This is the way, walk in it,' when you turn to the right or when you turn to the left" (Isaiah 30:21).

LORD, I FEEL SO ALONE STANDING HERE AT THIS CROSSROADS. HOLD MY HAND. LEAD ME, PLEASE. I CHOOSE TODAY TO BELIEVE THAT YOU CAN PROVIDE UNDERSTANDING BEYOND ANYTHING I CAN CONCEIVE. AMEN.

On the Way

*While I was speaking in prayer, the man Gabriel, whom
I had seen in the vision at the first, came to me in swift
flight at the time of the evening sacrifice. He made me
understand, speaking with me and saying, "O Daniel, I have
now come out to give you insight and understanding. At the
beginning of your pleas for mercy a word went out, and
I have come to tell it to you, for you are greatly loved."*

DANIEL 9:21–23

Silence—what with alarms, traffic, lawn mowers, music at gas pumps, ringtones, toddlers, sirens, and the list goes on, we all crave a little peace and quiet at times. But there's one area of our lives where we usually never want to hear silence: our prayers. God's silence is deadening. In that silence, we can easily forget that God hears our prayers and that He's at work answering them.

Did you catch the first words of Daniel 9:21? *"While I was speaking. . ."* Daniel hadn't finished praying, and Gabriel appeared. So when he began praying, or even before, God heard and sent an answer. Isaiah says of God, "Before they call I will answer; while they are yet speaking I will hear" (Isaiah 65:24). Our God is not too distant to hear the faintest voice; He is not too busy to handle one more request or listen to one more word. He is our heavenly Father, caring and close, so much so that He knows what we need even before we ask it (Matthew 6:8).

Today, wherever you need encouragement, boldness, resources;

whatever your desires, thoughts, troubles—you name it—God knows your heart. Don't hold back, but approach your Father in openness and humility. Gabriel's message to Daniel included the why of God's answer: "for you are greatly loved." God anticipates, hears, and answers His children's prayers because we are greatly loved. You are greatly loved. When your prayers seem to disintegrate before they reach the ceiling, let alone heaven, say the words to yourself (it's okay if you feel silly!): *I am greatly loved*. Rest in His love. Rest in the knowledge that He is awesome enough to answer prayers before they are prayed.

How many times do we think of God in heaven listening to our words and then saying, *"Hmm, interesting. I'll give that some thought and get back to you"*? Deeper than faith that God will respond, let's begin to have faith that He is working even while we are still speaking.

FATHER, I BOW MY HEAD TODAY IN AWE OF WHO YOU ARE. YOU HEAR EVERY PRAYER. FILL ME WITH ASSURANCE IN THE SILENCE THAT YOU HAVE BEEN AND ARE AT WORK. AMEN.

It's a Promise!

And I am sure of this, that he who began a good work in
you will bring it to completion at the day of Jesus Christ.
PHILIPPIANS 1:6

Have you ever met anyone who leaves things unfinished? (Maybe you're among the ranks of the start-but-don't-finish-ers.) A hand-knitted sock that has no mate. A novel deserted halfway through. Clean laundry left in the basket. The pristine gardening supplies on a shelf. Beginnings aren't always hard, but following through can be tough, especially when we get tired, discouraged, distracted, or busy.

While being a finisher isn't all-important in every aspect of life (that gym membership might not have been the greatest idea anyway), when it comes to what really matters, we're glad when we, and others, finish what we start. You'd be in trouble if your mechanic did only half an oil change. You'd be upset if you worked all week and your boss didn't pay you. You'd be disappointed in yourself if you bailed on plans with a friend for no good reason, or filled out but never submitted your tax return, or never achieved a dream. Finishing equals completion, closure. It's the well-earned sigh that comes at the end of a task, big or small.

When you believed in Jesus, your faith journey began. Since then God has been at work, transforming you to be more like His Son. For now we're unfinished. But with all the ups and downs of growing in Christ, the end, your salvation, is secure. Paul wrote in

Colossians 3:3–4, "For you have died, and your life is *hidden* with Christ in God. When Christ who is your life appears, then you also will appear with him in glory" (italics added). And again Paul wrote, "In him you also, when you heard the word of truth, the gospel of your salvation, and believed in him, were *sealed* with the promised Holy Spirit, who is the *guarantee* of our inheritance until we acquire possession of it, to the praise of his glory" (Ephesians 1:13–14, italics added). Think about those words: *hidden*—kept safe from harm; *sealed*—no one can alter it; *guarantee*—for certain.

Surrounded by what's yet unfinished in this life, we may naturally feel uncertain. But whether God will finish what He has begun isn't up in the air. He is faithful. He did not give us the promise of eternal life only to leave loose ends, the job half done. Having sacrificed His Son, God will not stop short of salvation. He "will bring it to completion."

GOD, FORGIVE ME FOR DOUBTING YOU. YOU'RE FOREVER FAITHFUL, AND YOU'LL NOT LEAVE UNFINISHED WHAT YOU'VE STARTED. THANK YOU FOR SALVATION, NOW AND FOR ALWAYS IN HEAVEN. AMEN.

For Our Good

And we know that for those who love God all
things work together for good, for those who
are called according to his purpose.

ROMANS 8:28

Maybe you have experienced a lot of rough waters in your life. You're a survivor; you've endured what many people couldn't imagine. But even if just a few hardships have come your way or tons of "little" things have plagued your steps, you might find yourself scratching your head after reading Paul's words in Romans 8:28. *"All things. . .for good." Really, Paul? Even cancer, violence, natural disasters. . . ? This world is so very broken. Everything can't eventually lead to sunshine and buttercups.*

Take a moment to think about Paul's life. After a miraculous conversion to Christianity, Paul went through tough times. He was falsely accused, beaten, imprisoned, and shipwrecked, to name a few. He was no stranger to suffering, both in his life and in the lives of those he loved. Yet he was also confident that God had good plans in and through the bad.

How can we adopt this optimism when life brings us to our knees and sometimes beats us into the ground? By looking up.

Just before his words of encouragement, Paul wrote, "For I consider that the sufferings of this present time are not worth comparing with the glory that is to be revealed to us" (Romans 8:18). There's so much *more* to come. By fixing our minds on heaven (Colossians

3:2), we as Christians realize that our lives don't end with our last breath on earth. Eternity awaits. God is working everything for good—in our earthly lives as well as our heavenly ones.

And there's so much *more* that God is working to accomplish. God is a big God; He has big plans. With our eyes focused on Him, we aren't so likely to see life centered in and revolving around us, but rather coming from God and for His glory. We aren't so likely to forget the one who commands the whole picture: "I am God, and there is none like me, declaring the end from the beginning and from ancient times things not yet done" (Isaiah 46:9–10). All of what God has in mind for His children we can't begin to fathom, but we can begin to have faith that what He has in mind is good.

So even while being battered by the winds, don't lose sight of the horizon. Blue sky is hidden behind those stormy clouds, just waiting for God to reveal it.

LORD, YOU TURN SORROW INTO JOY, WEAKNESS INTO STRENGTH, BAD INTO GOOD. YOU ARE AMAZING! INCREASE MY FAITH THAT YOU ARE WORKING ALL THINGS FOR GOOD. AMEN.

Sweet Coffee Surprise

The sweetness of a friend comes from his earnest counsel.

PROVERBS 27:9

I'm convinced that some of the popularity of coffee shops is the promise of conversation to which they allude. Somehow, hidden in the marketing, is perhaps the subliminal message *If you drink our coffee, you will have great relationships*.

Most of us value friendship. And what better way to talk to a friend than over a fragrant cup of coffee?

I've had a few coffee shop meetings about which I wasn't sure. Maybe I was meeting someone whom I didn't know very well. Maybe I was meeting to discuss a delicate topic. Maybe I was just in a rush that day and didn't want to take the time for a coffee chat. But many times I've been surprised by the blessing of those meetings. Taking time to get to know someone better is an investment, but it usually rewards more than it requires.

The proverb writer is correct: great counsel from a friend is a sweet gift.

I remember the days before coffee became a social phenomenon. People drank coffee, of course, but it was not a life event when they did. They didn't take pictures of their coffee mugs, stand in line for coffee, plan their shopping trips around coffee shops, and all the other things we do today. There were collectible coffee mugs, but they were usually just screen-printed ones from the local restaurant or souvenir ones from vacation spots. There was coffee to buy in the grocery stores but not all the glamorous flavors on the shelves today and certainly not in so many different forms. Grandma and Grandpa drank plain old coffee, probably with a little milk. Restaurants served basic brew with the powdered creamer in packets. But, even then, coffee meant conversation. Friends gathered in kitchens and drank coffee from Corelle cups and talked about life and supported one another and prayed for one another. Coffee was the excuse they needed to gather. And it still is at times.

Maybe you're not a coffee drinker. You can still discover the sweetness of good counsel in friendship. Make the first move. Invite a friend to get iced tea or lemonade with you somewhere and lean into the opportunity to develop your friendship. You never know what unexpected delights you'll discover.

GOD, EVERY GOOD GIFT COMES FROM YOU, AND THAT INCLUDES FRIENDS AND COFFEE AND TEA AND LEMONADE. THANK YOU THAT I CAN SHARE THESE DELIGHTS WITH MY FRIENDS. AMEN.

The Emergency Brake

Whoever is slow to anger is better than the mighty,
and he who rules his spirit than he who takes a city.

PROVERBS 16:32

My grandfather used to say, "Patience is the ability to idle your motor when you feel like stripping your gears."

Ah yes, patience. That elusive phantom control we long for. We blame many things for its absence—environment, genetics, mood, hormones, family, weather, and more. And there are many contributing factors, to be sure.

But when it comes down to the nitty-gritty of life, patience is an action, not a feeling, and it is only truly possible with the enabling power of the Holy Spirit at work in our personalities. He empowers us to respond appropriately even if we feel differently. We often do not choose to let Him help us. We find it more satisfactory to react to the insult or irritation or provocation. But we display holy growth when we submit in the moment and respond not out of self-centeredness but out of mature, godly love.

In this way, we can show unexpected mercy to those whom God has placed in our lives. Those around us have been conditioned to expect retaliation from others, withdrawal, the "cold shoulder," the "silent treatment." What if, instead of following the appetites of the carnal mind, which Romans 8:7 says is against God, we purposefully daily follow the will of the Spirit? What if we affirmed our big moment of total surrender with a lifetime of daily surrender?

An emergency brake is a mechanical brake system that completely bypasses the hydraulics of the regular vehicular brakes. In the event of a failure in the normal braking system, the emergency brake can help you get your vehicle safely stopped.

All of us have moments when our normal, calming techniques fail. In that extremity, we need a power that bypasses our human limitations. The writer of Proverbs knew about this, for he wrote that one who can rule over her own spirit is a mightier warrior than the conqueror of a city.

Let's take up the challenge today. Let's embody the unexpected mercy that God gives through us. Let's smile at the slow cashier, not honk or glare at the irritating driver, be kind to the forgetful waitress, swallow the sarcastic retort to our spouse, hug our moody teenager, love our world through patience. The old adage is true: "People need loving the most when they deserve it the least."

Be the "unexpected" in someone's life today.

FATHER GOD, YOU LOVED ME BEFORE I KNEW YOU, GAVE GRACE TO ME WHEN I WAS A REBEL, AND HAVE HAD MORE PATIENCE WITH ME THAN I COULD EVER MERIT. I ASK YOU TO ENABLE ME TO CHOOSE YOUR WAY IN MY MOMENTS OF IRRITATION TODAY. I WANT MY LIFE TO BE A DAILY WALK OF SURRENDER AND BEAUTIFUL RESPONSE TO YOUR WAY. IN JESUS' NAME, AMEN.

The B-I-B-L-E

*All Scripture is breathed out by God and profitable for
teaching, for reproof, for correction, and for training in
righteousness, that the man of God may be complete.*

2 TIMOTHY 3:16–17

What is the Bible? To some, the Bible is a history book. To others,
a collection of stories. To Christians, the Bible is so much more. It
is the Word of God, and through it He speaks to believers.

How you view the Bible can make a tremendous difference
in how you approach reading it. If Bible reading becomes just
another item on a to-do list, our eyes will take in the words, but
those words won't reach deep inside. We'll miss an opportunity to
grow in our faith. But if instead we begin our quiet times inviting
God to speak through His Word, He will. By opening our Bibles
with a willingness to hear, we'll open the door to a powerful source
of wisdom: "For the word of God is living and active, sharper
than any two-edged sword, piercing to the division of soul and of
spirit, of joints and of marrow, and discerning the thoughts and
intentions of the heart" (Hebrews 4:12). Unlike any other book in
print, out of print, or yet to be printed, the Bible transforms us in
real, lasting, to-our-core ways. Paul likely was thinking about the
radical results of God's Word when he wrote to the Thessalonians,
"And we also thank God constantly for this, that when you received
the word of God, which you heard from us, you accepted it not as
the word of men but as what it really is, the word of God, which

is at work in you believers" (1 Thessalonians 2:13).

That same Word of God is at work in believers still, deepening their faith as they grow more Christlike day by day. So wherever you need God's hand in your life, open your Bible. Make Bible reading as essential to you as the oxygen that flows into your lungs with every breath.

Maybe you feel distant from God. Maybe it has been awhile since you've dusted off the cover of your Bible, or maybe personal Bible study has never been a part of your daily routine. When you begin to read, the words. . .are just words. Don't give up. Pray. Let God know how you're feeling—your frustration, your desire to hear, your need for His help.

God gave us His Word for a reason. As we do our small part in the process, He is faithful to work in us.

LORD, YOUR WORD IS POWERFUL, AND I
WANT TO EXPERIENCE THAT POWER FOR
MYSELF. OPEN MY SPIRITUAL EYES AS I
OPEN THE BIBLE AND READ. AMEN.

Unplanned Stop

"For as the heavens are higher than the earth, so are my ways higher than your ways and my thoughts than your thoughts."

ISAIAH 55:9

Picture this: A lonely road out in the middle of nowhere, both ends extending far into the distance. You stand beside your car, which is pulled off to the side where it limped to a halt. You're stranded. Temporarily stuck between points A and B. Imagine that this is an unexpected event on a carefully planned road trip. For weeks, maybe months, you pored over maps and guidebooks, meticulously plotting the route you'd take, the places you'd stop. You might have spent years dreaming of a trip just like this and where you'd end up. . .except, of course, for this moment. When will you be on your way again? Will you have to make a detour? Will you reach your destination at all?

Now apply this scenario to your life's journey. Do you feel stalled somewhere? Were you hoping to earn a college degree, but you've had to put your education on hold? Did you think you'd be married by now? Have you been praying for a child for years? There are lots of places where we can feel stuck. No matter how long we've dreamed, planned, worked, or prayed, sometimes we're going nowhere fast. Where we've been is behind us, and where we want to be is still out of reach.

In these moments, it's easy to forget that with all the dreaming and planning, working and praying, God is ultimately in control.

Proverbs 16:9 says, "The heart of man plans his way, but the LORD establishes his steps." Yet even if we wholeheartedly yield to God's road map for our lives, we still may wonder what He's up to. We perceive no purpose in the in-between—but God does. He sees what's taking place in our lives from the heights; He understands what's going on with a depth unreachable to us without Him. As the words of Isaiah proclaim, His ways are higher, His thoughts are higher, so much higher than our own.

For whatever reason, God has you here now. Standing on the roadside of life, remember: you're not stranded forever and without purpose. Your great and loving Lord is the one who said, "For I know the plans I have for you. . .plans for welfare and not for evil, to give you a future and a hope" (Jeremiah 29:11). He holds the itinerary. Can you trust Him?

GOD, I'VE BEEN PLOTTING MY OWN WAY FOR
A WHILE, AND NOW I'M STUCK. HOWEVER
LONG I'M HERE AND WHEREVER I'M HEADED
NEXT, I CHOOSE TO TRUST IN YOU. AMEN.

Exploding People

In the morning, when the wine had gone out of
Nabal, his wife told him these things, and his heart
died within him, and he became as a stone.

1 SAMUEL 25:37

Some people have a short fuse, we say. They are especially challenging to figure out. And often they surprise us with their rapid temper.

Abigail was married to just such a man. Nabal, whose name means "fool," was undisciplined and undiscerning. How they came to be married scripture doesn't say. Since arranged marriages were the norm in that time, it is likely that she hadn't had much choice in the matter. Whatever the reason, she was the mistress of a large estate with many animals and servants.

David and his band of men offered volunteer protective service to the landowners and once a year asked for donations of food as a form of payment. Most were happy to help in gratitude for protection from thieves throughout the year. Nabal, however, was surly and impolite to the delegation from David and turned them away empty-handed.

David was furious and filled with revenge. He told his men to strap on their swords and prepare for battle. They were going to kill every male in the household of Nabal.

But along the way, they were met with a delegation from the other side. It was Abigail, who had heard what had happened and arranged a donation and brought it with her. Her words and her kindness caused David to see that he had been on the brink of committing a terrible sin in God's sight. He took the food and returned to his camp.

Back home, Nabal had been drinking and partying. He didn't know anything about Abigail's trip. The next morning, she told him, and he became so enraged that the Bible says his heart became like a stone. Scripture may be describing a stroke here. His anger actually damaged his body, and ten days later he died.

There isn't a lot of happiness in this story, is there? But there is a lesson. Explosive people will explode. But those of us who are in their lives, however we came to be there, have the opportunity to mitigate some of the damage they do. Of course, we can't take full responsibility for another person's actions, but we can arrange a few "donations" once in a while that might avert something that would hurt all of us.

GOD, I KNOW AN EXPLOSIVE PERSON. TO BE HONEST, HE [OR SHE] FRIGHTENS ME. I'M ASKING FOR YOUR WISDOM TO KNOW HOW TO HANDLE THOSE HEATED SITUATIONS AND FOR THE STRENGTH TO FILL MY PLACE IN HIS [OR HER] LIFE. AMEN.

The Pits

So when Joseph came to his brothers, they stripped
him of his robe, the robe of many colors that he wore.
And they took him and threw him into a pit.

GENESIS 37:23–24

Put yourself in Joseph's place, down in that pit. How would you respond? Would you shout in anger? Would you stare at the sky, waiting, hoping it was all a joke? Would you frantically search for a foothold, trying to climb up and out? Would you slump in a heap and cry? Would you think, *Hey, God must be using this experience to shape me. If I'll just hang in here, something wonderful will unfold!*

The Bible is silent on Joseph's time in the pit. We don't know if he fidgeted or fretted or fumed. Maybe he prayed. But we can see the results of what must have been a confusing and hurtful experience. As in the lives of Sarah, Ruth, David, Mary, and so many others, we know where each rocky path led and how God was at work every step of the way.

You see, the pit was just the beginning. In the years that followed, Joseph met with good and bad, sometimes very bad. He became a slave, proved his worth in Potiphar's household, then was falsely accused and imprisoned. He interpreted dreams, managed long-term famine, and ultimately forgave. Somewhere along the rocky path, Joseph understood that God was molding him into the man he needed to be. God was directing the events of his life for greater good. As he reunited with the very brothers who had thrown him into the pit, he said, "Do not fear, for am I in the place of God? As for you, you meant evil against me, but God meant it for good, to bring it about that many people should be kept alive, as they are today" (Genesis 50:19–20).

Looking back, you see God's hand in your life. Through the good and bad, and sometimes very bad, you can pinpoint where you were headed and how God was shaping you each moment. The trouble is seeing while you're in the middle of life, in the pit. With the walls towering around you, the sky only a patch overhead, how can you imagine something better *beyond*? It takes faith. "Now faith is the assurance of things hoped for, the conviction of things not seen" (Hebrews 11:1). Have faith that God is present. Have faith that He is at work, even when you can't see Him moving. He has shown Himself faithful over the centuries and won't change now.

GOD, EVEN IN THE PIT I WILL HAVE FAITH.
PLEASE HOLD MY FAITH STEADY WHEN
IT WAVERS. KEEP MY EYES FOCUSED
ON YOU UNTIL I CAN SEE. AMEN.

Do What?

"Be still, and know that I am God. I will be exalted among the nations, I will be exalted in the earth!"

PSALM 46:10

Look through some advice books and you likely won't find many that instruct, "Stop. Do nothing." There are steps to take, changes to implement, things to *do*. Surely we must foresee, plan, act, tweak. . .get our hands dirty as we grapple with and guide our lives. If we had to walk this earth under our own steam, that mindset would be logical. Who else will take charge if not us? But as Christians, we don't lead our lives alone.

Of the many lessons in the Bible, a big one is recognizing that no matter how well we're handling things—no matter how much we think, *I've got this!*—our control is under God's control. For some, that idea might be irksome (*What about free will?*). But for those of us who realize, even for brief moments, that we don't have it all together, it's sweet relief. Whether life seems manageable or out of hand, God is still God—and He's got this.

God is in control even through the worst threats of the earth and the nations. As Psalm 46 attests, "Though the earth gives way, though the mountains be moved into the heart of the sea" and while "the nations rage" (verses 2, 6), God is present. In and around the descriptions of disaster, God is at work: "God is our refuge and strength, a very present help in trouble" (verse 1); "God is in the midst of [Jerusalem]; she shall not be moved; God will help her when morning dawns" (verse 5); "Come, behold the works of the LORD. . . . He makes wars cease to the end of the earth; he breaks the bow and shatters the spear; he burns the chariots with fire" (verses 8–9). And at the end of the psalm, we hear His words ringing clear: "Be still, and know that I am God" (verse 10).

All the *doing* is God's. Our part is to stop, to be still, to rest in Him. The New American Standard Bible phrases verse 10 this way: "Cease striving and know that I am God," or the footnoted translation: "Let go. . .and know that I am God." It's okay to take our hands off this life and leave it to God's control. Know that the one who "utters his voice, [and] the earth melts" (verse 6) is God. He is mighty to act. And He is at work in the lives of believers.

LORD, I GRASP FOR WHAT LITTLE CONTROL
IS WITHIN REACH. BUT YOU ARE ALWAYS
IN CONTROL. TEACH ME TO BE STILL AND
KNOW THAT YOU ARE GOD. AMEN.

Don't Fight over Pebbles

"By this all will know that you are My disciples,
if you have love for one another."

JOHN 13:35 NKJV

I once was in a daily situation with someone who was on the hunt to catch me making mistakes. Ever been there? This individual was critical of my Christian walk and took delight in anything that might prove I was doing something wrong. I don't have to tell you that this is never the attitude of someone who follows Christ. You and I are called to a different level of interaction with those around us.

Jesus lived for thirty-three years on this earth with fallen people, people who made mistakes every day. How do you think He responded to that? We know that He was the perfect Son of God. I don't know if that means He never made an error in learning as a child. I do know it means He never transgressed the laws of God; He never sinned.

Sin and mistakes are like boulders and pebbles. Often when we hear the Christian community speak about showing grace to those around us, we hear them lump together willful sin and human error. True, both are short of perfection. But it is also true that motive is significant. If my toddler knocks over her glass of milk while eating, my response is different than if she looks me in the eye and pours out her milk in defiance. The result is the same—spilled milk, a mess—but motive makes a big difference.

Motive makes a big difference in our relationship with God too and in our relationship with others. Our response to those who grieve us should be grace no matter their motives, but the pebbles probably don't even merit our attention.

Our world is very unforgiving. I've heard people complain and gripe about small insults that they should just step over. "If she wants me to be nice to her, she'd better apologize—I'll tell you that!" Really? If a big boulder is blocking communication in the relationship, then address it and try to get it removed. But can you really not ignore the pebbles littering the path?

Relationships are hard enough; don't clutch those little pebbles for dear life. The other person might not even realize what happened. And probably their motive was never to hurt you.

What makes a Christ follower different is the love she shows. That's what Jesus said. Can you show unexpected mercy today in a way that will point others to Him? Ignoring the pebbles will make you stand out in any crowd you're in.

GOD, I KNOW THAT HUMANLY I TEND TO BE SELF-PROTECTIVE. I ASK YOU TO GIVE ME THE POWER TODAY TO IGNORE THE PEBBLES IN MY RELATIONSHIPS SO THAT YOUR LIGHT CAN SHINE UNEXPECTEDLY THROUGH ME. IN JESUS' NAME, AMEN.

First and Foremost

The saying is trustworthy and deserving of full acceptance, that
Christ Jesus came into the world to save sinners, of whom I am
the foremost. But I received mercy for this reason, that in me, as
the foremost, Jesus Christ might display his perfect patience as
an example to those who were to believe in him for eternal life.

1 TIMOTHY 1:15–16

You've heard of the apostle Paul? The guy who persecuted Christians and then went on to write large chunks of the New Testament? Considering his early life, he would be the worst candidate for the Lord's work, yet he was exactly the man God wanted for the job. Why? Because God is out to save sinners—the foremost and the least.

From the very beginning, when Eve then Adam helped themselves to the forbidden fruit, we humans have been following our desires instead of God's commands. Consequently, we've been ousted from the garden, parted from our close relationship with God. But through Jesus, God made a way back to the garden, back to a restored relationship with Him. And His love is so immense, His sacrifice so perfect, that all of us can find redemption at the cross: "For 'everyone who calls on the name of the Lord will be saved' " (Romans 10:13).

So as Paul (called Saul before his conversion) was headed to Damascus, "still breathing threats and murder against the disciples of the Lord" (Acts 9:1), the Lord met him on the road and transformed him inside and out. Despite Paul's sin, God had plans for his life. As the Lord told Ananias, "[Saul] is a chosen instrument of mine to carry my name before the Gentiles and kings and the children of Israel" (Acts 9:15). With Paul as an example, God demonstrated just how powerful He is to save.

Maybe you believe there's no way you can be an example to others. If that's the case, think about these words of Paul: "For consider your calling, brothers: not many of you were wise according to worldly standards, not many were powerful, not many were of noble birth. But God chose what is foolish in the world to shame the wise; God chose what is weak in the world to shame the strong; God chose what is low and despised in the world, even things that are not, to bring to nothing things that are" (1 Corinthians 1:26–28). God called you, He redeemed you, and now He chooses to use you—whoever you are—for His glory.

LORD, YOU ARE PATIENT AND MERCIFUL TOWARD
EVEN THE WORST OF SINNERS. MAY MY LIFE,
LIKE PAUL'S, BE PROOF THAT YOU SAVE. AMEN.

Uphill

"May the LORD our God be with us, as He was with our
fathers. May He not leave us nor forsake us, that He may
incline our hearts to Himself, to walk in all His ways,
and to keep His commandments and His statutes and
His judgments, which He commanded our fathers."
1 KINGS 8:57–58 NKJV

Eyes focusing straight ahead, fingers gripping the handlebars, legs pumping the pedals around and around—she's determined to reach the summit. Losing steam, growing weary, she's almost there. . .the top, the relief—and now the reward. Wind cooling her hot face, muscles relaxed, legs outstretched as the bike glides down the other side of the hill. If only the ascent were as sweet as this!

Does your faith walk resemble the uphill push more often than not? You strain to follow God—to walk in His ways, to keep His commandments—only to come up short. Your flesh is always present, pulling you down even as you seek to go up. You recognize yourself all too clearly in Paul's words: "For I do not understand my own actions. For I do not do what I want, but I do the very thing I hate" (Romans 7:15). The reality is no matter how much we pressure ourselves to live uprightly, we won't succeed. Paul wrote of himself what is true for all believers: "Nothing good dwells in me, that is, in my flesh. For I have the desire to do what is right, *but not the ability to carry it out*" (Romans 7:18, italics added). We can't obey God on our own. We lack the ability.

Before you're tempted to ditch the bike and camp out on the side of the hill, consider this: the desire to follow, "to do what is right," is itself from God. He is already at work. When King Solomon, the wisest man ever to live, blessed Israel, he asked that God would be with His people and "incline [their] hearts to Himself." Only then would the Israelites "walk in all His ways." We *can* triumph over the flesh, but we need to rely on God—first for leading us to follow, then for empowering us to follow through. Our outward following and victory result from His leading and power within.

Whatever uphill battles we face, let's not start pedaling without going to God. The one who draws our hearts close to Himself will be by our side giving us the extra boost we need to reach the summit and sweet reward.

GOD, I TRY AND TRY TO DO THE RIGHT THINGS,
BUT SO OFTEN I FEEL LIKE I'M PEDALING UPHILL.
I KNOW YOU'RE CALLING ME TO WALK IN YOUR
WAYS—PLEASE HELP ME OBEY. AMEN.

Erupting Volcanoes

But the people did not receive him, because his face was set toward Jerusalem. And when his disciples James and John saw it, they said, "Lord, do you want us to tell fire to come down from heaven and consume them?" But he turned and rebuked them.

LUKE 9:53–55

During His time on earth, Jesus mentored and discipled the twelve men He had chosen to be close followers. He gently exposed their weaknesses and pointed them to the grace of God to help them.

Thomas needed faith. Peter needed restraint. Judas needed integrity. And James and John? They needed mercy.

When the Samaritan village did not receive them, the brothers were incensed. How dare anyone refuse to host Jesus? They wanted to give the townspeople their due, immediately. But Jesus rebuked them and showed mercy. They got a nickname out of it, though. The Gospel of Mark calls them the "Sons of Thunder" (Mark 3:17).

Maybe we could think of them as being like a volcano, smoldering deep within the fissures of the earth. Then one day, a shift in the landscape, even something minor, causes the right combination of combustion, and the lava spews forth, killing the living things around it.

What character flaw is Jesus refining in your life? Do you have a nickname based on a negative trait you often display? There is no better place to bring your uncontrolled responses than to the power of Jesus. While He will not conquer it for you, He will empower you through His Spirit to make godly choices in your daily life.

The many manifestations of anger boil over and onto others—sarcasm, cynicism, harshness, negativism. At the first bubble of anger, we should turn to Him so it can be defused.

LORD, THANK YOU FOR WORKING ON ME. I'M GLAD
THAT NO TEMPTATION TO DISPLAY SELFISHNESS
CAN DEFEAT ME IF I AM ABIDING IN CHRIST AND
CHOOSING IN EVERY SITUATION TO FOLLOW
THE DIRECTION OF THE HOLY SPIRIT. AMEN.

Potter and Clay

But now, O LORD, you are our Father; we are the clay,
and you are our potter; we are all the work of your hand.

ISAIAH 64:8

If you've ever watched a potter at a potter's wheel, you know that the process of transforming a lump of clay into a vessel takes time. The potter's skilled hands coax the clay up and then press it down, up and down, softening and molding and smoothing it into the intended shape. Sometimes the potter seems to undo work already done, but each movement builds on the previous one until the vessel is complete.

Just so, our heavenly Father is the Master Potter, and our lives are clay in His hands. We are "the work of [His] hand," as Isaiah says. Over time, God forms our lives, working them into vessels for His glory. He is even powerful enough to take a "ruined" pot and re-form it. In Jeremiah we read:

> This is the word the LORD spoke to Jeremiah: "Go down to the potter's house, and I will give you my message there." So I went down to the potter's house and saw him working at the potter's wheel. He was using his hands to make a pot from clay, but something went wrong with it. So he used that clay to make another pot the way he wanted it to be.
>
> Then the LORD spoke his word to me: "Family of Israel, can't I do the same thing with you?" says the

LORD. *"You are in my hands like the clay in the potter's hands."* (Jeremiah 18:1–6 NCV)

Israel had abandoned God's ways, and as a result God warned that judgment was coming. Yet if Israel repented, God would halt judgment and instead reshape the nation, restoring Israel to His favor. Like the Israelites, our lives can become misshapen and marred because of sin. Hope is not lost, though. In His mercy, God offers us the chance to repent and be reshaped just as He wants us to be.

Alone, we would never produce the beautiful vessel God has in mind. We can't. We aren't the potter. But as clay in the Potter's hand, our lives become new. As we yield to Him, He daily fashions us into His daughters. Even when the pot looks like a lump on the wheel, we never need to doubt the Potter's skill. He envisions the end before He begins. He softens, molds, and smooths with precision, and He won't leave the pot unfinished.

FATHER, FORGIVE ME WHEN I WANDER FROM YOUR WAYS. I HEAR YOU CALLING. PLEASE DRAW ME BACK TO YOU AS CLAY READY TO BE SHAPED. AMEN.

Where God Leads

But Ruth said, "Do not urge me to leave you or to
return from following you. For where you go I will
go, and where you lodge I will lodge. Your people
shall be my people, and your God my God."
RUTH 1:16

Ruth was one radical woman. After her husband died and her widowed mother-in-law, Naomi, made plans to return to Bethlehem,
Ruth could have gone back to her hometown. She could have gone
back to familiar faces and gods. She could have gone back to a
more thriving marriage pool. But she didn't.

Why? No one would have blamed Ruth for leaving Naomi. It
was the sensible thing to do, after all. Naomi even encouraged Ruth
to accompany her sister-in-law on the trip back to Moab. Yet Ruth
remained firm. She chose following Naomi and her God over all
else. She chose faithfulness to others and faith that God would be
faithful in return. Ultimately, Ruth stood out for her commitment,
so much so that when Ruth met Boaz, her future husband, Boaz
said to her, "All that you have done for your mother-in-law since
the death of your husband has been fully told to me, and how you
left your father and mother and your native land and came to a
people that you did not know before. The LORD repay you for what
you have done, and a full reward be given you by the LORD, the
God of Israel, under whose wings you have come to take refuge!"
(Ruth 2:11–12). God *did* reward Ruth, first with provisions and

safety, then with marriage and a son. But God had bigger plans still. Beyond earthly blessings, Ruth's willingness to follow led her to the privilege of becoming a lasting part of God's kingdom work. Ruth and Boaz were the great-grandparents of King David, in the lineage of Jesus Christ.

At the outset, Ruth didn't know where following would lead. Even at the end of her life, she likely didn't know how God would use her faithfulness to bless countless others. She had to take each day one after the other, trusting God to take care of the rest. Are we willing to throw ourselves under the protection of God's wings and entrust what's to come to Him? Wherever He has us today and wherever He might lead us tomorrow, one thing is certain: He is present and active. And He can do great things with our willingness to stick close to Him.

LORD, MY LIFE FEELS A LITTLE LIKE RUTH'S.
I DON'T KNOW WHAT WILL HAPPEN AS I TAKE
THESE NEXT STEPS IN FAITH, BUT I TRUST YOU TO
DO WONDERFUL THINGS THROUGH ME. AMEN.

With His Help

And next to him was Shallum the son of Hallohesh, leader of half
the district of Jerusalem; he and his daughters made repairs.
NEHEMIAH 3:12 NKJV

It was a monumental task. Jerusalem's walls were heaps of rubble.
And here came Nehemiah, rallying the Jews to rebuild. Work began,
but so did the taunts: "When Sanballat heard [that the Jews] were
rebuilding the wall, he was very angry, even furious. He made fun
of the Jewish people. He said to his friends and those with power
in Samaria, 'What are these weak Jews doing? . . . Can they bring
stones back to life from piles of trash and ashes?' Tobiah the
Ammonite, who was next to Sanballat, said, 'If a fox climbed up on
the stone wall they are building, it would break it down' " (Nehemiah
4:1–3 NCV). How did Nehemiah respond to such mockery? He
prayed. But even though the work continued, Jerusalem's enemies
only upped the hostility. Opposition soon forced the people to work
with one hand and hold a weapon with the other (Nehemiah 4:17).
In short, the task was crazy. It was bold. It could only happen if
God worked through His people.

Faith in their God brought together Jews from all walks of life
and kept them going despite mounting trouble. And at the completion of the project (in a mere fifty-two days), no one could doubt
who was behind the success. Nehemiah recounted, "When all our
enemies heard of it, all the nations around us were afraid and fell
greatly in their own esteem, for they perceived that this work had

been accomplished with the help of our God" (Nehemiah 6:16). Without God, the mockers would have had the last word. Without God, the walls would have remained rubble.

Church families today sometimes undertake what seem like monumental tasks. We send missionaries to areas firmly resistant to the gospel. We raise large amounts of money to plant churches. We minister to communities facing unimaginable crisis. Whatever the task, one mindset is paramount: the work happens as God works through His people. Without God, ears are deaf to the good news, funds run out, needs go unmet. But with God. . .we can do the impossible (Matthew 17:20).

What monumental task is before you and your church today? Begin by asking God to work through you. God is just as mighty as He was in Nehemiah's day, and as we join together with fellow believers, He works through us to achieve even the impossible.

GOD, YOU KNOW WHAT WE ARE SETTING OUT TO DO. BE WITH US. WORK THROUGH US. MAY WE ACCOMPLISH BIG THINGS IN YOUR NAME. AMEN.

Not Straight Lines

You number my wanderings.

PSALM 56:8 NKJV

I like to drive on country roads. They meander and curve and laze around hills and dip by wooded hollows and climb onto ridges. Driving in the country is a pleasure, an adventure, a sensory treat. And though interstate highway driving is straight and fast, it brings little joy.

The shortest distance between two points, they say, is a straight line, which is mathematically proven to be true. But often God refuses to put us on the straight path and chooses for us the curvy one instead.

When we zoom from one life experience, one season, one victory straight to another, we can become arrogant, content, and comfortable. So God shakes up the map, and we discover the delight of bends in the road and forced deceleration in speed.

The word *wandering* generally carries a negative tone. People of purpose do not wander. The Bible does not speak well of those who wander. The Israelites wandered in the desert for forty years as discipline for their rebellion and lack of faith. The wisdom literature of the Bible tells us that wandering is not a desirable state of being either emotionally or spiritually. Yet at times, God lets us wander. And it is for our good.

From wandering, we learn that it's okay not to know the entire route we're walking. From wandering, we learn that some lessons are best understood when we seem to go in circles. From wandering, we learn that God is Lord of every journey and that He decides how quickly to get us to our destination.

One of the delights of driving on a country road are the landmarks—old school buildings, white wood-sided churches, faded barns, glorious farmhouses, vintage roadside parks, and historical sites. They're more than eye candy. They're stories in visual form. Behind every one of them is a tale of life, love, and learning, of hardship, sacrifice, and joy. Someone cared enough to carve out a place to live, a place to share with others, a place with meaning.

And these unexpected vignettes are what God uses in our spiritual journey too. When you feel like you can't find the "yellow brick road" to Oz, God may be letting you wander a bit so He can teach you wonderful, unexpected things along the way.

Stay on the journey. The sidetrack you're taking right now has a purpose.

HEAVENLY FATHER, I KNOW I CAN TRUST YOUR LEADERSHIP. IF I FOLLOW YOUR VOICE, YOU WILL GET ME TO THE PLACE I NEED TO BE AND TEACH ME NEW THINGS ALONG THE WAY. AMEN.

Press On!

*Not that I have already obtained this or am already
perfect. . . . But one thing I do: forgetting what lies behind and
straining forward to what lies ahead, I press on toward the
goal for the prize of the upward call of God in Christ Jesus.*

PHILIPPIANS 3:12–14

Maybe you're familiar with this frightening feeling. You pull into
your garage after a long day at work and realize you don't really
remember the drive home. You're so used to the route that your brain
went on autopilot, and voilà, here you are. Equally as dangerous
is becoming so consumed by what's in your rearview mirror (like
the vehicle glued to your bumper) that you stop looking forward.

Rearview driving can be disastrous.

Rearview living can be detrimental too. According to Philippians,
when it comes to the Christian life, the best advice is to forget what's
behind us and focus on what's ahead. But what are we to forget
and what are we to focus on. . .and why?

"Forgetting what lies behind" applies both to past sins that can
weigh us down with guilt and to past good works that can puff us
up with pride. Letting go of these former failures and successes
allows us to take hold of what God has planned next. After all,
the first thing God does in a Christian's life is exchange old for
new. "The old things have gone; everything is made new!" says
2 Corinthians 5:17 (NCV). And God continues transforming us for
good (Philippians 1:6). Our energy goes toward becoming more

like Christ in this moment and in a glorious future in heaven. Day in, day out, we turn our eyes to God and focus on Him. We tune our hearts to His Spirit so we can follow His ways. We open our lives to what God is fulfilling through us.

What is He doing in you today? Where can you shift your attention from the rearview mirror and instead look forward and press on? If forgetting the past and pursuing Christlikeness seems too daunting, remember: ultimately God is our means, and He is our reason. It is Christ's work on the cross that redeems us fully. It is Christ's work in us that produces righteousness. Paul wrote, "I press on to make it my own, because Christ Jesus has made me his own" (Philippians 3:12). We owe our present and future to Christ, and through Him we can live lives unburdened by the past.

LORD, MY MIND IS STUCK IN THE PAST. REMIND ME THAT YOU ARE ALWAYS GREATER THAN MY SIN, THAT YOU ARE THE SOURCE OF MY SUCCESS. HELP ME PRESS ON. AMEN.

Right on Time

*But do not overlook this one fact, beloved, that with the Lord
one day is as a thousand years, and a thousand years as
one day. The Lord is not slow to fulfill his promise as some
count slowness, but is patient toward you, not wishing that
any should perish, but that all should reach repentance.*

2 PETER 3:8–9

Late. Late payments are bad. Late starts are frustrating. Most people hate running late (except for being fashionably late to a party). Something that's a long time coming is better late than never. But sometimes it's too little, too late. Even the Rabbit from *Alice in Wonderland* is frantic: "I'm late! I'm late! For a very important date! No time to say hello, good-bye! I'm late! I'm late! I'm late!" Is *late* ever good, really?

When we think about God's promises, it's tempting to shout toward heaven, "You're late!"—particularly when we think about Christ's second coming. It's tempting to believe the scoffers whom Peter wrote about: "They will say, 'Where is the promise of his coming? For ever since the fathers fell asleep, all things are continuing as they were from the beginning of creation' " (2 Peter 3:4). But, as Peter urged, it's important to keep God's promises in perspective. God is so immense that even what seem like the longest spans of time to us are mere blips to Him. Eons are moments. Eternity is a speck within His hands.

Reflect on this: It took a long time to get from the Fall to Jesus.

For generations, God's people waited for the promised Messiah. Wouldn't it have been better for God to speed things up? Why wait? Yet in all that time, God was not idle. He was shaping history with precision. Every event that transpired, each person who lived, led to the fulfillment of His perfect plan. Jesus said before His baptism, "God's work, putting things right all these centuries, is coming together right now" (Matthew 3:15 MSG).

God today is the same God as then. In all these years, He has not been idle. He is shaping our days with precision. And what He has promised He will bring about. Meanwhile, this waiting period has purpose. God is not late, but patient. He gives His children time to come to Him. Let's model our heavenly Father and not grow impatient; let's use this time to share what God has done and what He continues to do. Slowly (to us) but surely, God will keep His promise.

GOD, YOUR TIMING IS BEYOND ME. BUT I'M
ETERNALLY GRATEFUL THAT YOU WAITED LONG
ENOUGH FOR ME TO TURN TO YOU. I PRAY THAT
MANY MORE WOULD DO THE SAME. AMEN.

A Spa for the Senses

He giveth snow like wool: he scattereth the hoarfrost like ashes.

PSALM 147:16 KJV

"Is it snowing?" The question is asked in eager tones by little children.

"Oh no! It's snowing." The statement is groaned out by adults.

The difference in perspective is amazing. And I know that children don't have to deal with the complications that arise from a snowstorm. All they can think of is a day out of school and a fun time playing in the flakes. But what if we looked at a snowstorm as a thing of rest?

Snow slows down the tempo of living. It just does. Traffic moves slower; events are delayed or postponed; plans are changed. It's an opportunity for an interlude of rest.

The Bible says that God gives snow. He *gives* it. Sure, it makes life a little more complex, but maybe it's okay if we just stay in. Maybe gazing across the field at the sea of white with a coffee cup in one hand and a quilt in the other is the kind of soul rest that's needed.

I hear you. Work must go on. There are no excuses for adults. That's true. But maybe after work you can clear your evening and take advantage of the atmosphere gentled around you by the swirling white.

The muffling effect of falling snow helps to tune out the daily noises. The monochromatic silvery tones of the snow and ice give the eyes visual rest from the bright lights and bold colors of marketing. The chill in the air invites burrowing under a plush throw, encouraging the body to relax and be warmed. The aroma of a hot drink beckons the palette and soothes the taste buds. Snow is a full-on spa for the senses.

So the next time the weather report indicates snow is arriving, start getting ready to rest! You might find that you look forward to snow days more than ever before! And I think that would make the Creator happy. He is the Giver, after all.

CREATOR GOD, THANK YOU FOR SNOW AND FOR THE PROMISED INTERLUDE OF REST. I WANT TO BE GRATEFUL FOR THE VARIETY OF WEATHER YOU GIVE TO THE EARTH. HELP ME TO TAKE ADVANTAGE OF THE REST FOR MY SENSES. AMEN.

Prove It

By this we shall know that we are of the truth and reassure our heart before him; for whenever our heart condemns us, God is greater than our heart, and he knows everything. Beloved, if our heart does not condemn us, we have confidence before God.

1 JOHN 3:19–21

A child beams as she shows off her pristine room, but is the mess just crammed under the bed? An employee types diligently at a computer, but is it Excel or Facebook that holds her attention? A gardener toils for hours, but is her thumb green? The proof is in the pudding. As in, *Mmm, that pudding looks delicious*, but is it? Results equal proof oftentimes. Clothes and toys are in their proper places, so the child cleaned. The spreadsheet is finished on time, so the employee worked. The flowers bloom, so the gardener succeeded. You taste the pudding, and it is indeed good.

Simple examples, but what about something invisible like your salvation? You say you're a Christian. You take God at His Word that He saves. Yet how do you know you're saved? Where's the proof in that pudding?

Read through the book of 1 John, and you'll likely catch on to a major theme. Some form of the word *love* appears nearly fifty times in just five short chapters. It's as if John is saying, "In case you missed it, let me repeat it: love, love, love." Because love is fundamental to Christianity. "For God so loved," we're told, that He made a way for sinners to find redemption through His Son (John

3:16). And it is by exhibiting love ourselves that we have proof of God's saving work in us. John wrote, "Beloved, let us love one another, for love is from God, and whoever loves has been born of God and knows God" (1 John 4:7).

On days when you feel less than confident about your salvation, look to your love. Where do you see love manifested? In acts of kindness, big or small. In compassion even for those who hate you. In the pull to reach out to others. . . All flow from a heart that is His. Still unsure? Rest in the words of 1 John: *God is greater*. He is greater than our doubts. He knows our hearts and who belongs to Him. "But God's firm foundation stands, bearing this seal: 'The Lord knows those who are his' " (2 Timothy 2:19).

God saves, and the proof is in our love.

GOD, MY CONFIDENCE IS A LITTLE SHAKY
TODAY. BUT I BELIEVE IN JESUS AND HOW HE
SAVES ME. REMIND ME, PLEASE, OF ALL THE
WAYS MY LIFE REFLECTS YOUR LOVE. AMEN.

Let the Flowers Bloom

For behold, the winter is past; the rain is over and gone.
The flowers appear on the earth, the time of singing has come.
SONG OF SOLOMON 2:11–12

Wildflowers spring up in amazing places. As I drive along the interstate, I am amazed at the beauty of random (to my eye) fields of wildflowers. Perhaps somebody sows the seeds at some time in an effort to keep our highways beautiful. But in some places they simply come up from some hidden richness below, bringing color and cheer to our world.

We must encourage flowers to grow in our hearts. Weeds of sin try to choke them out, and pollutants in our souls work to kill them at the roots. We must cultivate the soil of our lives to be fertile and receptive.

I remember a time in our family's life when we had been hurt by a ministry situation. The circumstances for our family's future were greatly changed, and all of us were devastated. Even our children were going through the sad process of giving away pets and saying goodbye to best friends as we prepared to move. My husband and I did our best to get through those difficult transitional months. We tried to process the disappointment properly and biblically. We knew that we had to allow the flowers to bloom again, so to speak. We were not going to be able to go back; we had to look ahead, to let happy feelings take root as we put positive patterns in place for our future health. We had cried long enough. The rainy days needed to be over and gone. It was time for flowers and singing.

We can choose to make our future brighter as we base our decisions not on our feelings but on the realization that God has called us to make choices that encourage growth in our spiritual lives. We can deliberately choose to put our hope in God even when we aren't feeling hopeful. We can purposefully clear away the weeds and let the flowers poke through.

I don't know what has happened in the field of your life, what unexpected calamity has brought a season of rain. But I do know that God calls us to open our eyes to the season of flowers. Let it come when it's time. Don't stay in the rain. Listen: the birds are starting to sing.

DEAR FATHER, I'M GLAD YOU UNDERSTAND
THE SEASONS IN OUR LIVES. THANK YOU FOR
BRINGING ME THROUGH A DIFFICULT TIME.
NOW I TURN TO THE TIME FOR FLOWERS AND
ASK YOU TO HELP ME CULTIVATE JOY AGAIN
IN MY LIFE. IN JESUS' NAME, AMEN.

What Do You Want?

*He has told you, O man, what is good; and what does
the LORD require of you but to do justice, and to love
kindness, and to walk humbly with your God?*

MICAH 6:8

Court is now in session. Micah 6 opens with the Lord's indictment of the people. He pleads His case, how He has been faithful through the years (verses 3–5). Yet despite His faithfulness, the people continued to walk their own way. Worse, their outward attempts at religion (even exaggerated ones) did nothing to change their insides. Micah rhetorically asked, "With what shall I come before the LORD, and bow myself before God on high? . . . Will the LORD be pleased with thousands of rams, with ten thousands of rivers of oil? Shall I give my firstborn for my transgression, the fruit of my body for the sin of my soul?" (Micah 6:6–7). Their pious offering of sacrifices was all for show. And the Lord was not convinced. He desired something deeper.

Back in Old Testament times, God's people strove to please Him by keeping the Law and offering sacrifices. But at every step, with every sin and sacrifice, it was clear that human efforts fell short. We needed God's ultimate sacrifice, His Son, to redeem us. Today we gladly accept God's grace. Still, how often do the sacrifices of the Old Testament morph into our efforts to *do* more for God? We attend Bible studies throughout the week. We cram in a community project or two. We spend Sundays juggling nursery duties, small groups, and worship services. If we aren't careful, our Christian lives begin to look like a one-woman band, this arm doing one thing, that knee doing another. . . .

Wait, what's wrong with those things? you ask. Nothing! In fact, good works are evidence of faith. As James put it: "Faith by itself, if it does not have works, is dead" (James 2:17). And again, "Show me your faith apart from your works, and I will show you my faith by my works" (James 2:18). The problem occurs if the "outer" takes precedence over the "inner"—if all the *doing* is done without first attending to the heart. God is not impressed by our activities alone, any more than He was impressed by Judah's attempts to cover up sinful habits with sacrifices. He wants something deeper: "For I desire steadfast love and not sacrifice" (Hosea 6:6). God has told us what is good, and it all starts with a relationship with Him.

LORD, LATELY I'VE OVERLOOKED THE ONE
THING YOU WANT MOST FROM ME. TODAY I
RECOMMIT TO LOVING YOU FIRST AND FOREMOST,
BEFORE I DO ANYTHING ELSE. AMEN.

Breaking the Cycle

Those who are God's children do not continue sinning,
because the new life from God remains in them. They are not
able to go on sinning, because they have become children of God.

1 JOHN 3:9 NCV

You've stumbled. You've slipped up. Sinned. In your mind's eye, you sit slumped on the ground. Dusty. Downtrodden. Discouraged. Will you ever get this right?

The concept of sin after salvation seems contradictory. The moment God saves us, the old self is "crucified" (Romans 6:6). We are made new, and with this newness comes a new allegiance. We no longer bow to sin but to God. Yet no matter how long we've been a Christian, we still struggle with sin. Our redeemed self still contends with our humanness—with the flesh and its desires. Paul wrote in Romans, "For I delight in the law of God, in my inner being, but I see in my members another law waging war against the law of my mind and making me captive to the law of sin that dwells in my members" (7:22–23). Our new nature perceives sin differently now. So begins the struggle. As we grow in our knowledge of God's holiness, we feel our sin more and more. Paul's sin was so evident to him that he cried out, "Wretched man that I am! Who will deliver me from this body of death?" (7:24). But just as quickly as Paul asks the question, he supplies the blessed answer: "Thanks be to God through Jesus Christ our Lord!" (7:25).

God rescues us from the cycle of sin. Although sin is present and we will stumble at times, sin is not the norm. The Holy Spirit is also present, and His presence makes it impossible for us to keep sinning endlessly. Patterns of righteousness replace patterns of sin with glorious results: "Little children, let no one deceive you. Whoever practices righteousness is righteous, as he is righteous. . . . By this it is evident who are the children of God" (1 John 3:7, 10). Christ's nature as God's Son is imparted to His children, allowing us to mirror Christ's righteous ways, however imperfectly.

First John 3:9 (NCV) tells us that we as God's children "are not able to go on sinning." If you find yourself slumped on the ground, take heart! God's grace and the new life He has given us empower us to pick ourselves up, dust ourselves off, and keep trying. Indeed, we *will* keep trying. We cannot do otherwise.

LORD, ON THE GROUND, IT'S EASY TO
FEEL STUCK IN SIN. THANK YOU FOR THE
REMINDER THAT SIN DOES NOT DEFINE MY
LIFE. YOUR RIGHTEOUSNESS DOES. AMEN.

Used to Be a Friend

And Samson's wife was given to his companion,
who had been his best man.

JUDGES 14:20

"With friends like that, who needs enemies?" an old saying goes.

I think Samson could identify. Yes, he had it coming because he was a jerk. I mean, he found a girl among God's enemies and demanded that his parents get her for him to marry. His parents tried to talk him out of it, to get him to see that he should choose a wife from among those who had faith in God, but he wouldn't have it! So, in some ways, it seems just that his wife was given in marriage to his best man. But still, that had to be a cruel form of betrayal even for a headstrong, unreasonable kind of man like Samson.

Again, we have to remember that we are discussing a story in the Old Testament when they had God's laws but not the power of the Holy Spirit to keep them. They did not have the understanding we have today or even a Bible to read. Scripture often records what happened but does not approve of it. This is one of those times.

Maybe you have had something happen in your life that is a little like what happened to Samson. Maybe you didn't contribute to the trouble like he did. Maybe, just out of the blue, you were betrayed by someone you thought was a friend. Nowhere is this more painful than in the breakup of a marriage. We know the stories of the "other woman" being the best friend of the wife, or maybe it's the husband whose best friend becomes involved with his wife. Like Samson, you are shocked, angered, humiliated. And maybe you feel like doing what he did when he discovered what had happened. Judges 15 says he caught three hundred foxes and tied them tail to tail, attached torches to their tails, and let them run through the fields and orchards of the Philistines, his ex-wife's people. Wow!

But remember, we are called by Jesus to love our enemies. This doesn't mean, of course, that we must conjure up warm fuzzies for a person who has damaged a marriage or has hurt us in some other destructive way, but it does mean that we "love" them by not enacting vengeance on them ourselves. We are not to make them pay. God will do that. And He has much better ways to keep track of what's going on.

When a friend unexpectedly acts in an unfriendly way, the hurt is real. In those moments, we must rely on the strength of our God who never betrays and whose steady love can uphold us in any surprise.

FATHER GOD, I'VE BEEN HURT BY SOMEONE WHO WAS SUPPOSED TO BE MY FRIEND. I NEED YOUR GRACE SO THAT I CAN FORGIVE AND NOT SEEK VENGEANCE. I ASK FOR STRENGTH AND PEACE AND HOPE. IN JESUS' NAME, AMEN.

Here and Now

"For if you keep silent at this time, relief and deliverance will rise for the Jews from another place, but you and your father's house will perish. And who knows whether you have not come to the kingdom for such a time as this?"

ESTHER 4:14

Put yourself in the book of Esther. Go ahead—immerse yourself. Read each word without anticipating the next sentence. Picture what's happening without rushing ahead to what's next. Take it moment by moment. Did you notice anything?

We have a tremendous gift in the Bible—the ability to see stories of faith played out. But as a result, we usually read about Abraham and Moses and Mary from a bird's-eye view of sorts. We witness the arc of events. We're privy to how the story ends. And through it all we watch God work. Looking at your own life, you might think, *If only things were so clear!* Of course, we don't have a bird's-eye view of our lives. We can't really see beyond this moment.

Neither could Esther. All along—from her arrival at the palace to twelve months of beauty treatments, from meeting the king to becoming queen—Esther, like us, had to live one day at a time. Moment by moment. And when she faced perhaps the biggest challenge of her life, she did not know with certainty whether she was the girl for the job or how it all would end. Yet she bravely sent her reply to Mordecai: "Go, gather all the Jews to be found in Susa, and hold a fast on my behalf. . . . Then I will go to the king, though it is against the law, and if I perish, I perish" (Esther 4:16). Without knowing the outcome, she did her part and then watched for the rest to unfold.

One major question concerning the book of Esther is God's apparent nonpresence. Unlike in other biblical accounts, He isn't a named participant. Yet, God is undeniably present. Esther's life reflects our experience. Even with faith, we can't always sense God's hand at work. We're restricted to this moment, without a clear view of what's to come. Still, let's never lose sight of God. He is orchestrating our lives with perfect timing, for all the "such a time" moments.

LORD, NO MATTER HOW MUCH I TRY TO
GLIMPSE TOMORROW, I CAN'T SEE BEYOND
NOW. RENEW MY FAITH THAT, IN THIS MOMENT,
YOU HAVE A PURPOSE AND A PLAN. AMEN.

A Person of Rest

I have calmed and quieted my soul, like a weaned child
with its mother; like a weaned child is my soul within me.

PSALM 131:2

Have you ever met someone who embodied rest, who made you feel calm just being in her presence?

Those people are unusual. I don't think I'm naturally one of them. But I want to learn how to become like them.

I am naturally an intense person, maybe what could be called high strung. Phlegmatic is not one of my temperament traits. But is it possible to learn to project calm and peace?

The psalmist said that he had "calmed and quieted [his] soul." It sounds like a deliberate action, a choice. A weaned child is one who has learned to be content without mother's milk; he or she has grasped the idea that comfort is still found in the presence of mother though the roles have changed. A weaned child is not fretful and restless but quiet and at rest.

To accomplish this in the spiritual life, one must follow the words of the first verse of the psalm: "O LORD, my heart is not lifted up; my eyes are not raised too high; I do not occupy myself with things too great and too marvelous for me."

The way to soul rest in the Lord is to refuse to get focused on matters that are out of our hands. We must not allow our minds to be occupied with outcomes that only come from God's throne. We must let Him keep the answers to the unsolvable earthly equations.

We must not lift up our hearts and imagine that we can sort things out; we must not elevate our eyes to the level where God reigns.

You may get the chance today to provide a moment of rest for someone. Our world is filled with people who are jostled by every kind of stress one can imagine. Maybe an encounter with you, filled with the Holy Spirit, could cause them to consider letting God rule. After all, if He can quiet you so you bring rest to others, He can use that rest to be a witness.

LORD, I'M GLAD FOR THE PROMISE OF REST.
LIKE THE PSALMIST, I WANT TO CHOOSE
PURPOSEFULLY TO BE CALM AND QUIET.
AND I WANT TO BRING UNEXPECTED REST
TO OTHERS. IN JESUS' NAME, AMEN.

Sans Words

*Likewise the Spirit helps us in our weakness. For we do not
know what to pray for as we ought, but the Spirit himself
intercedes for us with groanings too deep for words.*

ROMANS 8:26

From dawn till dusk, the day had been a struggle. Now with heavy limbs and a heavy heart, she kneels to pray. But despite the flurry of thoughts in her mind, words won't come. A sigh is all that escapes. Have you ever been to that place of silence? You can likely think of many effects of a stop there: frustration, weariness, doubt, helplessness, dismay, numbness. . . Your first thoughts might not be too encouraging. In fact, being on your knees and at a loss for words seems anything but positive. Yet it can be.

The Bible is full of promises about prayer:

- "Ask, and it will be given to you; seek, and you
  will find; knock, and it will be opened to you"
  (Matthew 7:7).

- "And this is the confidence that we have toward
  him, that if we ask anything according to his will
  he hears us" (1 John 5:14).

- "Therefore I tell you, whatever you ask in prayer,
  believe that you have received it, and it will be
  yours" (Mark 11:24).

Reading just a few of these promises, we may see prayer as

first an action on our part. We *ask*. We *speak*. Right? Sometimes. Prayer is a beautiful communion between the Father and His children. In His love, He listens to our words; He welcomes our prayers. First Peter 3:12 says, "For the eyes of the Lord are on the righteous, and his ears are open to their prayer." But it is through God's Spirit that we have assurance to kneel at our heavenly Father's knee: "You received the Spirit of adoption by whom we cry out, 'Abba, Father' " (Romans 8:15 NKJV). And this same Spirit who emboldens us to pray also enables us to pray when we cannot utter a word. He intercedes with the Father on our behalf, and because He and the Father are one, no words are required. "He who searches hearts knows what is the mind of the Spirit," we're told in Romans 8:27. Unspoken prayer reaches the Father's ear through the Spirit. What we leave unsaid, the Spirit in us conveys. So when you find yourself in that place of silence, remember that you are not on your own. Sometimes we speak. Sometimes we let Him do the talking as only He can.

GOD, I DON'T KNOW WHAT TO SAY. BUT YOU KNOW WHAT'S ON MY HEART, AND THE HOLY SPIRIT KNOWS JUST HOW TO EXPRESS IT WITHOUT WORDS. THANK YOU! AMEN.

Sure-footed

*For who is God, but the LORD? And who is a rock, except
our God?—the God who equipped me with strength
and made my way blameless. He made my feet like the
feet of a deer and set me secure on the heights.*

PSALM 18:31–33

It's mind blowing. It's a hold-your-breath, grip-the-edge-of-your-seat kind of experience. It's. . .well, *Nature* and footage of goats traversing cliff faces. But in all seriousness, their ability to maneuver up and down and across nearly vertical spaces is remarkable. Even at dizzying heights, their hooves are secure.

If you've ever been hiking, you know how important firm footing is. Loose pebbles on steep paths or jumbles of exposed roots can make difficult hikes even harder. One misplaced step and your feet slip from under you, or your head precedes your heels down the trail. At times, life can seem just as precarious. One wrong move or unexpected event and you lose your balance; your world turns upside down.

King David certainly knew the meaning of precarious. Just a cursory glance at his psalms reveals a life punctuated by fleeing and hiding, enemies and struggles. With all that uncertainty, David's words could have overflowed with insecurity. But David also knew what it felt like to be secure even when life was not. In Psalm 18, he used the image of a deer, hooves "secure on the heights," to describe the sure-footedness that characterized his walk. You see, through all the precariousness, David knew where to go for ultimate security: to God, his rock. It was God who set David's feet firmly on paths that otherwise would have been his downfall. He wrote earlier in Psalm 18:2–3, "The LORD is my rock and my fortress and my deliverer, my God, my rock, in whom I take refuge, my shield, and the horn of my salvation, my stronghold. I call upon the LORD, who is worthy to be praised, and I am saved from my enemies."

If the path ahead of you seems precarious, focus instead, as David did, on all the ways that God makes His children secure. Need protection? God is our shield. Overwhelmed? Find refuge in Him. See no way out? He is our deliverer. Think all hope is lost? God is salvation. Feeling unsteady? Stand firm on the solid rock. God, who is like no other, will equip us and steady us, making our feet secure even on the roughest paths.

GOD, YOU ARE ONE OF A KIND, WORTHY OF ENDLESS PRAISE. I'M HEADING UP A STEEP TRAIL RIGHT NOW. WITH EACH STEP, PLANT MY FEET FIRMLY ON THE ROCK. AMEN.

Stay Awhile

But the Lord answered her, "Martha, Martha, you are
anxious and troubled about many things, but one
thing is necessary. Mary has chosen the good portion,
which will not be taken away from her."

LUKE 10:41–42

Martha had too many plates in the air. The Lord had arrived, and she was busily preparing the meal. Were bread and roasting meat competing for space over the fire? Was her worktable cluttered with half-prepped dishes? Was she frantically dashing from kitchen to table? The Bible doesn't flesh out the scene, but it does say that Martha was focused on serving to the point of distraction (verse 40). Lest we think this short account applies only to our next dinner party, consider how crammed our lives have become—and how often the many details distract us from the one thing that's necessary.

Next to her sister, Mary provides a beautiful example for us of centering our lives on the one thing: Jesus. It's not that what Martha chose was bad. Hospitality is a blessing to others and is encouraged in the Bible (Hebrews 13:2). And Mary more than likely did not neglect her share of the work every minute of every day. But when it mattered, Mary chose to shift all her attention to her Lord. She chose to sit at His feet while the lesser things faded for a time.

Think of someone dear to you: husband, boyfriend, friend, sibling, parent. . . What if you only spent a few minutes with that person each week? Wouldn't there eventually be a distance in your relationship? You might even begin to feel like strangers. As believers, we have the amazing privilege of a personal relationship with almighty God. God offers us the chance to get to know Him. Hear Jesus' words "Martha, Martha" not as a scold, but as a wish: He longs for us to choose "the good portion"—and for a very good reason. We need it. In order to deepen our relationship with the Lord and grow in our faith, we have to draw near. We have to spend time at His feet—worshipping, listening, soaking up His love.

Paul once wrote, "I think that all things are worth nothing compared with the greatness of knowing Christ Jesus my Lord" (Philippians 3:8 NCV). What "nothings" distract us from getting to know Jesus? Where do we funnel our energy to the exclusion of quiet moments at His feet? We have much to gain from choosing the good portion. And what we gain we'll never lose.

LORD, I'M DISTRACTED. A TIME OF STILLNESS WITH YOU IS THE LAST THING ON MY MIND. FORGIVE ME. NOTHING IS OF GREATER VALUE THAN YOU. AMEN.

Enjoy the Drive

The heart of man plans his way,
but the LORD establishes his steps.

PROVERBS 16:9

Ever had your vacay plans changed? The cruise is canceled, the flight is delayed, the destination suffers a disaster, the family gets sick, or a death occurs and the funeral must be attended—all of these things can derail our plans for a fun getaway.

Things take us by surprise, and we have to adjust accordingly. It's part of the way life on earth goes sometimes. We can't predict what will happen when we make the reservations months ahead of time and schedule the week off work. Only God has foreknowledge.

God often is in the changes, though. Not just in a week away but on the larger scale. As we navigate life, detours sometimes take us down different career roads or ministry paths than we had on our personal map. But the God who led Abraham to an unknown land and guided the Hebrews into Canaan is the one who directs our steps. He made a way through the Red Sea and brought them through the wilderness into the land of promise. He surely knows how to lead us through the twists and turns that seem so confusing.

I love to drive on country roads; they're much more interesting than city streets. They wind and bend around ridges and valleys, pass by quaint farmhouses and pastures, and meander through little villages. The delight is that you're on an adventure and never can tell what lies around the next turn.

God's map for our lives is sometimes like that. And we can find joy in trusting Him and hanging on for the ride! I know that we like to know the details and figure out where we're going, but sometimes that just isn't possible. We don't always know how long we'll stay in one location. But He does! And we can know that whenever He brings us to an unexpected crossing, He already knows exactly where we need to go next. And He'll get us there!

FATHER, I DON'T KNOW EXACTLY WHERE I'M GOING IN LIFE, BUT I TRUST YOUR LEADING. I GIVE YOU MY ANXIOUS THOUGHTS AND FEARS AND DESIRE TO CONTROL THE FUTURE. LEAD ME FOR YOUR NAME'S SAKE. AMEN.

"I Know You!"

I praise you, for I am fearfully and wonderfully made.
Wonderful are your works; my soul knows it very well.

PSALM 139:14

Like a turtle knows its shell. Like a bird knows its nest. Like a goldfish knows its bowl. God knows us like the back of His hand.

Close your eyes and picture yourself. How clearly can you see the shape of your face? The contours of your body? Each freckle on your skin? Years of living mean we know ourselves pretty well. But as much as we know the waves in our hair or the flecks in our eyes, God's knowledge goes deeper. The psalmist said of God, "For you formed my inward parts; you knitted me together in my mother's womb" (Psalm 139:13). God's knowledge is more than passive familiarity with how we look. He knows everything that makes us who we are because He formed us, inside and out, "fearfully and wonderfully."

"That's great!" you say. "But now what?" How does what God did in the past apply to our present? Well, God didn't stop at our physical beings. Before we existed, He put in place His design for us: "Your eyes saw my unformed substance; in your book were written, every one of them, the days that were formed for me, when as yet there was none of them" (Psalm 139:16). Our heavenly Father has planned our days—from the major ones to the mundane—as intricately and with as much knowledge of who we are as when He formed our bodies. Today has purpose.

What about the days that are calendars away? God will know us just as deeply then, and His plans still stand. Jesus told believers, "Even the hairs of your head are all numbered. Fear not" (Luke 12:7). As these lives of ours unfold, we never need to fear. We have the promise of God's good will for us: "I know the plans I have for you, declares the LORD, plans for welfare and not for evil, to give you a future and a hope" (Jeremiah 29:11). Today and tomorrow, rest in the sovereignty and goodness of God. He who formed us and planned our days from the beginning continues to watch over us throughout our earthly lives, right down to the end. "He knows our frame; he remembers that we are dust," we read in Psalm 103:14. God has a perfect plan for eternity too, one He set in motion long ago.

God knows us. Like the back of His nail-pierced hand.

GOD, HOW WELL YOU KNOW ME! HOW PERFECTLY YOU HAVE FORMED MY LIFE! I PRAISE YOU FOR THE WONDERFUL THINGS YOU DO. AMEN.

Walking Blind

And I will lead the blind in a way that they do not know,
in paths that they have not known I will guide them. I will turn
the darkness before them into light, the rough places into level
ground. These are the things I do, and I do not forsake them.

Isaiah 42:16

She heads down the sidewalk. The curb to her right and the building to her left become her guides, keeping her straight. Her cane skims the pavement—back and forth, back and forth—as she searches for anything in her path. She approaches the intersection and listens for the signal, listens to the hum of engines in the traffic on the street.

If you're not blind yourself, just imagining daily activities like walking in your town or crossing a familiar street may be terrifying. Even more so is the thought of maneuvering in an unknown place. There, the fear is real—you wouldn't know which way to turn; you wouldn't know what to expect. That's the scene painted in Isaiah 42:16—the blind and the unknown road ahead. Only the blind in the verse aren't walking alone. They have God at their side, lighting the way, leveling the path.

God has a long history of leading His people in unknown territory. Take the exodus. God used clouds and fire to lead Israel through the wilderness: "And the Lord went before them by day in a pillar of cloud to lead them along the way, and by night in a pillar of fire to give them light. . . . The pillar of cloud by day and the pillar of fire by night did not depart from before the people" (Exodus

13:21–22). Later in Psalms we read, "[God] led out his people like sheep and guided them in the wilderness like a flock. He led them in safety, so that they were not afraid" (Psalm 78:52–53). Day and night, God's guiding presence was near. He kept His people safe. He kept them from fear.

Maybe you're facing a wilderness of your own. You don't know which way to turn; you don't know what to expect. When you envision your future, the vision is blank, blurry at best. Remember the words of Isaiah 42: "These are the things I do, and I do not forsake them." God is present. God is leading. He is actively reversing our fears—lighting the way, leveling the path. So link your arm with His and wait to see where He takes you.

LORD, NOT SEEING WHAT'S AHEAD HAS
MY FEET GLUED IN PLACE. BUT I KNOW
YOU WILL BE WITH ME EACH STEP I TAKE.
REPLACE MY FEAR WITH FAITH. AMEN.

Those He Loves

My child, do not reject the LORD's discipline, and don't get
angry when he corrects you. The LORD corrects those he
loves, just as parents correct the child they delight in.

The seconds crawled. Each minute was excruciating. Never in her young life had she suffered so terribly. There—on a stool, in a corner, staring at the wallpaper—the child was stuck in time-out. But her mother knew one thing: the suffering would make her daughter stronger. The unpleasant discipline would yield beautiful results.

In our Christian lives, God's discipline is a topic we'd rather not think about. Why focus on the negative? We need a renewed perspective on this topic. Eventually, discipline has a *positive* effect on our lives. All of us stray from the standards of our heavenly Father at times—standards that protect us and enable us to thrive. Discipline corrects our course; it trains us while we grow as God's daughters. Consider these verses:

> *So hold on through your sufferings, because they are like*
> *a father's discipline. God is treating you as children. All*
> *children are disciplined by their fathers. . . . It is even*
> *more important that we accept discipline from the Father*
> *of our spirits so we will have life. Our fathers on earth*
> *disciplined us for a short time in the way they thought*
> *was best. But God disciplines us to help us, so we can*
> *become holy as he is. We do not enjoy being disciplined.*

It is painful at the time, but later, after we have learned from it, we have peace, because we start living in the right way. (Hebrews 12:7, 9–11 NCV)

Of greater value still than the way discipline transforms us is what discipline tells us about God. Through it, God displays His boundless love. What loving parent would turn a blind eye to behavior that will hinder or, worse yet, hurt their child? God loves us immensely more, and He will not neglect to guide us—for our good.

Everything God does is aimed at restoration. Ever since the Fall, God has been bringing us back to communion with Him. Even in His discipline—the correction that seems to tear us down—God's goal is to build us up. "Blessed is the man whom you discipline, O LORD," the psalmist said (Psalm 94:12). We have so much to gain as we allow the Lord's discipline to do its work. Let's not reject His blessing.

LORD, THOSE YOU LOVE, YOU CORRECT. FROM NOW ON, I CHOOSE TO FOCUS ON THE LOVE BEHIND THE DISCIPLINE—ON THE WAY YOU ARE DOING SOMETHING BEAUTIFUL IN ME. AMEN.

Gifted

Then Moses said to the people of Israel, "See, the LORD
has called by name Bezalel the son of Uri, son of Hur, of
the tribe of Judah; and he has filled him with the Spirit
of God, with skill, with intelligence, with knowledge, and
with all craftsmanship, to devise artistic designs, to work
in gold and silver and bronze, in cutting stones for setting,
and in carving wood, for work in every skilled craft."

EXODUS 35:30–33

Take a look around your church congregation some Sunday, and you might be fascinated by the sea of people. Tall and short. Young and old. No shade of hair or skin or eyes exactly the same. And that's just on the surface. God equips each of His children with unique abilities too. One plays an instrument during worship; another greets visitors with a bubbly personality. One plans crafts for Sunday school; another organizes a food drive. One makes repairs around the building; another uses nursing skills on a mission trip. And on the list goes.

God has been equipping His people uniquely for generations. Like Bezalel. Back in Moses' day, Bezalel was one of two named artisans who were involved in the construction of the tabernacle. Based on the description in Exodus 25–30, the project was no small feat. From the curtains to the altars, from the lampstands to the ark, the tabernacle itself and everything in it required great skill to complete. But God, being God, knew what His people would be up against, and He prepared them ahead of time. God "filled [Bezalel] with the Spirit of God, with skill, with intelligence, with knowledge, and with all craftsmanship"—with everything necessary to do the job—abilities that he likely developed over the course of his life. When it was time to begin, Bezalel was ready.

Behind every individual ability is God. Paul wrote to the church in Corinth, "Now there are varieties of gifts, but the same Spirit; and there are varieties of service, but the same Lord; and there are varieties of activities, but it is the same God who empowers them all in everyone" (1 Corinthians 12:4–6). The God who worked through Bezalel works through us today. Each of us is Spirit filled with unique abilities, prepared in us ahead of time. "For we are his workmanship," we read in Ephesians 2:10, "created in Christ Jesus for good works, which God prepared beforehand, that we should walk in them." How has God gifted you? What has He been preparing you to do?

GOD, MY EXPERIENCES, MY EDUCATION, MY TALENTS. . .THEY'RE NO ACCIDENT. THROUGH THEM, YOU ARE PREPARING ME TO DO YOUR WORK. USE MY GIFTS FOR YOUR GLORY. AMEN.

God Chose to Rest

And on the seventh day God ended His work which He had done, and He rested on the seventh day from all His work which He had done. Then God blessed the seventh day and sanctified it, because in it He rested from all His work which God had created and made.

GENESIS 2:2–3 NKJV

Is there anything more unexpected than the all-powerful, ever-constant Creator taking a break?

That's what the second chapter of Genesis tells us took place on the seventh day of creation. God finished His work with the creation of humankind. And on the seventh day, the Creator rested. He didn't rest because He was tired. The kind of resting He did was a cessation of work; it was a pattern He established for us from the very beginning—a day of rest in the week.

That in itself is intriguing. God lives outside of time and space. But He created time for us, for earth. And He confined Himself to the space of a twenty-four-hour day so that He could show us what kind of rest we should do.

Rest is a biblical theme from the beginning. We see it continued all throughout scripture. It is listed in the fourth commandment given to Moses. It was strictly observed in the nation of Israel, and in Jesus' day, it had become so important to the strict religious leaders that "resting" was almost tiresome with all the extra restrictions. God's intent, however, was that we should have a day to rejuvenate our minds and stop our work. Remember, He instituted a day of rest even before the fall of man and woman, before sin entered our world and twisted the way things work.

Jesus affirmed God's loving plan for rest when He said in Mark 2:27 that the "Sabbath was made for man." It is a gift, made for mankind's good. Hebrews 4 speaks of the importance of the concept of rest—both in a literal sense and in a spiritual, eternal sense.

So don't be surprised that God would rest! Delight in the fact that He provided this pattern for us, and plan it into your week. You can't imagine the rewards you'll get from it.

DEAR FATHER, I NEED REST, AND I THANK YOU FOR SHOWING ME THE WAY TO PUT THAT INTO MY WEEK. YOU GIVE US GOOD THINGS, AND A DAY OF REST IN THE WEEK IS ONE OF THOSE. HELP ME TO BE PURPOSEFUL IN KEEPING IT. IN JESUS' NAME, AMEN.

Impossible!

He did not weaken in faith when he considered his own body,
which was as good as dead (since he was about a hundred years
old), or when he considered the barrenness of Sarah's womb.
No unbelief made him waver concerning the promise of God,
but he grew strong in his faith as he gave glory to God, fully
convinced that God was able to do what he had promised.

ROMANS 4:19–21

You sit down to your morning coffee and paper and read these headlines: MAN SURVIVES THREE DAYS IN WHALE'S BELLY; LOCAL FISHERMAN WALKS ON WATER; ENTOMBED MAN RAISED TO LIFE; RED SEA SPLITS IN TWO; SACK LUNCH FEEDS THOUSANDS; BLIND SINCE BIRTH—NOW HE SEES! "Impossible!" you say. In most contexts, you'd be correct. But in the Bible, these are only some of the "impossible" things that occurred. Jonah survived being swallowed by a big fish. Peter walked on water briefly. Jesus brought Lazarus back to life after four days in a tomb. God's people crossed the Red Sea on dry ground. Five thousand people feasted on five loaves of bread and two fish. A little mud plus Jesus' touch equaled sight for a man born blind.

The account of Abraham and Sarah is another example of impossibilities happening. God promised Abraham that he would have a son and that, through Isaac, Abraham would become "the father of many nations" (Romans 4:18). One-hundred-year-old Abraham and ninety-year-old Sarah were hardly candidates for such a promise. Yet that's exactly what God promised and exactly what He fulfilled. The key was believing that *God* would do the impossible. "God was able to do. . . ," we read in Romans 4:21, and Abraham was "fully convinced" of that fact. Later, in Hebrews 11:11, we read that "by faith Sarah herself *received* power to conceive" (italics added). Without God in the picture, there would be no promise, let alone fulfillment. But with God at work, the impossible was indeed possible.

Whenever God leads you into the realm of the "impossible," remember: what would be impossible for us alone isn't with God at our side. The angel said to Mary, "Nothing will be impossible with God" (Luke 1:37). Jesus told a demon-possessed boy's father, "All things are possible for one who believes" (Mark 9:23). And speaking of the most impossible thing, the saving of ourselves, Jesus declared, "With man this is impossible, but with God all things are possible" (Matthew 19:26). The one who makes the promise is faithful (Hebrews 10:23), so let's believe in our hearts, even when our heads say, "Impossible!"

GOD, YOU KNOW WHAT I'M FACING, AND IT'S
IMPOSSIBLE! BUT ONLY WHEN I FACE IT ALONE.
WITH YOU, IT'S NO LONGER IMPOSSIBLE. AMEN.

What's Wrong?

Search me, O God, and know my heart: try me,
and know my thoughts: and see if there be any wicked
way in me, and lead me in the way everlasting.

PSALM 139:23–24 KJV

While each of us may be guilty of fishing for compliments at one time or another, few of us fish for criticism. We want the spotlight on our good side, not the bad. We generally put our best foot forward; we don't ask someone to identify our missteps. "Show me my faults!" is rarely the cry of our hearts. And it's certainly not something we'd relish from the God of the universe, the one who knows absolutely everything about us. Psalm 139 opens, "O LORD, you have searched me and known me! You know when I sit down and when I rise up; you discern my thoughts from afar. You search out my path and my lying down and are acquainted with all my ways. Even before a word is on my tongue, behold, O LORD, you know it altogether" (verses 1–4). If we ask God to tell us what's wrong, He's not going to miss one word, one action, one thought. Yet asking God to tell him what's wrong is precisely what David does. The psalm he begins by declaring God's omniscience, he ends by inviting God to reveal his faults. Why? Because David knew that hiding from God was futile and that God would reward a humble heart.

On the flip side, those with hearts closed to His instruction will find no place at His table. Jesus told the Pharisees, the religious elite who held tight to self-righteousness, "Those who are well have no need of a physician, but those who are sick. I came not to call the righteous, but sinners" (Mark 2:17). When we seek the Great Physician's care, asking Him to examine us, He will poke and prod and point out where sin still festers inside. It takes humility, and some guts, to open ourselves to God, to face the unpleasantness of our faults. James wrote, "Submit yourselves therefore to God. . . . Cleanse your hands, you sinners, and purify your hearts, you double-minded. Be wretched and mourn and weep. Let your laughter be turned to mourning and your joy to gloom" (James 4:7–9). Ugh. But don't overlook the results. "Humble yourselves before the Lord," James continued, "and he will exalt you" (verse 10).

When we approach the God of the universe and say, "Show me my faults!" He will show us favor (Proverbs 3:34).

SEARCH ME, GOD. SHOW ME WHERE I AM WRONG— AND WHERE YOU CAN MAKE ME RIGHT. AMEN.

Heavenly Friends

Do not forget to entertain strangers, for by so
doing some have unwittingly entertained angels.

HEBREWS 13:2 NKJV

It's been a favored theme of authors and screenwriters for centuries—the heavenly being who steps in to assist the beleaguered main character. From Dickens's Ghost of Marley to Frank Capra's Clarence in *It's a Wonderful Life*, angels have been a great addition to the plot. While not all of these angelic friends have traits that are authentically biblical, the Bible does remind us that sometimes strangers are really God's messengers. We are commanded by the inspired writer to show them hospitality.

Few of us imagine that we have made friends with an angel, but it seems to be possible. The way God works in our world is mysterious and known fully only to Him. There are times when it seems we see evidence of supernatural help or protection, and we've heard the stories of those who heard a voice or saw a hand pointing or in some other way were assisted by an otherworldly friend.

Most of the time, God uses what is already in place in our lives to work out His will. But occasionally we might be surprised if we realized just what was happening.

With the increasing lack of true biblical understanding and the growing reliance on personal interpretation as truth, people today often attribute unexplainable events to angels and even call diseased loved ones "my angel." However, we know that God's messengers only do things consistent with God's character and Word. Moreover, our dear departed do not become angelic but rather go either to a place of comfort or torment, depending on whether they accepted or rejected Christ when they were on earth. Still, we must acknowledge this verse that says that angels do show up at times on our earth.

I am not encouraging you to become mystic. But I am reminding you that God has His hosts ready at a second's notice if He wills to use them in your life. You are never out of His thoughts or His reach. Someday He might send a heavenly helper to aid you in a moment of crisis, and if He does, it will be Him working out His plan for you out of His love. No one is more present in our unexpected moments than our great God, who "makes his angels spirits, and his servants flames of fire" (Hebrews 1:7 NIV).

HEAVENLY FATHER, YOU ARE THE COMMANDER OF THE HOSTS OF HEAVEN. THANK YOU FOR SENDING THEM TO EARTH WHEN YOU HAVE A TASK FOR THEM TO COMPLETE. I MAY NEVER REALIZE I HAVE SEEN ONE OF THEM, BUT I KNOW I CAN TRUST YOU IF EVER I NEED THE ASSISTANCE OF A HEAVENLY FRIEND. AMEN.

Portrait of a Woman

Who can find a virtuous woman?
for her price is far above rubies.

PROVERBS 31:10 KJV

Proverbs 31:10 is the first verse of a poem written by a wife and mother. This model of womanhood might intimidate you or irritate you, but God can use these verses to shape us. If you've never read them (or haven't in a while), time to refresh your memory!

Who can find a virtuous woman? for her price is far above rubies. The heart of her husband doth safely trust in her, so that he shall have no need of spoil. She will do him good and not evil all the days of her life. She seeketh wool, and flax, and worketh willingly with her hands. She is like the merchants' ships; she bringeth her food from afar. She riseth also while it is yet night, and giveth meat to her household, and a portion to her maidens. She considereth a field, and buyeth it: with the fruit of her hands she planteth a vineyard. She girdeth her loins with strength, and strengtheneth her arms. She perceiveth that her merchandise is good: her candle goeth not out by night. She layeth her hands to the spindle, and her hands hold the distaff. She stretcheth out her hand to the poor; yea, she reacheth forth her hands to the needy. She is not afraid of the snow for her household: for all her household are clothed with scarlet. She maketh herself coverings of

tapestry; her clothing is silk and purple. . . . She maketh fine linen, and selleth it; and delivereth girdles unto the merchant. Strength and honour are her clothing; and she shall rejoice in time to come. She openeth her mouth with wisdom; and in her tongue is the law of kindness. She looketh well to the ways of her household, and eateth not the bread of idleness. Her children arise up, and call her blessed; her husband also, and he praiseth her. . . . Favour is deceitful, and beauty is vain: but a woman that feareth the LORD, she shall be praised. Give her of the fruit of her hands; and let her own works praise her in the gates.
(Proverbs 31:10–22, 24–28, 30–31 KJV)

What describes the Proverbs 31 woman? Words like *dependable*, *savvy*, *diligent*, *strong*, *openhanded*, *fearless*, *joyous*, and *caring*. Her crowning glory? Reverence for God. She is a woman of faith, which brings her praise. If you look, you can see aspects of her reflected back at you in the mirror. And as you seek God each day, you'll see her more and more.

GOD, PLEASE WORK IN ME SO THAT I HAVE
THE HEART OF A VIRTUOUS WOMAN. AMEN.

The Root of Worry

"And which of you by being anxious can
add a single hour to his span of life?"
MATTHEW 6:27

The rent is due, but your bank account is empty. You're waiting for the doctor's call. Your car breaks down miles from home. You've sent out dozens of résumés and still don't have a job. Your child is heading off to college. You watch footage of yet another disaster. Add worry to any of these situations and what do you get? Headaches, lost sleep, a frazzled mind, sapped joy. . .more worry. Worry just doesn't work. In the moment, worry feels constructive, but it's useless to bring about the positive outcome we hope for. Being anxious won't pay the rent or make the phone ring. Being anxious won't fix a flat or land you a job. Being anxious won't safeguard your child or save the world. As our Lord put it, "Which of you by being anxious can add a single hour to his span of life?"

Bottom line: worry is powerless—but our God is powerful. Near the beginning of His earthly ministry, Jesus called His twelve apostles, and as part of their marching orders, He warned them that they would encounter persecution. "I am sending you out as sheep in the midst of wolves," He said (Matthew 10:16). If ever words could cause anxiety, those could. But Jesus also told the apostles not to worry: "And do not fear those who kill the body but cannot kill the soul. . . . Are not two sparrows sold for a penny? And not one of them will fall to the ground apart from your Father. But even the hairs of your head are all numbered. Fear not, therefore; you are of more value than many sparrows" (Matthew 10:28–31). God controlled everything, even down to a tiny sparrow's death; He would certainly watch over His own.

When worry grips our lives, it's a sure sign of misplaced focus. We focus too much on ourselves and not enough on God. We forget all God can do for us and in us. Paul preceded his oft-quoted verse on worry—"Do not be anxious about anything, but in everything by prayer and supplication with thanksgiving let your requests be made known to God" (Philippians 4:6)—with five crucial words: "The Lord is at hand" (4:5). Because God is near, we do not need to be anxious. Because God is in control, we do not need to fear.

LORD, I CONFESS, I'M A WORRYWART.
FORGIVE ME. FORGIVE ME FOR TRYING TO TAKE
CONTROL OF WHAT ONLY YOU CAN CONTROL.
I LEAVE MY ANXIETY WITH YOU. AMEN.

Lights On!

"You are the light of the world. A city set on a hill cannot be hidden. Nor do people light a lamp and put it under a basket, but on a stand, and it gives light to all in the house. In the same way, let your light shine before others, so that they may see your good works and give glory to your Father who is in heaven."

MATTHEW 5:14–16

A child wakes up in the night. Shadows lurk around the room. Shapes loom in the darkness. But with the glow of a night-light, the shadows disperse, and the shapes transform into her sturdy dresser, her plush chair. A woman sits in a dark campsite. Every sound is amplified. It's as if a murky curtain surrounds her, blocking her sight. But with the light of a fire, she sees the canopy of majestic trees, branches rustling in the wind. Introduce light into darkness, and everything changes.

Before we knew Christ, we lived in spiritual darkness. We were blinded by sin and unable to see our way out. But God, "the Father of lights" (James 1:17), did not leave us in the dark. He called us, and He offered His light. In one of his letters to the Corinthians, Paul wrote, "For God, who said, 'Let light shine out of darkness,' has shone in our hearts to give the light of the knowledge of the glory of God in the face of Jesus Christ" (2 Corinthians 4:6). When God's light enters our hearts, when spiritual truth once veiled becomes visible, everything changes. God works a total transformation in us. Sinful to righteous. Old to new. Dark to light. "For at one time you were darkness, but now you are light in the Lord" (Ephesians 5:8).

Our role? "Walk as children of light (for the fruit of light is found in all that is good and right and true)" (Ephesians 5:8–9). God's enlightening produces fruit in us, and as our transformed lives reflect the good and the right and the true, others are drawn like moths. God uses our light to shed light, to "proclaim the excellencies of him who called [us] out of darkness into his marvelous light" (1 Peter 2:9).

Our world is a dark one, and the darkness often causes us to shrink back. Hiding our light—fitting in instead of standing out—is easy to do. But Jesus called believers "the light of the world," and then He told us to let the light shine. He held nothing back to bring us light. Let's shine for Him!

LORD, I WANT TO BE LIGHT IN DARKNESS,
SO BRIGHT THAT NO ONE MISSES YOU. AMEN.

A Fake Love

When the Lord saw that Leah was unloved, He opened her womb;
but Rachel was barren. So Leah conceived and bore a son, and
she called his name Reuben; for she said, "The Lord has surely
looked on my affliction. Now therefore, my husband will love me."

GENESIS 29:31–32 NKJV

When a woman marries, she expects to be happy. Usually. At least in our modern culture. But not so much in biblical times. Arranged marriages were the norm, and romantic feelings were not necessarily part of the equation. But girls knew that was the way things were. Still, they had anticipation of a ceremony and then a new home and babies someday.

So, imagine what Leah's wedding day was like. She was married incognito. The man in the ceremony thought she was her sister. And all the affection he showered on her and the sweet things he whispered to her that night were not really hers; they were sentiments for another woman. Can you comprehend how painful that was?

The Bible says that Leah had weak eyes (Genesis 29:17). Maybe she was nearsighted; maybe she was unattractive in some way. Whatever the reason, the verse goes on to say, "but Rachel was beautiful in form and appearance." Leah was the negative contrast to her lovely sister.

And after the wedding night, Jacob discovered that he had the wrong woman. "And in the morning, behold, it was Leah!" (Genesis 29:25). The wording of that verse doesn't sound like it was a welcome discovery. Think of the embarrassment that was for Leah, to see her new husband's eyes widen and his expression change from adoration to shock to maybe recoil. Probably Leah had no say in the deception; she had to follow the will of her father as the custom was. Maybe she was secretly glad that she was getting a desirable husband because her chances weren't good otherwise. Maybe she felt terrible that she was getting the man her sister was pining for. Maybe she hated every minute of a wedding that didn't really belong to her. We don't know.

We do know that she was unloved. The Bible says so. The unexpected pain in Leah's life was that she was used by others and not appreciated as herself. The scripture says that after she had borne her first child, she believed that her husband would love her.

I hope you haven't experienced that kind of pain. But our God sees the pain you do have, and He cares, just like He cared for Leah. I know He wants to help you bear up under the sadness you're carrying. You may not find acceptance and respect from others, but to your Creator, there is no person like you. Bring your story to Him, and you may be surprised by the love you find.

HEAVENLY FATHER, I'VE HAD UNWANTED NEGATIVE REACTIONS FROM OTHERS. I'M AFRAID TO TRUST, BUT I BRING MY STORY TO YOU AND ASK YOU TO HELP ME FIND MY BALANCE IN YOU. THANK YOU FOR LOVING ME. IN JESUS' NAME, AMEN.

Cradle to Grave

"Listen to me, O house of Jacob, all the remnant of the house of Israel, who have been borne by me from before your birth, carried from the womb; even to your old age I am he, and to gray hairs I will carry you. I have made, and I will bear; I will carry and will save."

ISAIAH 46:3–4

We begin getting older from the moment we are born. Up to a certain age, aging is a reason to celebrate. Babies receive joyous applause as they learn to crawl then walk. Children look forward to each birthday party. Teenagers count down the days till sweet sixteen. College students can't wait to head off to school and freedom! . . . But at what age does aging lose its luster? When our twenties (or thirties, or forties. . .) are past tense? When we spot that first gray hair? When our batteries run down faster than they charge up? When the kids we used to babysit have kids? When we're ma'am, not miss, to almost everybody? When our high school photos look dated? When we realize we're getting *older* and there's nothing we can do about it?

While there's nothing we can do to keep ourselves from aging—nothing we can do to stop the dates on the calendar from coming and going—there's still good news. God's care has no expiration date. As the Lord promised to Israel in Isaiah 46, He is the same God year in, year out. Just as He cared in the past, He will continue to care.

The psalmist who wrote Psalm 71 knew what it meant to rely on God's faithfulness even when confronted with this ugly kicker: passing time doesn't exempt us from troubles. Despite being older, the psalmist had enemies to deal with, enemies who sought his life (verse 10). Yet he remained confident of God's care. He knew God would stand by him no matter how old he was: "Even to old age and gray hairs, O God, do not forsake me. . . . Your righteousness, O God, reaches the high heavens. You who have done great things, O God, who is like you? You who have made me see many troubles and calamities will revive me again; from the depths of the earth you will bring me up again. You will increase my greatness and comfort me again" (verses 18–21).

No matter what your age, cling to God's promise: He will revive and comfort. He will carry and save.

GOD, SOMETIMES THE THOUGHT OF AGING
IS OVERWHELMING. SO I'LL THINK OF
YOUR PROMISES INSTEAD. AMEN.

Lives That Talk

*Many Samaritans from that town believed in him because of
the woman's testimony, "He told me all that I ever did."*

JOHN 4:39

God could never use me! Has that thought ever crossed your mind?
*My past is too complicated. My present is too frayed. My act just isn't
together.* If asked if God could use her, the Samaritan woman in
John's Gospel might have felt the same. She was an outcast with a
past. Would she ever have guessed that God would handpick her
for a special role in His kingdom work? That is, in fact, exactly
what He did.

We're introduced to the Samaritan woman on a journey from
Judea. Jesus and His disciples were on their way to Galilee, and
Jesus, tired from all the walking, sat down at a well. A woman
showed up toting her water jar, but the meeting was no accident.
John's statement that Jesus "had to pass through Samaria" (John
4:4) implies intention. Our Lord chose the road through Samaria
with a purpose, and it wasn't to save time, although that particular
route was a well-established shortcut. He was on a mission from
His Father that included this lone Samaritan woman. As with all
that God does, the timing was perfect. When the woman arrived,
Jesus was waiting. Immediately, He bucked expectations by asking
for some water. Here was a Samaritan woman with a bad reputa-
tion, and Jesus—a Jewish religious leader—speaks with her. No
cultural barrier and nothing from her past would prevent Him from

104

reaching out. Then, over the course of the conversation, He would confront the woman with her sin, discuss theological truth, offer living water, and reveal Himself as Messiah. Far from dismissing her, Jesus was calling her to Himself. The disciples, returning just in time to hear Jesus' declaration of who He was, "marveled" at what they witnessed (John 4:27). But God was not amazed or surprised. It was all part of His plan.

The one who was an outcast God wanted to use to spread His message. He took the ragged bits and began making them whole, and in response, the woman abandoned her water jar and rushed to town to boldly share her experience with those who, until then, had rejected her. So powerful was God's work in her that her testimony caused a domino effect as "many more" sought Jesus and believed (John 4:41).

God was only getting started using the Samaritan woman's life to inspire others. He's still using it some two thousand years later.

GOD, CAN YOU USE ME? MY LIFE SEEMS LIKE SUCH A MESS. BUT I FORGET THAT YOUR WORK WITHIN ME IS WHAT MAKES MY MESSY LIFE BEAUTIFUL. AMEN.

Great Expectations

Now unto him that is able to do exceeding abundantly above all that we ask or think, according to the power that worketh in us.

Ephesians 3:20 KJV

Are you an expecter? Expecting things comes naturally. When you go on vacation, you expect to have a good time. When you purchase something, you expect to get what you pay for. When your kids are running late, you expect them to let you know. When your friend wants to stop by for a visit, you expect her to call first. When your brother makes a promise, you expect him to follow through. Life is full of expectations. In fact, while whatever else we bring to a given situation may vary, we usually come with expectations—of what's going to happen, of how we're going to feel, of what someone else is going to do. . . We're glad when our expectations are met, but how do we respond when they're not? And what about our expectations of God?

Too often we have low expectations of God, and the fault stems from our humanity. We tend to frame what's possible using our human lens. What we pray for, what we expect to happen, is limited if we aren't viewing the situation from the perspective of our limitless God. God isn't just able to meet our expectations. He isn't just able to exceed them either. Ephesians 3:20 says He is able to do "exceeding abundantly" more. So how do we claim this truth for ourselves? To understand the how, backtrack a handful of verses to the beginning of Paul's prayer:

For this cause I bow my knees unto the Father of our Lord Jesus Christ, of whom the whole family in heaven and earth is named, that he would grant you, according to the riches of his glory, to be strengthened with might by his Spirit in the inner man; that Christ may dwell in your hearts by faith; that ye, being rooted and grounded in love, may be able to comprehend with all saints what is the breadth, and length, and depth, and height; and to know the love of Christ, which passeth knowledge, that ye might be filled with all the fulness of God. (Ephesians 3:14–19 KJV)

It all comes back to "the power that worketh *in us.*" If we are to know "exceeding abundantly" firsthand, self has to step aside and let God work. It's the Holy Spirit strengthening. It's Christ indwelling. It's God's love rooting. And as we are filled to the brim with God, His power overflows in us—far exceeding our expectations.

FATHER, FORGIVE MY LOW EXPECTATIONS.
YOU ARE ABLE TO DO EXCEEDINGLY ABUNDANTLY
MORE THAN I COULD EVER IMAGINE. AMEN.

The Prodigals We Love

*A foolish son is a grief to his father
and bitterness to her who bore him.*

PROVERBS 17:25

A popular saying goes that being a mother is like forever carrying your heart around outside your body. It's true. Mother's hearts are made of strong stuff—they have to be. They carry the burdens of their children and never give up. Yet they are also fragile enough to break when the child is rebellious and irresponsible.

One of the most painful, unexpected situations in our lives is the discovery that a child is in trouble through bad, maybe even sinful, life choices. In a moment of time, a son or daughter chooses a path that puts them in a life of regret for years to come—alcohol use, illegal drug consumption, pornography, rash loans, credit card debt, relocation, hasty marriage, sex outside marriage, rejection of faith, not attending church, body-altering procedures.

Some of these have an easier solution than others. Some of them are life scarring. Some have consequences that affect many others. The proverb writer had it right. A foolish child breaks his mother's heart. Why does this happen?

Remember that adult children are their own responsible party. Regardless of whom they would like to blame, ultimately they make their own life decisions. Only those severely mentally or emotionally impaired live off the decisions of others.

Remember that individual temperament can affect the disparity between the choices of one child and those of another. Some are born with rebel spirits. Thus the hard work of teaching submission must be done in the early years. But at times we fail to do so. And some children have such strong wills that God must finally bring them to a crisis to get them to surrender. "Those who will not learn must feel," goes the old saying.

And remember also that God specializes in bringing prodigals home. Don't give up hope on yours.

If you have a young child in your home right now, stay on the job and put into place the framework that will reap the rewards of good choices in the years to come.

FATHER IN HEAVEN, WORK IN THE HEART
OF MY "FOOLISH CHILD" TODAY. AWAKEN
MY CHILD TO THE TRUTH. HELP ME LOVE
AND HOPE AND TRUST IN YOU. AMEN.

What's the Plan?

The heart of man plans his way, but the Lord establishes his steps.

PROVERBS 16:9

Interviewer: *Where do you see yourself in five years?* Applicant: *In five years. . .* Although we may dread (or mentally roll our eyes at) this cookie-cutter interview question, it's a good one, really. Having plans or goals shows that we're motivated and forward-thinking. It reveals our priorities. Plus, knowing where we're headed helps us get there. But when, as Christians, we plan the next year or decade or beyond, we need to follow one simple rule: Don't leave God out of the equation.

Don't leave God out of the equation? Is it possible *to* leave Him out? He is almighty God, after all, the one of whom Isaiah wrote: "The Lord of hosts has sworn: 'As I have planned, so shall it be, and as I have purposed, so shall it stand. . . .' This is the purpose that is purposed concerning the whole earth, and this is the hand that is stretched out over all the nations. For the Lord of hosts has purposed, and who will annul it? His hand is stretched out, and who will turn it back?" (Isaiah 14:24, 26–27). On one level, we know God is in all things and controls all things. Yet how often do we act, perhaps unconsciously, as if we can run our lives without Him? Instead, we should take our cue from Jesus. When speaking to the crowd at Capernaum, Jesus said, "For I have come down from heaven, not to do my own will but the will of him who sent me" (John 6:38). Later, when the hour was drawing near for His crucifixion,

Jesus prayed, "My Father, if it be possible, let this cup pass from me; nevertheless, not as I will, but as you will" (Matthew 26:39). If Christ, who is one with God, bent His will to the Father's—even in the most bitter of circumstances—how much more should we?

The next time you make plans, keep these instructions in mind: "Come now, you who say, 'Today or tomorrow we will go into such and such a town and spend a year there and trade and make a profit'—yet you do not know what tomorrow will bring. . . . Instead you ought to say, 'If the Lord wills, we will live and do this or that' " (James 4:13–15). Place God first before the plan. Include Him in the process. You'll find that when you partner with God, you succeed (Proverbs 16:3).

FATHER, I HAVE SO MANY PLANS!
TODAY I HAND THEM OVER TO YOU.
MAY YOUR WILL BE DONE, NOT MINE. AMEN.

Powered by the Spirit

If we live by the Spirit, let us also keep in step with the Spirit.

GALATIANS 5:25

We see examples of it every day. Electricity makes a lightbulb burn. Wind makes a kite fly. Water makes a blade of grass green. Fire makes a marshmallow toast. Gasoline makes an engine run. One thing powers another. A similar phenomenon takes place in us as Christians. The Holy Spirit is our fuel—a high-octane fuel.

The Holy Spirit, being one with God, is powerful—so powerful that He raised Christ from the dead (Romans 8:11). As believers, we have access to the Holy Spirit from the moment of salvation when the Holy Spirit enters our beings. Paul explained in Ephesians, "In him you also, when you heard the word of truth, the gospel of your salvation, and believed in him, were sealed with the promised Holy Spirit" (Ephesians 1:13). The outgrowth of the indwelling Spirit is power (Acts 1:8). How much power? A mind-boggling amount. Zechariah's fifth vision is just one of many illustrations in the Bible of the power available to believers through the Spirit. Following the captivity in Babylon, Israel returned home and began rebuilding the temple, but the work stalled. Zechariah's vision functioned as reassurance to Zerubbabel, a civil leader, to keep on with the work because even what wasn't humanly possible was attainable when accomplished by the Spirit. The angel told Zechariah, "This is the word of the LORD to Zerubbabel: Not by might, nor by power, but by my Spirit, says the LORD of hosts. Who are you, O great mountain?

Before Zerubbabel you shall become a plain" (Zechariah 4:6–7).

The power that flattened mountains—or rebuilt temples—is our power too, to live a godly life. Without the Holy Spirit, we are susceptible to sin, all the "works of the flesh" listed in Galatians 5:19–21. But with the Spirit, we have supernatural power to overcome and a bounty of good fruit that He produces in our lives: "Walk by the Spirit, and you will not gratify the desires of the flesh. For the desires of the flesh are against the Spirit. . . . But the fruit of the Spirit is love, joy, peace, patience, kindness, goodness, faithfulness, gentleness, self-control" (Galatians 5:16–17, 22–23). Given these benefits, what stops us from tapping into our fuel source every day? The results are powerful when we spend time in the Word and on our knees, when we walk side by side with the Spirit.

HOLY SPIRIT, YOU ARE MY FUEL: YOU COUNSEL ME,
YOU FORTIFY ME, YOU COMFORT ME, YOU EMPOWER
ME. . . .FOR ALL YOU DO, I GIVE THANKS. AMEN.

Looking Ahead

"Remember not the former things, nor consider the things of old. Behold, I am doing a new thing; now it springs forth, do you not perceive it? I will make a way in the wilderness and rivers in the desert."

ISAIAH 43:18–19

"Remember when. . ." It's the familiar chorus that begins reminiscences. "Remember when we used to spend summers at the lake?" "Remember when we stayed up all night cramming for that exam?" "Remember when Dad got me a puppy for my birthday?" "Remember when we had that lemonade stand?" "Remember when we took those ski lessons?" Remembering old times can bring smiles among friends and family. In terms of our faith, remembering what's come before and what God has done can buoy us in rough waters. So why does the Lord tell His people to "remember not the former things, nor consider the things of old"?

God had a long history of delivering Israel in astonishing ways. Just think of the string of plagues followed by the grand finale of the Red Sea splitting in two that freed the nation from Egyptian rule. But as much as God wanted His people to remember His previous mighty acts, He also wanted them to know that He was not finished delivering them. "Therefore, behold, the days are coming, declares the LORD, when it shall no longer be said, 'As the LORD lives who brought up the people of Israel out of the land of Egypt,' but 'As the LORD lives who brought up the people of Israel out of the north country and out of all the countries where he had driven them' " (Jeremiah 16:14–15). If the Israelites thought God's deliverance from Egypt was something, it was nothing compared to God's deliverance from Babylon. And still greater things were yet on the horizon. When the Lord says, "Remember not the former things," it is because He is "doing a new thing"—ushering in Messiah and drawing Israel ever closer to ultimate restoration.

Looking back over your life, where have you seen God work mightily on your behalf? Where can you say, "Remember when God. . ."? Memories of God's faithfulness are beautiful blessings. Gain confidence from all God has done. Allow His track record to build up your faith. *But* don't stop looking forward. Keep your eyes trained on how God is working in you today. . .and tomorrow. Anticipate the "new thing" He is doing, because greater things are yet to come.

GOD, WHEN I SURVEY THE LIFE I'VE LIVED
SO FAR, I CAN SEE YOUR FINGERPRINTS
ALL OVER IT. REVEAL TO ME ALL THE NEW
THINGS YOU ARE DOING TOO. AMEN.

Wounds in the Body

I entreat Euodia and I entreat Syntyche to agree in the Lord.

PHILIPPIANS 4:2

The jokes about church "bosses" and conflict in the church are sadly often reflective of truth. Anywhere there is a group of people working together, there will be conflict. The question is, how will it be handled and resolved?

Unbelievers fight for their individual way and rights. The "natural man" is more concerned with winning than anything else. But Christians are called to a higher plane, a better way.

Jesus said, "By this all people will know that you are my disciples, if you have love for one another" (John 13:35).

What marks Christians is not the absence of conflict but the way in which we handle it. The love we have for one another is to outshine our desire to win. In fact, if the desire to have our own way is so dominant, we may need to seriously examine our surrender to the Spirit's control in our lives.

In his letter to the Philippian church, the apostle Paul urged two Christian women to reconcile in the name of Jesus. Any disagreement we have cannot be more important than our ties as sisters in God's family. That is an eternal bond. The things we debate and champion down here will mostly fade away when this earth is dissolved with fervent heat (2 Peter 3:12). But the kingdom of God and the work we do for Him will last.

Perhaps you have been surprised by wounds you received in

church, in the place that was supposed to be safe, in the environment where you thought everyone would always agree. Remember that people in the family of God are still works in progress but that Christ never condones unkindness or grudges. Remember that what is most important is how we handle conflict. And remember that love heals wounds.

FATHER GOD, YOUR CHURCH, YOUR BODY, SOMETIMES EXPERIENCES DIVISIONS. JESUS PRAYED FOR BELIEVERS TO BE UNIFIED IN THEIR LOVE FOR YOU AND FOR EACH OTHER. HELP ME TO BE PART OF THE SOLUTION. AND LET ME RESPOND WITH KINDNESS WHEN I RECEIVE UNEXPECTED WOUNDS. IN JESUS' NAME, AMEN.

A Piece of Advice

Keep me from looking at worthless things.
Let me live by your word.
PSALM 119:37 NCV

You can find advice around every corner, it seems. From billboards to magazines to the internet to your aunt Louise, there's no shortage of sources if you want to learn the "secret" of living well. Want to be happier? There's a top-ten list of tips to try. Want to reboot your mind, body, or spirit? There's an array of diet plans to follow. Want to succeed? There's a successful person's book that will tell you how. Want to breathe better? Yes, there's a book on that too. While much of this advice can be helpful, it shouldn't be the Christian's first resort. If we want to find life—thriving, abundant life—we need to go to the source.

God is our source of life, and He has given us His Word as the source of wisdom on living well. Shortly before Moses' death and before the people entered Canaan, Moses reminded Israel of all God had told him throughout the years in the wilderness. Some of his final advice was "Take to heart all the words I have solemnly declared to you this day, so that you may command your children to obey carefully all the words of this law. *They are not just idle words for you—they are your life.* By them you will live long in the land you are crossing the Jordan to possess" (Deuteronomy 32:46–47 NIV, italics added). God's words to His people were not hollow; they were essential to living the life of fullness God desired for them.

The nation was to cling to God's law as if its life depended on it, which, of course, it did.

Believers today receive life—that is, eternal life to come in heaven—through believing in the Word, Jesus Christ; and they also receive life—spiritual nourishment and growth—through ingesting God's Word, the Bible. When the devil tempted Jesus, he first used Jesus' hunger. After forty days and nights without eating, Jesus was hungry (Matthew 4:2), but He had a means of subsistence that was even more valuable than physical food. He said, "It is written, 'Man shall not live by bread alone, but by every word that comes from the mouth of God' " (Matthew 4:4). God's Word is a powerful resource in our lives. Now, just as in the psalmist's day, our prayer should be to have eyes turned from the world and focused on the Word. Our life depends on it.

LORD, WHEN MY LIFE IS A JUMBLE OF
SELF-IMPROVEMENT, SHIFT MY ATTENTION
BACK TO YOUR WORD. AMEN.

Running to Win

Therefore, since we are surrounded by so great a cloud of witnesses, let us also lay aside every weight, and sin which clings so closely, and let us run with endurance the race that is set before us, looking to Jesus, the founder and perfecter of our faith.

HEBREWS 12:1–2

The runner took her mark as the crowd of curious spectators watched. Decked in clunky, loosely tied boots, baggy pants, and dangling jewelry, she looked like a running disaster waiting to happen. Either she'd trip on her laces or she'd catch her arm in her necklace. Even if she managed to escape those perils, the excess material of her pants would surely slow her down. She needed to get ready for the race. The author of Hebrews used a race as a metaphor for entering and pursuing the Christian life. Athletes in ancient times would remove any unnecessary garments before competing. With no extra weight and with nothing to trip them, they could run to win. Applying the metaphor to our lives, we too need to get ready for the race.

The Christian "race" is no easy sprint down the track. Our Lord guarantees tribulation (John 16:33), and the apostles' lives certainly reflected that troubles are a fact of the Christian life. Paul wrote the Corinthians, "For we do not want you to be unaware, brothers, of the affliction we experienced in Asia. For we were so utterly burdened beyond our strength that we despaired of life itself" (2 Corinthians 1:8). Each of us knows from our own experience that temptation and trials are inevitable. The Christian race, then, is more of a cross-country, long-distance obstacle course. So how do we prepare?

One way is by drawing inspiration from "the cloud of witnesses" mentioned in Hebrews; the Bible is filled with examples of faithful men and women whose lives pump us up to keep going. Another way we prepare is by ridding our lives of anything that hinders us. What distracts us from the race? What slows us down? What sins do we cling to that will only cause us to stumble? By letting these go, we're running to win. "Do you not know that in a race all the runners run, but only one receives the prize?" Paul wrote. "So run that you may obtain it. Every athlete exercises self-control in all things. They do it to receive a perishable wreath, but we an imperishable" (1 Corinthians 9:24–25). We're running an imperfect race right now, but Jesus—the perfecter of our faith—will bring us across the finish line to receive an imperishable prize.

LORD, PLEASE HELP ME RUN
THIS RACE TO WIN. AMEN.

"I Don't Understand!"

As you do not know the way the spirit comes to the bones in the womb of a woman with child, so you do not know the work of God who makes everything.

ECCLESIASTES 11:5

Some things we humans just can't explain. As much as science has advanced, God's creation is greater still. Even things we can explain are amazingly intricate. Think about all that has to happen for you to read these words—how the eyes work with the brain to make sense of marks on a page. Wise King Solomon—whom God gifted with "wisdom and understanding beyond measure, and breadth of mind like the sand on the seashore" (1 Kings 4:29)—recognized that there is a limit to what God's children are able to understand about His creation and, by extension, how He works, and Solomon shared his insight with us in Ecclesiastes 11:5. Just as we don't fully comprehend how a baby grows in the womb, we don't comprehend how God works. Or, using the footnoted wording of the verse, just as we "do not know the way of the wind," we do not know God's ways.

Is God working in your life in a way that you don't understand? Maybe you've been running in circles and wish things would straighten out. Maybe you've lost a loved one. Maybe you've received an unwanted medical diagnosis. Maybe a relationship or your job or your bank account is giving you a headache. Maybe you've stepped out on a limb for God and think you hear a crack.

Your heart cries out, *What's going on here, Lord?* Things aren't always so clear on the front line of life. We can't always make sense of what seems senseless. In the moments when we lack clarity, though, we can rest in God's omniscience. He declares, "For as the heavens are higher than the earth, so are my ways higher than your ways and my thoughts than your thoughts" (Isaiah 55:9). We may not be able to understand the how and why of what's happening, but God is able. What's more, He is in control and working for our good (Romans 8:28).

There's something else we can rest in, something else that's beyond human understanding: God's love. Paul prayed that believers would begin to understand through the Spirit "what is the width and length and depth and height—to know the love of Christ which passes knowledge" (Ephesians 3:18–19 NKJV). Yes, God works in ways we humans just can't explain, but He also loves us more than we'll ever know.

GOD, I DON'T UNDERSTAND ALL
THAT'S HAPPENING IN MY LIFE,
BUT I'LL REST IN YOU. AMEN.

Loneliness Turned to Laughter

You have turned for me my mourning into dancing;
you have loosed my sackcloth and clothed me with gladness.

PSALM 30:11

Loneliness isn't usually a setting for laughter. When we think of laughter, we think of happy gatherings with friends and food and fun; we imagine sharing lighthearted moments with those whose company we enjoy.

The man who wrote Psalm 102 knew what it was to be lonely. "I am like a desert owl of the wilderness, like an owl of the waste places; I lie awake; I am like a lonely sparrow on the housetop" (verses 6–7). He used vivid imagery to describe his feelings—an owl in waste places and a lonely sparrow on the housetop. These are not the descriptions of a joyful person. And certainly not the setting in which we expect to find laughter.

Can one laugh alone?

Actually, yes, if you have something to laugh about. Psalm 30, written by David, was used for the dedication of the temple. He exulted about the things the Lord had done for him, how God had come through for him time after time. He praised Him for His mighty deeds and great power.

These are things we can be joyful about even when alone. Celebrating the triumphs of our God is always appropriate—alone or with others. And it can include laughter. The book of Exodus records how Moses and Aaron's sister, Miriam, led the Israelites in a joyous celebration after the Lord brought them through the Red Sea. "Then Miriam the prophetess, the sister of Aaron, took a tambourine in her hand, and all the women went out after her with tambourines and dancing. And Miriam sang to them: 'Sing to the LORD, for he has triumphed gloriously; the horse and his rider he has thrown into the sea' " (Exodus 15:20–21).

Our God specializes in turning the negative into positive. If we focus on Him and His power, we can be surprised by the joy He brings to our hearts and the life we feel in our spirits. Circumstances may be the same, but the awareness of our faith in the one who is ever present and all-powerful makes all the difference in the world.

JEHOVAH GOD, YOU ARE THE GREAT ONE. YOU SEE ME IN MY ALONENESS. YOU HAVE RESCUED ME IN THE PAST. YOU WILL DO IT AGAIN. I TRUST YOU, AND I CHOOSE TO LAUGH ALOUD BECAUSE OF THE VICTORY I KNOW I HAVE IN YOU. AMEN.

Cause for Boasting

But he said to me, "My grace is sufficient for you, for
my power is made perfect in weakness." Therefore
I will boast all the more gladly of my weaknesses,
so that the power of Christ may rest upon me.

2 CORINTHIANS 12:9

Why would anyone boast in weakness? To boast is "to puff one-self up,"** after all. Our boasting goes hand in hand with our pride. We use it to show off our strengths. We don't generally drag our weaknesses into the spotlight and gush over them. They don't puff us up. So why is Paul, in his letter to the Corinthians, so glad when he's weak? Perspective is the key.

At the time Paul was writing, he was concerned about the church at Corinth. False apostles were discrediting him and undermining the Corinthians' faith by preaching a false gospel. Hoping to put an end to the threat, Paul first defended his ministry (2 Corinthians 10), and then he used the false apostles' boasting against them. What, he sarcastically questioned, could any of them boast about that he could not outdo? He was a Hebrew, a descendant of Abraham, a servant of Christ, and a better one at that, because his track record far surpassed their own (2 Corinthians 11:16–29). Yet Paul knew that such boasting was foolishness. The root of the false apostles' boasting was self; they wanted to show off what made them look good. Paul flipped this reason for boasting on its head and instead boasted in what made him look weak—like the time he made a grand escape. . .in a basket lowered through a window (2 Corinthians 11:32–33). Why the switch? The false apostles' boasting said "Look at me!" Paul's boasting said "Look at Him!" The times he was weakest pointed directly to the one who gave strength. "For the sake of Christ, then, I am content with weaknesses, insults, hardships, persecutions, and calamities," Paul wrote. "For when I am weak, then I am strong" (2 Corinthians 12:10).

Paul's view of weakness wasn't limited to its downside. The weakness itself wasn't enjoyable, but Paul saw the potential for God's power to work through him in his weakness. God told Paul, and He tells us today, that His power "is made perfect in weakness." The weaker we are, the more plainly we see how powerful God is to use even our weaknesses to His glory. Our God is mighty, and that's a reason to boast.

GOD, I HATE BEING WEAK. BUT WHEN I FEEL LITTLE, I'M REMINDED OF JUST HOW BIG YOU ARE. USE MY WEAKNESSES TO SHOW OFF YOUR STRENGTH. AMEN.

*Merriam-Webster's Collegiate Dictionary, 11th ed. (2014), s.v. "boast."

The Long Way Around

When Pharaoh let the people go, God did not lead them by
way of the land of the Philistines, although that was near.
For God said, "Lest the people change their minds when
they see war and return to Egypt." But God led the people
around by the way of the wilderness toward the Red Sea.

EXODUS 13:17–18

He called it "taking the scenic route." Wherever they were headed, the quickest way from point A to point B was not the way they went. Instead, they took back roads and made frequent stops. When the girl was young, she didn't understand what went through her father's head as he mapped out their course. Why not arrive at their destination faster? Why the delay? But as the years passed, she grew to treasure the trip. Every byway. Each roadside stand. Flat tires and all. She learned from her father as she traveled by his side. She formed memories that accompanied her no matter where life led next.

The Israelites probably didn't consider their forty-year journey through the wilderness "the scenic route." It was long, monotonous, difficult. Why not arrive at the Promised Land faster? Why the delay? While we'll never understand all that goes through God's mind (1 Corinthians 2:11), He reveals glimpses into the wisdom of His ways through the Bible. The seemingly roundabout journey to Canaan had purpose. One purpose was to ready God's people for their new lives in the land He had promised; the wilderness was a training ground in obedience and trust, among other things. Another purpose was to ensure that Israel reached their destination. The shorter route was shorter, yes; but it was also riskier. One encounter with the Philistines, and the people would have been tempted to turn back. God was preparing a place for His people, and He would make sure they got there (Exodus 23:20).

The line between where we start and where we end up in any stage of our lives isn't always the shortest. Sometimes God takes us the roundabout way. We may wish we'd reach wherever we're headed faster. We may not even know where we're going. But once the journey is over, what a joy to look back and see God's mastery and care in action. Every road traveled, each experience, trials and all, has purpose. Even on the most winding path, we can have faith that God has a destination in mind, and He will make sure we get there.

GOD, JUST THINKING ABOUT THE PAST FEW YEARS, I'M AMAZED BY HOW YOU GOT ME FROM WHERE I WAS TO WHERE I AM. THANK YOU FOR THE MASTERFUL WAY YOU GUIDE ME. AMEN.

Good Question

The angel of the LORD found her by a spring of water
in the wilderness, the spring on the way to Shur.
And he said, "Hagar, servant of Sarai, where have
you come from and where are you going?"
GENESIS 16:7–8

The child stomps to her room, propelled by huffs of displeasure and indignation. Once there, she stuffs her small suitcase with the essentials: her pajamas, her collection of seashells, her stuffed ostrich, and her stash of candy. She enters the kitchen, head held high, and declares to her mother, "I'm running away!" Maybe you starred in your own version of this scenario when you were young, or maybe you've seen it played out on TV so many times that it makes your eyes roll. Either way, most of us can identify with the child. When life chucks something at us that we're not ready—or don't want—to handle, running away seems like a pretty good option.

Hagar ran away too, but her problem was more serious than the fictitious child's. God had promised Abram and Sarai a son. Ten years later, there still was no son, so Sarai devised her own plan to fulfill God's promise. She offered her servant, Hagar, to her husband. All went according to plan; Hagar became pregnant. But what Sarai did not anticipate was Hagar's response: Hagar looked down on her. The situation continued to devolve as Sarai confronted Abram, and Abram told Sarai to do as she wished with Hagar. Sarai used this freedom to mistreat Hagar so harshly that Hagar fled.

Here's where the angel of the Lord comes in. He appeared and, rather than immediately commanding Hagar to return to her mistress, asked her a question: "Where have you come from and where are you going?" In the middle of her emotions and an unbearable set of circumstances, Hagar had seen running as the best option. God asked her to pause and think it over. Of course, He already knew the answer. He knew where she had come from— and He knew where she was going. God had plans for Hagar, and He wouldn't let her stray too far from them. He saw her in the wilderness and lovingly guided her in the right direction. Hagar's response: "So she called the name of the LORD who spoke to her, 'You are a God of seeing,' for she said, 'Truly here I have seen him who looks after me' " (Genesis 16:13).

Is God asking you to pause and listen for His direction?

LORD, LATELY I'VE BEEN ON THE RUN, BUT YOU AREN'T THROUGH WITH YOUR PLANS FOR ME. I'M PAUSING NOW TO HEAR FROM YOU. . . .

Focus!

Set your minds on things that are above,
not on things that are on earth.

COLOSSIANS 3:2

Her limbs trembled like wind-ruffled leaves on a tree. Her hands were damp clamps gripping the ropes, trying both to anchor herself and to squeeze out the fear. *Stop being so silly*, she thought. *It's only a rope bridge.* But she couldn't get over how far apart the boards were, and how old the ropes looked, and how the bridge swayed with each gust of wind. Then she looked down. *Yeah, right.* The river seemed miles below. Just as she was about to turn on her heels and retreat, she heard her friend's voice: "Don't look down. Keep your eyes focused on the end of the bridge and take it one step at a time."

Having a focal point is helpful if not crucial. Peter, for one, could attest to that. When he saw Jesus walking on the water, he asked to join Him, and with his eyes locked on Jesus, Peter did the impossible. Once he looked away, however, he saw the wind, his faith faltered, and he began to sink (Matthew 14:28–30). While we don't walk on water a whole lot, having a focal point in our Christian lives is still essential. Paul advised believers, "Set your minds on things that are above, not on things that are on earth." Why? Because Paul saw firsthand the destruction that focusing on earthly things would cause. If, instead, believers followed the example of those who pursued Christlikeness and focused on heaven, they could anticipate glorious results: "Join in imitating me, and keep your eyes on those who walk according to the example you have in us. For many, of whom I have often told you and now tell you even with tears, walk as enemies of the cross of Christ. Their end is destruction, their god is their belly, and they glory in their shame, with minds set on earthly things. But our citizenship is in heaven, and from it we await a Savior, the Lord Jesus Christ, who will transform our lowly body to be like his glorious body" (Philippians 3:17–21).

In heaven, we'll be transformed, perfected. Until then, we strive to model our Savior as best we can. The earth will always be full of distractions and pitfalls, but with minds focused on "things that are above," we are filled with God's power that shapes us as His daughters day by day. Don't look down. Keep your eyes focused on heaven.

LORD, WHEN I TAKE MY EYES OFF YOU,
I FALTER. SO WHY DO I LET MYSELF LOSE
FOCUS SO EASILY? PLEASE HELP ME SET
MY MIND ON THINGS ABOVE. AMEN.

Laughing with Joy

When the Lord saw her, He had compassion on her and said to her, "Do not weep." Then He came and touched the open coffin, and those who carried him stood still. And He said, "Young man, I say to you, arise." So he who was dead sat up and began to speak. And He presented him to his mother.

LUKE 7:13–15 NKJV

When someone dies unexpectedly, it often feels surreal that he or she is really gone, especially if the person was young and healthy. You'll have moments when you have to remind yourself of the grim reality because it seems like a horrible nightmare from which you will surely awaken. It must have been so for the mother of this man in Luke 7. He was her only son, her pride and joy, as well as her security in her old age. She was a widow, and now no one was left for her.

Have you been there? Maybe at a funeral or maybe in a cemetery of extinct hopes, a place where there is no life, no future. You watched your tomorrows pass before you on a funeral bier. There are all kinds of deaths and all kinds of loss. Yours may feel as agonizing to you as the widow's was to her.

Someone has said that Jesus disrupted all the funerals He ever attended. What a happy fact! As He and His disciples approached the city gate, the funeral procession was leaving. This was common enough. But Jesus was touched by the mother's grief. Perhaps He thought of His mother and His approaching death. Maybe there was some particular characteristic about this death or this mother that moved Him. We do know that Jesus was always filled with compassion for the people around Him, the suffering ones, the sinful ones, the separated ones.

I can imagine Jesus laying a gentle hand on the woman's shoulder as He said, "Don't cry." Maybe she looked up at Him and wondered why He would say that. Then He walked to the coffin, touched it, and spoke to the dead man. And the man sat up and began to talk. I wonder what he said!

I am always thrilled that Jesus speaks to those who are dead as though they can hear. They can. His voice penetrates even the veil of death, and life springs forth when He calls. Imagine the joy, the laughter of that mother and her son, as they walked back home together. Together!

You may be grieving today. Jesus is passing by. Let Him speak comfort to your sorrow and life to your loss. Watch Him work, and hear the laughter as you join the procession that isn't going to the cemetery now!

DEAR LORD JESUS, YOU ARE LIFE AND PEACE.
I BRING TO YOU THE DEAD HOPES OF
MY LIFE AND ASK YOU TO REVIVE MY
SPIRIT WITH YOUR POWER. AMEN.

Our Defense

Submit yourselves therefore to God. Resist the devil, and he will flee from you. Draw near to God, and he will draw near to you.
JAMES 4:7–8

Peter did not mince words when he warned believers about a danger of the Christian life: "Be sober-minded; be watchful. Your adversary the devil prowls around like a roaring lion, seeking someone to devour" (1 Peter 5:8). Paul too wrote in strong terms of the opposition confronting believers: "For we do not wrestle against flesh and blood, but against the rulers, against the authorities, against the cosmic powers over this present darkness, against the spiritual forces of evil in the heavenly places" (Ephesians 6:12). *Okay then.* Like it or not, we're at war—in a spiritual battle. There's a reason Satan and his forces are called the enemy. His goal is to see us defeated.

Not coincidentally, we often feel the devil strike the hardest when we are doing our best to live a godly life. If a person is already straying from God, she's right where the devil wants her. But when she's walking God's way? The devil aims to slow her down, detour her, or stop her in her tracks. Sometimes it seems as if making a decision to follow God more closely opens the door for an all-out assault as the devil tries to undermine our efforts.

One of his tactics is to convince us through lies that God is not present. Maybe you've heard some of them: "Still waiting on an answer to that prayer? That's because God isn't listening"; "All

the 'bad' in your life right now just proves that God doesn't care";
"Why would God bother to do anything for *you*?" Lies, every last
one. So how do we fight them?

Our defense against any and all of Satan's tactics comes from
almighty God: "Be strong in the Lord and in the strength of his
might. Put on the whole armor of God, that you may be able to
stand against the schemes of the devil" (Ephesians 6:10–11). Daily
we put on God's armor. Daily we resist the devil. Daily, even hourly,
we choose to say, "I trust in God." If you think you're not up to the
fight, remember, the one who is in us is far greater than the devil
(1 John 4:4). God is with us each time we face the enemy, each time
we say, "I trust in You." When we place ourselves in God's hands,
taking a stand against the devil, the devil has no choice but to run.

FATHER, I'M AFRAID OF THE BATTLE, BUT YOUR
WORD ENCOURAGES ME. WITH YOU AS MY DEFENSE,
I DON'T HAVE TO FIGHT THE DEVIL ALONE. AMEN.

Even That One

He is the propitiation for our sins, and not for ours
only but also for the sins of the whole world.

1 JOHN 2:2

The dishcloth had been in commission for years. After rinsing the last of a sink full of pots and pans, the woman looked down at the grimy, soppy, ratty piece of cloth. To wash or to toss? Into the trash can it went; it was beyond redemption. Sin can make us feel like that dishrag at times. Whether because of sin that caught us unawares or a temptation we've struggled with over and over, we may wonder if we're beyond redemption. Surely God won't forgive *this one*.

Where does this type of thinking come from? It begins with an inflated view of ourselves and a deficient view of Christ's sacrifice. To think that we were slightly more redeemable before one sin or another is to give ourselves credit we don't deserve. To think that Christ's death covers some sin but not all is to limit His righteousness. In reality, we all fall short of God's holy standard (Romans 3:23), and to fall short by even the slightest margin makes us unworthy of heaven. But Jesus' death is sufficient to save everyone, completely: "For Christ also died for sins once for all, the just for the unjust, so that He might bring us to God" (1 Peter 3:18 NASB).

Still not convinced? Consider these words from Paul: "We ourselves were once foolish, disobedient, led astray, slaves to various passions and pleasures. . . . But when the goodness and loving kindness of God our Savior appeared, he saved us, not because of works done by us in righteousness, but according to his own mercy, by the washing of regeneration and renewal of the Holy Spirit, whom he poured out on us richly through Jesus Christ our Savior" (Titus 3:3–6). God, in a gesture that displayed His vast love for us when we were far from worthy, reached down and offered salvation. He offered to remove our sin—to wash us, renew us—through the righteousness of His Son. We were never too grimy, soppy, or ratty for God to make us clean and whole.

We're still not. God's forgiveness is always available. "If we confess our sins," says 1 John 1:9 (KJV, italics added), "he is faithful and just to forgive us our sins, and to cleanse us from *all* unrighteousness." God is faithful to forgive. . .even that one.

GOD, I'VE SINNED. RIGHT NOW I FEEL SO
UNDESERVING OF YOUR FORGIVENESS.
BUT I KNOW I AM YOUR CHILD; CHRIST'S
RIGHTEOUSNESS IS MY OWN. FORGIVE THIS
SIN. PLEASE WASH ME CLEAN AGAIN. AMEN.

You 2.0

Therefore we do not lose heart. Though outwardly we are
wasting away, yet inwardly we are being renewed day by
day. For our light and momentary troubles are achieving
for us an eternal glory that far outweighs them all.

2 CORINTHIANS 4:16–17 NIV

Nothing lasts forever, it's true; and our earthly bodies are no exception. They are prone to illness and injury. Joints stiffen, skin wrinkles, hair grays, muscles weaken with age. The troubles that go along with living bruise us time and again. But as Paul told the Corinthians, don't lose heart. As Christians, we know this body—this life—is not the end. We don't have a handful of years on earth and then nothing. We look forward to an eternity of years in heaven.

Although these physical bodies—the flesh and blood and bones that make us human—are only temporary, God still cares about them. Jesus, who experienced all the frailties of a human body, has compassion for us, and He often healed physical ailments as part of His earthly ministry. Yet the physical healing was just the beginning and a symbol of something greater. Matthew wrote of Jesus' healing, "This was to fulfill what was spoken by the prophet Isaiah: 'He took our illnesses and bore our diseases' " (Matthew 8:17). Jesus' death allowed us to be healed body *and* soul. "He was pierced for our transgressions; he was crushed for our iniquities; upon him was the chastisement that brought us peace, and with his wounds we are healed" (Isaiah 53:5). Because of Jesus, we have a cure for the sickness inside—the invisible disease called sin that leads to death—and the promise of perfected bodies in heaven, where both sin and sickness will be eradicated.

Paul had more to tell the Corinthians: "In this [tent, our physical body] we groan, earnestly desiring to be clothed with our habitation which is from heaven. . . . For we who are in this tent groan, being burdened, not because we want to be unclothed, but further clothed, that mortality may be swallowed up by life. Now He who has prepared us for this very thing is God, who also has given us the Spirit as a guarantee. So we are always confident" (2 Corinthians 5:2, 4–6 NKJV).

For now we have these bodies to deal with—the outer self and its wasting away. But we don't lose heart. God is renewing our inner self. Through this life He is preparing us for something greater.

LORD, THANK YOU FOR CARING ABOUT THE WHOLE ME. WHEN I'M HURTING PHYSICALLY, YOU HEAR MY PRAYERS TO HEAL THIS BODY OF MINE. BUT FAR BETTER THAN THAT—YOU HAVE ALREADY HEALED MY SOUL. AMEN.

Laughing in the
Human Moments

Then our mouth was filled with laughter,
and our tongue with shouts of joy.

PSALM 126:2

I don't like to laugh at myself. It's one of my worst flaws. I love the strong sense of self people possess who can do it, but it's something I'm still working on.

Perhaps it's hard to laugh at ourselves because it makes us feel foolish for doing something laughable. Goofs always seem to look worse on us than on others.

We often comment on our "humanness." It certainly is a reason for our errors in judgment, social skills, and sometimes just blind spots. But it is also the lovable part of us.

When we unexpectedly commit a faux pas, we indicate that we are part of the human race, not something extraordinary, not someone above everyone else, but just normal like the rest of the folks around us. There is something warming about that.

Personally, I think Jesus had a sense of humor and liked to laugh. Now, He never sinned in any way and He had perfect judgment, but I wonder if He laughed at the little things that happened around Him. I think He and His disciples had relaxing, enjoyable moments as they traveled and camped together and ministered together. When a group of people live in close proximity for any length of time, funny things happen. And there is opportunity for pranks and banter. I don't know that Jesus ever had a need to laugh at Himself, but He certainly identified with the humanity in us that needs light moments from time to time.

Some of my most embarrassing moments have been the result of my words coming out wrong or an error in spatial judgment causing me to bump into something or fall. At such times, others find their mouths filled with laughter as the verse says, but I am more likely to feel my face burning with humiliation.

The delicate balance is learning to laugh at our humanness and yet not guffaw the loudest at the gaffe of a friend. Today you may have the opportunity to practice this. Do it well.

LORD, THANK YOU FOR LAUGHTER AND FOR THE COMMON HUMAN BOND I SHARE WITH THOSE AROUND ME. HELP ME TO BE MATURE ENOUGH TO SMILE AT MY OWN GOOFS AND YET GIVE GRACE TO THOSE OF PEOPLE IN MY LIFE. AMEN.

"Tell Me What to Say"

*"Do not be anxious beforehand what you are to
say, but say whatever is given you in that hour,
for it is not you who speak, but the Holy Spirit."*

MARK 13:11

At a loss for words. Have you ever been there? A situation is so surprising, overwhelming, or intimidating that when you open your mouth, all you can manage is silence?

The disciples likely could imagine a time when they wouldn't know what to say. Peter, James, John, and Andrew were on the Mount of Olives with Jesus, and Jesus had just foretold the destruction of the temple. In response, the disciples asked about the end times. What Jesus divulged would make even the bravest believer tremble in his sandals. Jesus spoke of false prophets, wars, earthquakes, famines, pestilences, and terrors (Matthew 24:4–8; Mark 13:5–8; Luke 21:8–11). On top of all that, there would be persecution. Believers would be abused and brought before religious and government leaders to bear witness (Mark 13:9; Luke 21:12–13). A blank mind—or, at the very least, doubt about the adequacy of their response—would be natural under the circumstances. Knowing that His words would cause concern, Jesus paired them with some instructions and a promise. Jesus told believers not to be anxious about what to say. Why? Because the Holy Spirt would speak through them. Again in Luke, Jesus said, "Settle it therefore in your minds not to meditate beforehand how to answer, for I will give you a mouth and wisdom, which none of your adversaries will be able to withstand or contradict" (Luke 21:14–15).

Jesus' assurance of divine assistance might have reminded the disciples of another incident from generations past. When God commissioned Moses to lead Israel out of Egypt, Moses had a number of excuses why he wasn't fit for the job, the fourth being that his lack of eloquence would fail to convince Pharaoh of anything. God's response nixed that argument: "Who has made man's mouth? . . . Is it not I, the LORD? Now therefore go, and I will be with your mouth and teach you what you shall speak" (Exodus 4:11–12).

Even if we don't face a pharaoh or the persecution Jesus spoke about, we still may worry that we'll be at a loss for words when it matters. What about defending our faith when others mock us? What about sharing the gospel with a dear friend? In those times, we have the Holy Spirit to help us find just the right words.

GOD, I WORRY THAT I WON'T KNOW WHAT
TO SAY ABOUT MY FAITH IF I'M PUT ON
THE SPOT. PLEASE REASSURE ME OF YOUR
PRESENCE AND POWER. AMEN.

Choose Your God

And Elijah came near to all the people and said, "How long will you go limping between two different opinions? If the LORD is God, follow him; but if Baal, then follow him."

1 KINGS 18:21

A carved wooden figure. An altar dedicated to a god of harvest, or fertility, or rain. . . That's what we think of as idols, right? We might even skim over the Bible's passages on idolatry and say, "Not for me!" Those passages were full of truth and relevance in Old Testament times, we don't doubt, but today? Not so much. Yet Israel's struggle isn't so far removed from our own.

Israel was on dangerous ground. Although they had not rejected God completely, as Baalism spread, God's people began combining worship of the Lord with worship of Baal. Enter Elijah. God sent the prophet to challenge Baalism, to warn Israel that they could not continue "limping between" two choices. Almighty God would not accept a part-time place on the throne of their hearts. If God was their God, they needed to follow Him alone.

God's warnings against idolatry are not reserved for the false gods of the Old Testament. It's just as vital for us today that God takes His rightful place in our lives. In the Sermon on the Mount, Jesus told the crowd, "No one can serve two masters, for either he will hate the one and love the other, or he will be devoted to the one and despise the other" (Matthew 6:24). As believers, we cannot hop between devotion to God and devotion to earthly things. We cannot split the role of "God" between God and our bank account—or our possessions, our romantic life, our family, our beauty, our career goals—and expect to get anywhere. If God is our God, we must follow Him alone, serving and worshipping Him exclusively.

"There are many 'gods' and many 'lords,' " Paul wrote the Corinthians, "yet for us there is one God, the Father, from whom are all things and for whom we exist, and one Lord, Jesus Christ" (1 Corinthians 8:5–6). He then issued a warning: "Let anyone who thinks that he stands take heed lest he fall. . . . Therefore, my beloved, flee from idolatry" (1 Corinthians 10:12, 14). Christians today are not immune to idols. If anything, they might be harder to spot since we don't often physically bow down to them. Before we dismiss the warnings as "Not for me," let's look closely at our lives. What is taking God's rightful place?

GOD, I'M SO ASHAMED. LATELY I'VE BEEN LIVING AS IF YOU AREN'T GOD IN MY LIFE. FORGIVE ME, PLEASE. DETHRONE MY IDOLS AND REIGN FULLY IN ME. AMEN.

Even in the Bad Times

A friend loves at all times.

PROVERBS 17:17 NKJV

"Fair-weather friends" we call them. These are the kind who are hard to find when the party is over and the cleanup begins. They're nice while they last, but you can't depend on them. You're never really sure if they'll be around or not. And, in fact, it's probably not accurate even to call them friends. They're just acquaintances.

A real friend doesn't just like what's happening around you; she likes *you*. She has committed to investing in the relationship whether you're serving steak or hot dogs. She comes to see you even if your laundry isn't done and your kitchen needs to be mopped and your windows are smudgy. She puts up with your bad moods and your flaws and your weird little ways. She talks you off the ledge during a crisis and brings you coffee on a Monday. She's there to stay.

You know you have one of these friends when the doorbell rings and she stands there and says, "What can I do?" Thanks to the Lord for friends like these!

But we are blessed so that we can, in turn, bless others. We are to be that kind of unexpected, exceptional friend to our friends.

In Luke 11:5–8, Jesus told the story of a man who needs that kind of friend. This man has company show up late at night, and what is worse is that he doesn't have food to offer the guest. What does he do? He thinks of his friend and hops on over to his house and wakes him up. We aren't told if he throws pebbles at the side of the house, calls out, or knocks, but he does something to let his friend know he's there.

The friend isn't very happy, actually. Basically, he says, "Go away; we've already closed everything up and put the kids to bed. I'm tired."

Well, maybe he wouldn't win the Best Friend of the Year Award! But the other guy persists. And so finally the man in bed gets up and gives him the snacks he needs.

We need to be the kind of friends who get up at the first knock. The kind who love at *all* times—even the sleepy times.

Today you may have the chance to be that kind of friend to someone. It will probably surprise them. They won't expect it. And that will make it all the sweeter.

GOD, I WANT TO BE A FRIEND AT ALL TIMES. GIVE ME THE LOYALTY AND THE GRIT TO STICK WITH MY FRIENDS IN THE HARD TIMES, THE INCONVENIENT TIMES, THE EMBARRASSING TIMES, AND THE UNPLEASANT TIMES. I KNOW YOU HAVE ALL THE GRACE I NEED TO DO IT. IN JESUS' NAME, AMEN.

Back to Him

[Hannah] was deeply distressed and prayed to the LORD and wept bitterly. And she vowed a vow and said, "O LORD of hosts, if you will indeed look on the affliction of your servant and remember me and not forget your servant, but will give to your servant a son, then I will give him to the LORD all the days of his life."

1 SAMUEL 1:10–11

Think about a time when you desperately asked for God to fulfill a deep need in your life. Not just a run-of-the-mill "It would be nice if God grants my request," but an honest-to-goodness "I'd give an arm and a leg for God to grant my request." In all your praying, did it cross your mind to offer back to God the thing you prayed for? If it didn't, you're not alone. We might think to offer something else. We might promise to do something in return. But release what we've prayed for? That says a great deal, and that's exactly what Hannah did.

Hannah desperately wanted a son. Although she had the love of her husband, Elkanah, her status as a woman in her culture hinged on the children she bore. Add to that the fact that her husband's second wife, Peninnah, regularly tormented Hannah because of her barrenness, and you begin to see what a son meant to Hannah. So on one of their yearly trips to Shiloh to worship and sacrifice, Hannah went to the temple to pray. There Hannah poured out her soul (1 Samuel 1:15). So intense was her plea that Eli, the priest at the temple, thought she was drunk. But she was only approaching her heavenly Father in raw humility and with deep faith.

Hannah's prayer was for a son, as one would expect, but her prayer was also a promise to take what God gave and give it right back to Him. Her blessings came from God, and back to God they would go. In all aspects of her life, it seems, Hannah recognized the source. Hannah left the temple that day heartened. The Bible says, "Her face was no longer sad" (1 Samuel 1:18). How could that be? On the surface, nothing had changed; she still did not have a son. But she had placed her need in the hands of her God, and Hannah trusted in His providence. The one who had closed her womb (verse 5) was in control and was completely capable of answering her prayer favorably with the birth of a son. And so He would.

LORD, SOMETIMES I LOSE YOU IN MY PRAYERS. I HYPERFOCUS ON ME AND FORGET TO LOOK BEYOND TO YOU. HOW CAN I GIVE BACK FROM ALL YOU'VE GIVEN ME? PLEASE SHOW ME. AMEN.

Laughing at Impossibilities

And Sarah said, "God has made laughter for me; everyone who hears will laugh over me." And she said, "Who would have said to Abraham that Sarah would nurse children? Yet I have borne him a son in his old age."

GENESIS 21:6–7

Sarah was old and her womb was withered. Dead. That's what the Bible says (Romans 4:19). She didn't expect to birth a child. And she certainly didn't expect to laugh. But she did both. In God's time.

The name Isaac means "laughter." And he certainly brought that to a hundred-year-old man and his ninety-year-old bride when he arrived. Those two elderly people laughed like they never had before as they watched a tiny baby boy wriggle and learn to crawl and give big grins and run around all over their nomadic camp. It was the fulfillment of God's promise. And Sarah knew her story would amuse people for all time. She knew we'd smile at the thought of her joy at finally receiving motherhood when she should have been sitting around in retirement.

I've always been interested in the fact that Sarah seemed to laugh in disbelief in the account told in Genesis 18 when the pre-incarnate Christ visited the tents of Abram and promised him a son. If I were God, I think I would have been indignant at the idea that a mere human would laugh at the promise. But God isn't like me. He is so far above us that He can see all the things we can't.

He surely understood that to Sarah it was like a joke. And because they didn't have His Word to read like we do, which tells of all the impossibilities He can accomplish, and because He hadn't spoken to her before of it, He could see the heartbreak behind the laugh and the desperate hope that it might be true.

What are you hoping for that seems impossible? Can you believe that God might bring it to pass? Can you imagine that someday you might be laughing in delight at the fulfillment of a promise? It might seem just as impossible as a postmenopausal woman giving birth, but God can do the impossible. "Is anything too hard for the LORD?" (Genesis 18:14).

Pray for God's will. Believe in His plan. And you might be laughing sooner than you think.

JEHOVAH GOD, YOU ARE THE ONE WHO CAN
BRING LAUGHTER INTO MY LIFE. I ASK YOU
TO BE AT WORK IN ALL THE IMPOSSIBILITIES
ABOUT WHICH I AM PRAYING. I TRUST
THAT YOU CAN DO ANYTHING. AMEN.

Fruitful

But the fruit of the Spirit is love, joy, peace, patience,
kindness, goodness, faithfulness, gentleness,
self-control; against such things there is no law.
GALATIANS 5:22–23

"If it looks like a duck, swims like a duck, and quacks like a duck, then it's probably. . .a duck!" Whether you've heard some version of this expression or not, the conclusion is obvious. If something is that something, it generally exhibits certain characteristics. That goes for people as well as ducks. Take, for instance, believers. If a Christian is a Christian, she will exhibit certain characteristics—what Paul called "the fruit of the Spirit."

When we become believers, God gifts us with the Holy Spirit (Acts 2:38), and the Spirit's presence is one way we can reassure ourselves of our salvation (1 John 4:13). He is much more than a token proof, though. The Holy Spirit becomes our power source to resist the flesh and live a godly life. The fruit—the love, joy, peace, patience, kindness, goodness, faithfulness, gentleness, and self-control listed in Galatians—is evidence of His working. Jesus, in His Sermon on the Mount, described the opposite when He warned the crowd to be on guard against those who claimed to know the way to salvation but did not. "Beware of false prophets, who come to you in sheep's clothing but inwardly are ravenous wolves," He said. How could they tell a true shepherd from a wolf? "You will recognize them by their fruits. Are grapes gathered from thornbushes, or figs from thistles? So, every healthy tree bears good fruit, but the diseased tree bears bad fruit. A healthy tree cannot bear bad fruit, nor can a diseased tree bear good fruit. . . . Thus you will recognize them by their fruits" (Matthew 7:15–18, 20). True believers, because of the Holy Spirit, will bear good fruit.

So what is a Christian like? She's loving—showing the kind of love Christ showed. She's joyful—possessing a sense of well-being from God no matter the circumstance. She's peaceful—resting in the calm of knowing God. She's patient—long-suffering through hardships. She's kind—treating others with care and concern. She's good—displaying the holiness fitting for one of God's children. She's faithful—proving herself trustworthy, devoted. She's gentle—having a spirit of meekness. She's self-controlled—taming the flesh while pursuing godliness.

However small the harvest, the Holy Spirit is producing what we could not produce alone. May it be our prayer that we bear more and more of that good fruit.

HOLY SPIRIT, I SEE THE FRUIT YOU YIELD IN MY LIFE. IT'S MY DESIRE TO BEAR A BOUNTY OF GOOD FRUIT—SO MUCH THAT OTHERS SEE ME AND SAY, "THAT'S A CHRISTIAN!" AMEN.

Share the Comfort

Blessed be the God and Father of our Lord Jesus Christ,
the Father of mercies and God of all comfort, who
comforts us in all our affliction, so that we may be able to
comfort those who are in any affliction, with the comfort
with which we ourselves are comforted by God.

2 CORINTHIANS 1:3–4

It's a friend who sits beside us for hours on the hard waiting-room chairs. It's the gentle embrace of Mom or Dad rocking us back to sleep when we were young. It's heads huddled together while we talk over our troubles. It's the outstretched hand that lets us know we don't have to walk alone. Comfort takes many forms, but it often involves the support of someone else.

In the Bible, another name for the Holy Spirit, our Comforter, is Paraclete. The name derives from the Greek word *Paraklētos,* which can be translated "advocate" or "intercessor." Like a lawyer who stands beside a defendant in a court case, the Holy Spirit comes alongside believers in life—counseling them, helping them. No wonder the word for "comfort" that Paul used in 2 Corinthians is related to the Greek paraclete. Paul had experienced intense struggle in Asia—to such a degree that he felt he had "received the sentence of death" (2 Corinthians 1:9). Yet through it all, Paul was convinced of God's presence—upholding him, encouraging him, and, ultimately, delivering him. He was convinced too of the surety of God's comfort, that even in the most intense situation,

God's comfort abounded both for himself and for fellow believers: "For just as the sufferings of Christ are ours in abundance, so also our comfort is abundant through Christ. But if we are afflicted, it is for your comfort and salvation; or if we are comforted, it is for your comfort. . .and our hope for you is firmly grounded, knowing that as you are sharers of our sufferings, so also you are sharers of our comfort" (2 Corinthians 1:5–7 NASB).

Paul knew one other truth about God's comfort. The benefits went beyond the immediate comfort itself. Each instance of God's comfort in the midst of suffering bolstered faith and united believers. And once comforted by God themselves, believers in turn could comfort others. The same rich layering of comfort continues to this day. In the midst of our sufferings, God comes alongside us— upholding us, encouraging us, and delivering us. We in turn have the joy of sharing the blessing of His comfort.

GOD, YOU NEVER STOP COMFORTING ME.
YOU ARE ALWAYS WITH ME TO HELP ME THROUGH
MY STRUGGLES. REMIND ME TO SHARE WITH OTHERS
THE ENDLESS WAYS YOU WORK IN MY LIFE. AMEN.

Cast Those Cares!

Casting all your anxieties on him, because he cares for you.

1 PETER 5:7

A belly of nerves has to be one of the most uncomfortable feelings there is. You're on edge. Your mind won't settle except on what you're uneasy about, which it cycles over and over. And the more you feed anxiety, the quicker you are to become anxious. When we're feeling anxious, we easily forget that anxiety itself isn't always bad. The sudden unease caused by a cracking twig when we're walking alone or an unfamiliar creak of the floorboards at night alerts us to potential danger. We're revved up for a reason. . .until the danger passes. But we simply aren't meant to be anxious about every little thing, every waking moment.

Yet we often are, and we're not the first generation to need an anxiety cure. Our propensity for anxiety is age-old. Back in Bible times, Jesus had a few words to say on the subject, and He also nudged us toward the solution: "Consider the lilies of the field, how they grow: they neither toil nor spin, yet I tell you, even Solomon in all his glory was not arrayed like one of these. But if God so clothes the grass of the field, which today is alive and tomorrow is thrown into the oven, will he not much more clothe you, O you of little faith? Therefore do not be anxious, saying, 'What shall we eat?' or 'What shall we drink?' or 'What shall we wear?'. . .Your heavenly Father knows that you need them all" (Matthew 6:28–32). What's the antidote to anxiety? Reminding ourselves of God's presence in our lives and trusting Him to take care of us.

"Blessed is the man who trusts in the LORD," God said. "He is like a tree planted by water, that. . .is not anxious in the year of drought, for it does not cease to bear fruit" (Jeremiah 17:7–8). No matter what our circumstances, we can trade the unsettledness of anxiety for the assurance of God's care. We can surrender our worries to the one who gives life. "Cast your burden on the LORD, and He shall sustain you" (Psalm 55:22 NKJV). Peter echoes the psalmist's words, telling believers to cast their anxieties on God. Don't miss the vivid language in these verses. *Cast* your burden, your anxieties. With each anxious thought, picture your heavenly Father and cast those cares over His shoulders. Because He knows what to do with them. Because He cares for you.

LORD, I CAST ALL THAT'S TWISTING ME UP INSIDE
ON YOU. YOU'LL TAKE CARE OF ME. AMEN.

Laughing at the Feast

A feast is made for laughter.
ECCLESIASTES 10:19 KJV

There are some places where you expect to laugh, right? A comedy show. A concert. A party. A reunion.

The wisdom writer said that feasts are exactly the right place for laughter. One is made for the other.

Ancient custom forbade a long face in the presence of the king. In fact, it might even be reason for an instant execution! One was supposed to show positivity of spirit and joy of countenance when approaching the throne. Some kings even employed their own entertainer, the court jester, to tell jokes or perform antics and keep the atmosphere jolly.

Remember the story of Esther? She was nervous about walking into the king's presence without an invitation. That was also forbidden on threat of death. Such was the strict regulation that controlled the palace in biblical times.

Our God sits on the throne of heaven. He reigns over our world and the galaxies beyond. Yet He allows us to approach Him with our raw emotions and with downcast faces.

Hebrews 4:16 says that we may approach God's throne boldly and find grace to help us in our time of need. Our God doesn't demand that we make Him feel good; He reaches out to us to bring us good.

Someday every believing child of God will be gathered in one place for the greatest feast of all. It's called the marriage supper of the Lamb (Revelation 19:9). There the King will celebrate the marriage of His Son, Jesus, to His bride, the church. And there will be great joy and laughter like we've never known. Laughter that lasts for eternity.

Who would ever have imagined that the God who made everything would throw a great feast and invite us to it? That's an unexpected welcome. But He did. And He doesn't want anyone to miss it.

FATHER, I'M SO GLAD YOU MADE ROOM FOR ALL OF US AT YOUR GREAT FEAST. THANK YOU FOR INCLUDING ME. BECAUSE I HAVE PUT MY FAITH IN CHRIST, I AM LOOKING FORWARD TO THE JOY AND LAUGHTER OF THAT DAY. AMEN.

Drastic Measures

"And if your hand or your foot causes you to sin, cut it off and throw it away. It is better for you to enter life crippled or lame than with two hands or two feet to be thrown into the eternal fire. And if your eye causes you to sin, tear it out and throw it away. It is better for you to enter life with one eye than with two eyes to be thrown into the hell of fire."

MATTHEW 18:8–9

What's the best policy when it comes to dealing with sin? Nip it in the bud. You've likely heard that expression before. It means to halt something early on and refers to new flower buds that a spring frost kills before they have a chance to grow.

Jesus used a more arresting depiction of how to deal with sin. And He used it more than once (Matthew 5:29–30; 18:8–9). If a person's hand, foot, or eye causes her to sin, it is better to lose that hand, foot, or eye than suffer the consequences of sin. Of course, He was exaggerating to make a point. He wasn't advocating that we harm our bodies to manage sin in our lives. Punishing the outside won't begin to touch the source of sin in our hearts. But when dealing with a temptation to sin, it is best to get rid of it completely rather than flirt with the temptation and risk sinning.

Whether we realize it or not, we Christians are at risk of adopting a destructive mindset. With Christ's death on the cross, He paid the penalty for our sins, every last one. If we sin and repent, God will forgive, every single time. So is sin still a big deal? Yes! Here's what Paul wrote on the issue: "What shall we say then? Shall we continue in sin that grace may abound? Certainly not! . . . Therefore do not let sin reign in your mortal body, that you should obey it in its lusts. And do not present your members as instruments of unrighteousness to sin, but present yourselves to God as being alive from the dead, and your members as instruments of righteousness to God" (Romans 6:1–2, 12–13 NKJV). Forgiveness is not a license to sin; neither is sin beneficial to a believer. If we want to be used by God to the fullest and grow in Him, we must deal with sin. Christ took drastic measures to free us. At the first sign of temptation, let's do the same and nip sin in the bud.

LORD, THE NEXT TIME I FACE TEMPTATION, REMIND ME OF YOUR SACRIFICE. HELP ME RID MY LIFE OF ANYTHING THAT CAUSES ME TO SIN. AMEN.

Just the Essentials

At that time the disciples came to Jesus, saying, "Who is the greatest in the kingdom of heaven?" And calling to him a child, he put him in the midst of them and said, "Truly, I say to you, unless you turn and become like children, you will never enter the kingdom of heaven. Whoever humbles himself like this child is the greatest in the kingdom of heaven."

MATTHEW 18:1–4

"That was just too easy! What am I missing?" she said.

What is it about simple things that makes us question them? Sometimes complexity only adds complexity. Just look at the reams of paper that are the US tax code. It's true for religion too. The Pharisees were famous for complicating God's law with added regulations. But when Jesus arrived on the scene, He preached a way to righteousness through faith that defied complexity.

It wasn't the outwardly religious but inwardly unchanged Pharisees, or even one of His devoted followers, to whom Jesus pointed in answer to the disciples' question of who was "greatest in the kingdom." It was a child. At another time, parents brought their children to Jesus so He could bless them. Although the disciples tried to turn them away, Jesus welcomed the children. "Let the children come to me," He said. "Do not hinder them, for to such belongs the kingdom of God. Truly, I say to you, whoever does not receive the kingdom of God like a child shall not enter it" (Mark 10:14–15). To Jesus, the child embodied what all the "stuff" of religion could never produce: the pure heart and faith of a child in relationship with the Father. A child with nothing to offer but everything to gain. A child full of trust in her Father for every need. A child content to rest at her Father's knee.

We, as God's children, should come to the Father in the same way. To deepen our faith, we must simplify our faith.

GOD, I'M TIRED OF RUNNING IN CIRCLES,
OF COMPLICATING FAITH AND FEELING NO
CLOSER TO YOU. TODAY I CALL TO YOU—
DAUGHTER TO HEAVENLY FATHER. AMEN.

A Ruth Opportunity

*Ruth said, "Do not urge me to leave you or to
return from following you. For where you go I will
go, and where you lodge I will lodge. Your people
shall be my people, and your God my God."*

RUTH 1:16

In the category of great relationships, mother-in-law and daughter-in-law are not usually at the top of the list. This is one of those bonds where historically there has been friction—two women loving the same man and wanting to be significant in his affections.

It is a wonderful surprise, then, that God's Word gives us the story of just such a relationship that was close and loving. The book of Ruth is a love story on many levels—the love of Ruth for Naomi, the love of Naomi for her homeland, and the love of Boaz for Ruth. We can learn from all the angles.

If you're married, you know that loving your husband's family is a choice you make, and it takes effort and commitment. Rarely are they like you. They are often from a very different kind of background, eat different foods, use different everyday vernacular, value different kinds of hobbies and celebrations, and may even be from a different culture. That was certainly the case in Ruth's story. Her husband, Mahlon, was a Hebrew, and though his family had been immigrants in Moab for years, no doubt they still retained some of their Jewish preferences. By the time he died, she was aware of most of the differences, I'm sure. Maybe that helped her make her decision. Maybe she thought she knew enough about the land of Israel that she wouldn't have such a difficult adjustment.

Whatever the reason, she begged her mother-in-law not to refuse her request to travel back to Bethlehem with her. Naomi must have been surprised, but the Bible record says that when she saw that Ruth was determined, she gave her consent.

Perhaps you have extended family members who are very different from you. Today, accept Ruth's challenge and look for ways to bond with them in healthy ways. Of course, one should never forsake God for pagan worship or adopt practices that violate His laws. But within those boundaries, why not see how you can surprise them with unexpected overtures of friendship? And who knows? It might open their hearts to Christ if they don't already know Him.

HEAVENLY FATHER, THANK YOU FOR CREATING DIFFERENT PEOPLE GROUPS ON THE EARTH. YOU HAVE INCLUDED SOME OF THEM IN MY FAMILY. I WANT TO REACH OUT TO THEM AND SURPRISE THEM WITH FRIENDSHIP THAT GOES BEYOND MERE TOLERANCE. I'M ASKING FOR WISDOM AS I LOOK FOR THOSE OPPORTUNITIES TODAY. IN JESUS' NAME, AMEN.

Times Infinity

"Judge not, and you will not be judged; condemn not, and you will not be condemned; forgive, and you will be forgiven; give, and it will be given to you. Good measure, pressed down, shaken together, running over, will be put into your lap. For with the measure you use it will be measured back to you."

LUKE 6:37–38

This had happened before. Like a bad dream on rerun, once more her friend had wronged her. She knew what to do—forgive. But she knew the feeling seeping into her heart too—hardness. She'd forgiven time and again; had she finally reached her limit?

Questions about forgiveness are nothing new. Even the disciples questioned just how far to extend forgiveness. When Peter asked Jesus to clarify, he also threw out a number that he must have thought generous: "Lord, how often shall my brother sin against me, and I forgive him? Up to seven times?" But Jesus' reply declared that seven times was just the beginning: "I do not say to you, up to seven times, but up to seventy times seven" (Matthew 18:21–22 NKJV). In other words, innumerable times. A limitless number.

Our model for limitless forgiveness is God's forgiveness. The debt we owed because of sin was unpayable, and we didn't deserve a pardon. But on the cross, Christ paid our debt in full. He called out for our forgiveness before we knew our need, just as He did for His tormentors at His crucifixion. Even in His agony, His hope for condemned sinners was forgiveness: "Father, forgive them, for they know not what they do" (Luke 23:34). By believing in Jesus, complete forgiveness from the final penalty for sin—eternity separated from God—is ours. Righteousness is ours. "We have been sanctified through the offering of the body of Jesus Christ once for all" (Hebrews 10:10).

Such total, blessed forgiveness is not the extent of God's forgiving nature, either. The one who has pardoned an unpayable debt continues to forgive us when we disobey. Even with the best intentions, we will still fail time and again, and time and again we can ask our Father's forgiveness without crossing our fingers that He'll forgive. He will. Hardening our hearts and refusing to offer forgiveness does not honor God's grace, and He won't overlook our stinginess, a scenario that Jesus illustrated in His parable of the unforgiving servant (Matthew 18:23–35). But when we forgive generously, limitlessly, as God does, we will get back an equal measure.

FATHER, YOU HAVE FORGIVEN ME TOO MANY
TIMES TO COUNT. WHEN I STRUGGLE TO FORGIVE
JUST ONE MORE TIME, HELP ME FORGIVE
AGAIN AND AGAIN. MAY MY FORGIVENESS
POINT THE WAY TO YOURS. AMEN.

Unknown Wonder

Then the rib which the LORD God had taken from man He made into a woman, and He brought her to the man.

GENESIS 2:22 NKJV

The best kind of love stories are the unexpected ones, the kind where two people meet by "chance" or where an ordinary happening results in extraordinary romance. We women never tire of this kind of story line. Perhaps it's because of the plot of the first romance on earth.

Her name was Eve. Her husband named her. And he had never seen a woman before. He didn't even know such creatures existed. Actually, she didn't until God made her out of his bone.

When he woke up from his nap (during which God performed surgery), Adam looked around and saw that the Creator had left him a surprise—her.

Think of what this love story was like. They must have both spoken the same language, whatever it was. He reached out to her. What did he say? Did he touch her smooth skin with wonder? With his perfect brain and reasoning, he must have known that God had given him a mate, a companion wonderfully suited for him and gloriously different at the same time. The awe of that first meeting of male and female had to be something glorious. And God said it was very good.

Every feminine heart longs for that kind of wonder. We yearn to be gazed at with amazement. It's the reason women spend so much money on cosmetics and so many hours at the gym. We want to recapture the glory Eve had, the indefinable attraction that entranced Adam.

The serpent and his temptation spoiled forever the enchanting romance in the garden. And hard as we try to regain the spark, something was distorted then that still haunts our love stories. But we know, deep in our souls, that we were made for that kind of wonder, and we long for it still.

Someday we will be given to Christ as His bride. The magnificence of that moment will outshine any other. For the garden awe is only a tiny glimmer of the eternal splendor. And the Creator who ordained earthly romance has something far better to reveal in that day.

FATHER, MY FEMININE HEART WAS MADE TO THRILL WITH ROMANCE. AND I AM SO GLAD THAT I AM PART OF THE BRIDE OF CHRIST THROUGH MY FAITH IN YOUR SON. UNTIL THAT DAY, KEEP MY AFFECTIONS FOCUSED ON YOU. THANK YOU FOR YOUR UNENDING LOVE. AMEN.

Take a Look Around

The heavens declare the glory of God,
and the sky above proclaims his handiwork.

PSALM 19:1

Want to hear about God? Step outside. The heavens are declaring, the sky is proclaiming the truth about the Creator. Nature shouts how awesome God is—from the tip-top of the sky to the deepest depths of the ocean.

What God reveals about Himself through His creation is called general revelation (as opposed to special revelation—what God reveals to individual people directly), and it is available to everyone, at every moment. David continued in his psalm, "Day to day pours out speech, and night to night reveals knowledge. There is no speech, nor are there words, whose voice is not heard. Their voice goes out through all the earth, and their words to the end of the world" (Psalm 19:2–4). Paul, when explaining why those who tried to suppress the truth about God and dwell in their sinfulness were without excuse, used nature's testimony. God's witness was all around people: "What can be known about God is plain to them, because God has shown it to them. For his invisible attributes, namely, his eternal power and divine nature, have been clearly perceived, ever since the creation of the world, in the things that have been made" (Romans 1:19–20).

If we take the time to listen and observe, we can't miss God speaking through nature. Jonathan Edwards, the theologian at the root of the Great Awakening, could attest to that. After his spiritual transformation, he saw ever more of his Creator in the world around him—he recognized God in the sun, moon, stars, clouds, trees, and more.

There's no better place to look for reassurance of God's presence and power than nature. Can we see the intricacy of a snowflake, the hues of a sunset, or the lush growth of plants without imagining a Creator? Can we hear the boom of thunder, the rush of waves, or the silence of a vast night sky without thinking of someone higher than ourselves? God's creation is shouting. The same almighty God at work in nature is at work in us.

GOD, IN MY MODERN LIFE, I'VE LOST SOMETHING
OF YOU. EVEN IF IT'S ONLY A FEW MINUTES,
I WANT TO SET ASIDE TIME EVERY DAY TO HEAR
WHAT YOUR CREATION HAS TO SAY. AMEN.

*George M. Marsden, *Jonathan Edwards: A Life* (New Haven, CT: Yale University Press, 2003), chap. 3.

Anywhere at All

*If I take the wings of the morning and dwell in the
uttermost parts of the sea, even there your hand shall
lead me, and your right hand shall hold me.*

PSALM 139:9–10

She sat on a park bench watching the pedestrians and drivers on the busy sidewalks and streets around her. Her brain began to churn: What were their names? What were their stories? Where were they headed? And this cityscape was only one small patch of the planet! In that moment, thinking of all the billions of other lives spread across the globe, she could have felt tiny, like just another face in humanity's crowd. But instead she felt a rush of wonder—because in that moment, she also thought of God watching over her.

Now and then, we can lose sight of God in our lives or even question whether He's there. When we fade into daily routine or face difficult times, we may think, *Does God see me?* Yet no matter what our heads say, we can reassure our hearts with the truth from God's Word:

Wherever we find ourselves, God hasn't lost track of us. Quicker than a breath, God can pinpoint His own—zooming in from heaven to our world to our country to our city to our street to a park bench—and He is intimately aware of everything in our lives. In Psalm 139—a testament to God's "omni-" attributes, His omniscience, omnipresence, and omnipotence—David wrote, "O LORD, you have searched me and known me! You know when I sit down and when I rise up; you discern my thoughts from afar. You search out my path and my lying down and are acquainted with all my ways" (verses 1–3).

Wherever we go, God is there. Nothing we do is out of God's sight because He is present everywhere. "Where shall I go from your Spirit? Or where shall I flee from your presence?" David asked. "If I ascend to heaven, you are there! If I make my bed in Sheol, you are there!" (verses 7–8).

And wherever God is, He is at work. David had sensed God forming his path throughout his life—"You hem me in, behind and before, and lay your hand upon me" (verse 5)—so he had confidence that even "in the uttermost parts of the sea," God's hand would guide and keep him (verses 9–10). That confidence is ours too. God's mighty hand is guiding us and will never let go.

GOD, I'M AWESTRUCK BY YOU! I'M ONLY ONE IN MANY BILLIONS, BUT YOU KNOW ME SO WELL. THANK YOU FOR WATCHING OVER MY LIFE—WHERE I AM TODAY AND WHEREVER I'LL BE TOMORROW. AMEN.

Still with Us

All this took place to fulfill what the Lord had spoken by the prophet: "Behold, the virgin shall conceive and bear a son, and they shall call his name Immanuel" (which means, God with us).

MATTHEW 1:22–23

Picture God. What image do you have in your mind's eye? Is He a white-haired, bearded man like the one in Michelangelo's fresco at the Sistine Chapel? Is He a nebulous form? Is He a blank? Your first thought might not have been a baby in a manger, a boy on the streets of Nazareth, a man on the way to the cross.

No one has seen God (John 1:18; 1 John 4:12), but in a miracle that humans could never dream up and only God could bring about, God made Himself known through Jesus—deity in a mortal body. Immanuel—God with us. John wrote in his Gospel, "And the Word became flesh and dwelt among us, and we have seen his glory, glory as of the only Son from the Father" (John 1:14). With the birth of Jesus, humanity had access to God like never before as the one who created everything spent time among His creation, as the embodiment of the fullness of God left heaven to walk this earth.

Jesus' earthly life was no vacation, a quick jaunt to look around. Fully God, He was also fully man, and He experienced what we experience. He felt joy and sorrow, health and sickness, comfort and pain, strength and weakness. But unlike us, He lived a perfect life from start to finish. He faced temptation and endured so that we could claim His perfection as our own. He hungered and thirsted and bled and died for our sake.

Each day, we walk this earth as imperfect beings. We're not yet who we'll be in eternity. But each day, we walk with the assurance that God, who was with us on earth, has compassion on us, and we can call on Him in our need (Hebrews 4:15–16). Even though Immanuel has returned to heaven for a time and no longer dwells among us, we are never without God. Before His final days, Jesus comforted His disciples with the promise of the Holy Spirit, and it is our promise too: "[The Father] will give you another Helper, to be with you forever, even the Spirit of truth, whom the world cannot receive, because it neither sees him nor knows him. You know him, for he dwells with you and will be in you" (John 14:16–17).

GOD, THANK YOU—FOR YOUR SON WHO
DWELLED AMONG US UNTIL HE MADE A WAY TO
YOU, AND FOR YOUR SPIRIT WHO DWELLS IN
US UNTIL WE'RE FOREVER WITH YOU. AMEN.

When the Worms Come

But when dawn came up the next day, God appointed
a worm that attacked the plant, so that it withered.

I don't like them, but they don't usually make me angry. Worms are a little icky to some of us. Yes, I can bait my own fishing hook, but I don't particularly care for the squishy little things. And I try to avoid stepping on them when they cover the church parking lot after a heavy rain. But I've never had an encounter with a worm like Jonah had. After his triumph of obedience in finally going to Nineveh to preach to the pagan fish worshippers there, the prophet of God had a spiritual battle over a plant and a worm.

Jonah must have felt sure that God would destroy the evil inhabitants of Nineveh. He was, at last, willing to preach to them, but he must not have expected God to forgive them and avert His judgment. This, in Jonah's mind, seemed unjust. And so he sat a distance away from the city and waited to see what would happen.

God allowed a plant to grow up as shade over Jonah's little shelter to give him relief from the heat. And then, just after he was comfortable, God sent a worm to nibble away at the green leaves and destroy the plant. Then He sent a strong, scorching wind that pummeled the prophet in addition to the blistering heat of the sun. And Jonah prayed to die.

It's interesting, isn't it, that the man who ran from God and almost died without wanting to was now asking for that very thing.

But God knew that the real problem was Jonah's lack of submission to anything other than what he thought should happen—the call to go to a place he didn't like, the pardon of people he wanted to be judged, the death of a plant that he liked for comfort. He wanted his way. And when he didn't get it, he was angry.

"But God said to Jonah, 'Do you do well to be angry for the plant?' And he said, 'Yes, I do well to be angry, angry enough to die' " (Jonah 4:9).

What makes you suddenly angry? Is it when something happens that goes against your "plans"? Is it the unexpected event that doesn't match your ideas of God and life? Is it a small thing like a worm eating a plant?

We don't know if Jonah changed his attitude. The Bible narrative ends with God's words to the prophet. But we can write the end of our own narrative today. Anger is a response to unmet expectations. It is a normal human emotion. But the way we channel it and manage it tells us if we are being controlled by the Holy Spirit or by our own willful attitudes.

CREATOR GOD, YOU MADE US WITH THE ABILITY TO FEEL A RANGE OF EMOTIONS, AND ANGER IS ONE OF THEM. PLEASE HELP ME TODAY NOT TO BECOME SUDDENLY ANGRY WITH THE WAY YOU CHOOSE TO DO THINGS IN MY LIFE. I WANT TO BE SPIRIT CONTROLLED, NOT ME CONTROLLED. IN JESUS' NAME, AMEN.

Get Ready

Now there was one, Anna, a prophetess, the daughter of Phanuel,
of the tribe of Asher. She was of a great age, and had lived with
a husband seven years from her virginity; and this woman was
a widow of about eighty-four years, who did not depart from the
temple, but served God with fastings and prayers night and day.
And coming in that instant she gave thanks to the Lord, and spoke
of Him to all those who looked for redemption in Jerusalem.

LUKE 2:36–38 NKJV

Jesus was only weeks old. In keeping with the law of Moses, Joseph
and Mary traveled from Bethlehem to Jerusalem to present Him
at the temple and offer a sacrifice. Waiting for them was Simeon, a
righteous and devout man with a promise: he would not die before
he had seen Christ. So on the day Joseph and Mary brought Jesus
to Jerusalem, Simeon was also there. The Bible says he "came in
the Spirit into the temple" (Luke 2:27). Spirit-led Simeon knew
right away who the infant was. In what must have been great joy,
Simeon "took him up in his arms and blessed God and said, 'Lord,
now you are letting your servant depart in peace, according to your
word; for my eyes have seen your salvation that you have prepared
in the presence of all peoples, a light for revelation to the Gentiles,
and for glory to your people Israel' " (Luke 2:28–32). While Simeon
was still praising and blessing, a woman entered the scene in the
perfect timing of her Lord. "Coming in that instant" was Anna.

It's just a guess, but Anna's life at eighty-four probably didn't look like what she had imagined as a young girl. Married then widowed after seven years, she now was a prophetess and lived at the temple. Evidently, Anna did not let early widowhood dampen her faith but continued to serve her Lord faithfully. Night and day, she fasted and prayed, readying her heart for what God called her to. And night and day, God was present behind the scenes in Anna's life and the lives of those around her. From Jesus' birth to Joseph and Mary's trip to Simeon's words, God was laying the foundation to bless and work through Anna at exactly the right moment—the moment when Anna saw the fulfillment of her faith in person and then went on to tell others that Messiah was here.

LORD, LIFE ISN'T ALWAYS WHAT I IMAGINED IT WOULD BE. BUT I'LL HAVE FAITH THAT YOU ARE PREPARING THE WAY FOR SOMETHING BETTER THAN I COULD IMAGINE. AMEN.

The Solid Kind
of Love

"But I say to you, love your enemies, bless those who curse you, do good to those who hate you, and pray for those who spitefully use you and persecute you."

MATTHEW 5:44 NKJV

Do you want to do something completely wild?

Love someone who doesn't like you.

That's right. The most unexpected, most Christlike gift you can give is to love those who mistreat you and hate you. No other amazement is quite like what your enemy will experience if you do.

We often think of unexpected blessings coming to us, but what if we are the source of unexpected blessing for someone else? That is when we are like our Father in heaven. He calls us to be like Him, and that includes patterning our interactions with others after the way He does things. The apostle Peter wrote that we can be "partakers of the divine nature" (2 Peter 1:4). What an astounding realization! Because of the Holy Spirit's work in us, we can imitate our Lord and actually have His nature inside us.

Sometimes at parties there is a white elephant gift exchange. This silly little game is simply the fun of exchanging corny, impractical gifts. One might be especially desirable, but generally none of them are worth much except for laughs. Part of the hilarity is tearing off the wrapping and discovering what ridiculous thing is inside.

But the kind of love we have to share with our enemies, while it might be surprising, is never frivolous nor silly. It is the most solid, genuine love there can be because it comes from the heart of God through us.

HEAVENLY FATHER, GIVE ME THE GRACE TO LOVE THOSE WHO MISTREAT ME. IN YOUR STRENGTH, I MAKE THE CHOICE TO BLESS THOSE WHO CURSE ME AND DO GOOD TO THOSE WHO HATE ME. I DEPEND ON YOUR LOVE TO FLOW THROUGH ME. IN JESUS' NAME, AMEN.

Faithful Giving

Whoever brings blessing will be enriched.

PROVERBS 11:25

Ready for a tough question? When it comes to giving of yourself—whether it's your time or your resources—where are you on the giving scale? Do you grip what you have to give and only let a little trickle out through your fingers? Do you offer everything with open hands? Maybe you're somewhere in between. If the number of times the Bible speaks of generosity is any indication, we all need to work on cultivating a generous heart.

Both Mark and Luke record a memorable lesson on giving (Mark 12:41–44; Luke 21:1–4). Jesus was watching the people bring their offerings, and among the rich with their large sums of money, He saw her: a poor widow who dropped a couple of small coins into the offering box. Jesus gathered His disciples and said, "Truly, I tell you, this poor widow has put in more than all of them. For they all contributed out of their abundance, but she out of her poverty put in all she had to live on" (Luke 21:3–4). The widow's offering did not amount to a day's wage, but Jesus honored her gift because great faith underlaid her generosity. She gave her last cent, trusting God to provide her every last need.

How do we cultivate generous hearts? By growing our faith. "The point is this," Paul wrote, "whoever sows sparingly will also reap sparingly, and whoever sows bountifully will also reap bountifully. Each one must give as he has decided in his heart, not reluctantly or under compulsion, for God loves a cheerful giver. And God is able to make all grace abound to you, so that having all sufficiency in all things at all times, you may abound in every good work. . . . You will be enriched in every way to be generous in every way" (2 Corinthians 9:6–8, 11). Believers would abound in every good work and be generous in every way because God would supply and God would enrich. The kind of wholesale giving Paul wrote the Corinthians about pointed to the one the giver relied on for the seeds to sow (verse 10). "It is a proof of your faith," he told them (2 Corinthians 9:13 NCV).

Put your faith in God and give generously and He *will* be faithful. "Test Me now in this," the Lord told Israel, "if I will not open for you the windows of heaven and pour out for you a blessing until it overflows" (Malachi 3:10 NASB).

GOD, FORGIVE ME FOR THE TIMES I'VE HELD ON TO BLESSINGS BECAUSE I'VE LACKED FAITH. YOU WILL ALWAYS GIVE MORE THAN I CAN GIVE AWAY. AMEN.

Quenched

And the LORD will guide you continually and satisfy your
desire in scorched places. . .and you shall be like a watered
garden, like a spring of water, whose waters do not fail.
ISAIAH 58:11

The land was all dust and dryness. A sea of sand-colored earth stretched out as far as sight. But across the parched ground were dots of color, splashes of life. Tiny wildflowers were blooming.

If you've ever seen plants growing in the desert, you might marvel at their ability to thrive in an arid climate. And if you are experiencing some sort of drought in your life—whether you're sapped physically or drained emotionally or dried up spiritually—you might envy them. With cracked dirt below, the glaring sun above, and so little rain falling between, how do they still grow?

The biblical writers often used images of plant life to describe a godly person, with an emphasis on an ability to thrive—to remain green and fruitful—even in difficult times. In the book of Psalms, the godly person "is like a tree planted by streams of water that yields its fruit in its season, and its leaf does not wither" (Psalm 1:3). Jeremiah compared the godly to "a tree planted by water, that sends out its roots by the stream, and does not fear when heat comes, for its leaves remain green, and is not anxious in the year of drought, for it does not cease to bear fruit" (Jeremiah 17:8). What is this source of water that keeps the godly man (or woman) growing? "His delight is in the law of the LORD, and on his law he meditates day and night," the psalmist said (Psalm 1:2). And "Blessed is the man who trusts in the LORD, whose trust is the LORD," wrote Jeremiah (Jeremiah 17:7).

God provides a constant source of life-giving water to the believer. Jesus declared, "Whoever believes in me, as the Scripture has said, 'Out of his heart will flow rivers of living water'" (John 7:37–38). God's living water both grants eternal life in heaven and supports spiritual life on earth through the Spirit. We as believers need water to grow just as we need air to breathe. Perhaps this truth is most obvious when we're in a dry spell. It's then that we cry out like the psalmist, "As the deer pants for the water brooks, so pants my soul for You, O God. My soul thirsts for God, for the living God" (Psalm 42:1–2 NKJV).

When you're thirsty, return to the source. Dip deeply into God's Word. Drink your fill of His presence.

HOLY SPIRIT, FILL ME TO THE
BRIM WITH LIVING WATER. AMEN.

Persistently Persistent

And he told them a parable to the effect that they
ought always to pray and not lose heart.

LUKE 18:1

"Daddy?"

Here it comes, thought the father while holding back a grin. "What is it, honey?"

"Can I have a surfboard?"

"Maybe."

"I'd take good care of it. Can't I get one, please?"

"Maybe."

"But I've asked a bazillion times. Please, please, please?"

"Ask me one more time and we'll see."

If you ever asked for something over and over as a child, you remember how difficult the waiting was, but you probably didn't hesitate to ask. Is the same true with your heavenly Father? Are you as bold to ask over and over in your prayers to Him?

Persistence in prayer isn't frowned upon in the Bible. In fact, Jesus encouraged it. He once told the disciples a parable about a persistent widow to urge them to keep praying (Luke 18:1–8). The widow needed justice, so she pleaded her case to a certain judge over and over. The judge was not a godly man and repeatedly refused to help the widow. Eventually, though, he gave the widow what she wanted to stop her from bothering him. Jesus' point? If this ungodly man would respond favorably to spare himself, God will most certainly answer the ones He loves. "God will always give what is right to his people who cry to him night and day, and he will not be slow to answer them," Jesus said. "I tell you, God will help his people quickly" (Luke 18:7–8 NCV). Again Jesus promised, "Everyone who asks receives, and the one who seeks finds, and to the one who knocks it will be opened. . . . If you then, who are evil, know how to give good gifts to your children, how much more will your Father who is in heaven give good things to those who ask him!" (Matthew 7:8, 11). God wants us to approach Him with our needs. And it's okay to be persistent, like the blind beggar along the road outside Jericho who called out to Jesus for mercy. Even though the crowds rebuked him, he called out the same words again, and Jesus responded, restoring his sight. Or like the Canaanite woman who sought healing for her daughter. At first Jesus remained silent; then He turned her down. But the woman asked again. This time Jesus answered, "O woman, great is your faith! Be it done for you as you desire" (Matthew 15:28).

Go ahead. Ask Him one more time.

FATHER, THANK YOU FOR LISTENING TO MY
EVERY REQUEST. EVEN IN THE ASKING, YOU ARE
BUILDING MY FAITH. SO I'LL KEEP ASKING. AMEN.

Spontaneous Actions

So she quickly emptied her jar into the trough and ran
again to the well to draw water, and she drew for all
his camels. The man gazed at her in silence to learn
whether the LORD had prospered his journey or not.

GENESIS 24:20–21

It's highly unlikely to receive a marriage proposal while you're watering animals. But that's what happened to Rebekah.

It was chore time. She was doing what women in the household did—going to the well for water. And her spontaneous act of kindness toward the stranger with the caravan of camels was the thing that secured her future.

Abraham had commissioned his trusted servant to find a wife for his son. He didn't want Isaac to marry a pagan woman from the Canaanites. And so the servant had a plan. And Rebekah did exactly as he had asked the Lord for her to do in order to give him a sign that she was the right woman for his master. And the rest, as they say, is history. After talking with her family and doing some deep thinking, she decided to return with the servant and marry a man she had never seen, the child of promise grown up, the beginning of the great Hebrew nation.

What were you doing when you met the man you would marry? Something menial? Something unusual? Did it have anything to do with the life you now share together?

I wonder if we would be more attuned to the significance

of everyday actions if we remembered that someone might be watching how we perform them for a specific reason. Perhaps our responses and offers of help guide others in knowing how God is leading them. Maybe they are watching us in silence like the servant did to see if God is showing up in this ordinary place.

They made the long journey back across the desert, and Rebekah's first glimpse of Isaac was of him walking in the field, meditating. She asked who he was and then veiled herself as propriety demanded in those days. Only a husband could view a woman unveiled. And Isaac took her as his wife and loved her. Her love brought him comfort after the death of his mother, Sarah.

She couldn't have dreamed when she went to the well that day that her life was going to change so drastically. You might not know how the events that are happening right now are changing your future. But God does. And He guides caravans and chore time and every other detail if we let Him.

GOD, YOU ARE THE ONE WHO SEES EVERY TINY DETAIL OF MY LIFE. I'M NOT SURE HOW MY TOMORROWS CONNECT WITH MY ACTIVITIES TODAY, BUT I TRUST YOU TO WORK ALL THINGS OUT IN YOUR TIME. IN JESUS' NAME, AMEN.

Die to Live

"Whoever finds his life will lose it, and whoever loses his life for my sake will find it."

MATTHEW 10:39

Lose your life to find it. *Shouldn't that be the other way around?* But Jesus' statement in Matthew is just one example of the Bible's sometimes backward-sounding logic. Truth is, without the Holy Spirit's help, much of God's Word doesn't make a whole lot of sense.

So what exactly does Jesus mean when He tells us that by losing our lives for His sake we will find them? His meaning is twofold. For some of Jesus' followers, professing faith in Him will lead to losing their lives literally—they will be martyred for their faith. For every believer, though, true faith in Christ involves dying to self to live for Christ (Galatians 2:20). It involves letting go of self to grab hold of Christ alone. Jesus said, "If anyone would come after me, let him deny himself and take up his cross and follow me" (Matthew 16:24). Taking up one's cross—living completely surrendered to God—echoes the complete sacrifice that Christ made for us on the cross. But Christ's sacrifice also brought life, and so does ours. When we choose Christ over self, when we forsake the world to follow Him, we gain abundant life now and eternal life to come. "Most assuredly," said Jesus, "unless a grain of wheat falls into the ground and dies, it remains alone; but if it dies, it produces much grain. He who loves his life will lose it, and he who hates his life in this world will keep it for eternal life. . . . And where I am, there

My servant will be also. If anyone serves Me, him My Father will honor" (John 12:24–26 NKJV).

LORD, YOU'VE GIVEN ME TRUE LIFE THROUGH THE CROSS—LIFE FOR MY SOUL NOW AND IN ETERNITY. EVERY DAY, SHOW ME MORE OF WHAT IT MEANS TO LOSE MY LIFE FOR YOU. AMEN.

"Shepherd Me!"

The LORD is my shepherd. . . . Yea, though I walk through the valley of the shadow of death, I will fear no evil: for thou art with me; thy rod and thy staff they comfort me.

PSALM 23:1, 4 KJV

At age five, it was the dark. At age nine, it was spiders. At age sixteen, it was her driver's license test (and spiders). At age twenty-seven, it was finances. At age thirty-four, it was a health scare. At age. . . No matter what our age, it seems fear is always with us. Yet no matter what we're afraid of, we always have a reason *not* to fear.

In his well-known psalm, Psalm 23, David identified God with an image that appears throughout scripture: the Lord as shepherd. Both Old and New Testament writers referred to God's guiding presence in believers' lives in terms of shepherding. For David, the Lord as his shepherd meant that even in the most frightening times—"the valley of the shadow of death"—he would not fear because God was with him. Like a shepherd fending off predators and gently leading the sheep with the tools of his trade, God was there, guarding and guiding David.

Without a shepherd, a sheep's life is hazardous. There are thickets and ditches that trap and wolves that devour. Sound familiar? Life is full of fears, the most threatening being death. But we believers have a shepherd and savior from our fears. Jesus said, "If anyone enters by me, he will be saved and will go in and out and find pasture. The thief comes only to steal and kill and destroy. I came that they may have life and have it abundantly. . . . I am the good shepherd. I know my own and my own know me. . .and I lay down my life for the sheep" (John 10:9–10, 14–15). Such a promise is reason enough not to fear.

Each of us as a believer is one of the Lord's flock. He knows us individually, calling us by name, and cares for us beyond anything we could imagine. He is our Good Shepherd, and we will not fear even the valleys because He is with us—guarding and guiding, shepherding us through life. "Now may the God of peace who brought again from the dead our Lord Jesus, the great shepherd of the sheep, by the blood of the eternal covenant, equip you with everything good that you may do his will, working in us that which is pleasing in his sight" (Hebrews 13:20–21).

LORD, WHEN I FACE MY FEARS, PLEASE REMIND
ME THAT I DON'T FACE THEM ALONE. YOU,
MY GOOD SHEPHERD, WALK BEFORE ME. AMEN.

Decelerating the Rage

He who is slow to anger is better than the mighty, and
he who rules his spirit than he who takes a city.

PROVERBS 16:32 NKJV

I am not given to loud outbursts while driving. But one day while driving somewhere with my teenage daughter (and probably trying to hurry), the Holy Spirit convicted me of my muttering about the car ahead of me. He seemed to whisper that I was not really modeling Christian grace to my teen, who is still picking up cues for her later adult life from me. Of course, I had to agree; the Spirit of God is always right.

Road rage is supposedly a modern complication of our stressful lives. Drivers who are already upset about their day and their obligations and commitments are "driven" to a sudden explosion of anger by a small error or inconsideration on the part of another driver.

I wonder if they had similar problems in Bible times. Most ordinary people didn't own chariots, so it probably wasn't as much of a problem. Animals used to carry things were slow, and everybody knew it. But you can be sure that there were factors that made people feel an emotion similar to road rage. The human psyche can only take so much before it boils over. That's why we need the controlling presence of the Holy Spirit in our everyday lives. When we have surrendered ourselves fully to His work in us, He empowers us to manage these trying situations in a way that doesn't bring harm to others.

Feeling irritation is admittedly a human response to something that isn't just or that hinders our ability to accomplish a goal or that doesn't meet our personal expectations. The emotion itself is clearly just a response. It is the manner in which we express it that becomes either a sin or a grace.

I admit that I often tap my fingers on the wheel when I'm in a hurry and I'm being blocked by other cars, or when I'm waiting at a traffic light. I guess I think that moving something helps a little! But we must be careful not to transfer these bits of impatience into our words and actions toward others.

The wisdom writer says that ruling one's spirit is a greater victory than conquering a city. I think that goes for driving to an appointment without yelling or staring at another driver. God in us wins the victory; our assignment is to give Him control.

LORD, I SURRENDER MY DRIVING HABITS TO YOU. LET ME SHOW GRACE AND FORBEARANCE TOWARD OTHERS, HOWEVER IRRITATING THEIR DRIVING SKILLS MAY BE. I ASK THIS IN JESUS' NAME, AMEN.

A Lesson in Humility

Humble yourselves, therefore, under the mighty hand
of God so that at the proper time he may exalt you.

1 PETER 5:6

The last months had been no picnic. She still believed she was where God wanted her to be, but the joy of following had led to a place of hardship. Sometimes she wished she could go back, plug her ears, and pretend she didn't hear God. Sometimes she desperately wanted to look for an escape route. Sometimes she was tempted to shake her fist at God and cry out, "Why? Why have You brought me here to suffer?" One thing she was sure of: God was working in her life.

God is continually working in our lives, using every moment to fulfill His plans. And He will fulfill them. "Have you not heard that I determined it long ago?" the Lord asked. "I planned from days of old what now I bring to pass" (2 Kings 19:25). When we're swimming in blessings, we cheer at those words. But what if God's plan involves molding us through hardship? What if His doing something better requires some bitterness along the way? Do we push against His mighty hand? Or do we humble ourselves and wait for Him to work?

Jesus knew what it meant to humble Himself. He left His throne in heaven to wash the feet of sinners. He tasted the bitterness of death for our sake. And His mentality is to be our own. Paul instructed believers in Philippi, "Have this mind among yourselves, which is yours in Christ Jesus, who, though he was in the form of God, did not count equality with God a thing to be grasped, but emptied himself, by taking the form of a servant, being born in the likeness of men. And being found in human form, he humbled himself by becoming obedient to the point of death, even death on a cross" (Philippians 2:5–8). The Son submitted to the Father. He made Himself low—until God lifted Him up. Paul continued, "Therefore God has highly exalted him and bestowed on him the name that is above every name" (Philippians 2:9).

God is continually working in your life. When in His sovereignty He brings you through challenging times, don't resist His mighty hand—He's using even the rough moments for your good and His glory. Instead, "give your[self] completely to God. . . . Humble yourself in the Lord's presence." And in due time "he will honor you" (James 4:7, 10 NCV).

GOD, I DON'T LIKE WHERE I AM RIGHT NOW,
BUT I WON'T FIGHT WHAT YOU'RE DOING IN MY
LIFE. I CHOOSE TO HUMBLE MYSELF BEFORE
YOU SO THAT YOU CAN LIFT ME UP. AMEN.

Relax–
It's the Sabbath

Jesus said to them, "The Sabbath was made for man,
and not man for the Sabbath. So the Son of
Man is Lord even of the Sabbath."
MARK 2:27–28 NASB

Sabbath. Sunday. The day of rest. We call it different names, and our opinions on it vary. Is it a day like any other, a catchall for the loose ends of the week, or a chance to catch up on some z's? Do we hit PAUSE on everything but worship and reflection? Our view on the Sabbath may be a jumble of tradition, practicality, and scripture. It may even become a source of tension. What are we supposed to do about the Sabbath?

The Pharisees, of course, had rules for the Sabbath, and one Sabbath, Jesus' disciples broke those rules. As they were traveling through a grain field, the disciples, who were hungry, began to pick off some heads of grain to eat. When the Pharisees pointed out this infraction, Jesus replied:

> *"Have you not read what David did when he was*
> *hungry, and those who were with him: how he entered*
> *the house of God and ate the bread of the Presence, which*
> *it was not lawful for him to eat nor for those who were*
> *with him, but only for the priests? Or have you not*
> *read in the Law how on the Sabbath the priests in the*

*temple profane the Sabbath and are guiltless? I tell you,
something greater than the temple is here. And if you
had known what this means, 'I desire mercy, and not
sacrifice,' you would not have condemned the guiltless."*
(Matthew 12:3–7)

While the Pharisees were shortsighted amid all their rules and the regulations they thought they knew, Jesus was looking toward "something greater." His death on the cross would bring the kind of rest that the Sabbath only represented—a rest for the soul from the toils of living up to the law (Matthew 11:28). Christ offered freedom from the regulations; He offered rest. After Christ, the Sabbath became what it was intended to be—a blessing, not a burden.

A final thought: God rested on the seventh day (Genesis 2:3). No regulation bound Him, but He set the pace for us. Will you join Him in some rest this Sabbath?

GOD, THANK YOU FOR REST—
REST FOR MY BODY EACH WEEK AND
REST FOR MY SOUL IN ETERNITY. AMEN.

"For God So Loved"

For God so loved the world, that he gave his only begotten Son, that whosoever believeth in him should not perish, but have everlasting life.

JOHN 3:16 KJV

You might be familiar with the children's book *Guess How Much I Love You.** It's the story of Little Nutbrown Hare and his father, Big Nutbrown Hare. Throughout the pages, Little Nutbrown Hare tries to show his father how much he loves him—as wide as his arms can stretch and as high as he can reach, up to the height of his hops and way out to the moon. But each time, the father shows he loves much more—as wide as *his* arms can stretch. . .way out to the moon and back.

John 3:16 (KJV) is one of the most well-known verses in the Bible, and for good reason. Using only about two dozen words, John encapsulated the gospel message. "For God so loved the world, that he gave his only begotten Son, that whosoever believeth in him should not perish, but have everlasting life." God so loved us that He sent His Son to save us. By believing in Him, we have eternal life. What love! But what makes that love even greater is the fact that God loved us when we were unlovable. Paul explained, "For while we were still weak, at the right time Christ died for the ungodly. For one will scarcely die for a righteous person—though perhaps for a good person one would dare even to die—but God shows his love for us in that while we were still sinners, Christ died for us" (Romans 5:6–8). We had nothing to offer in our sinful state—not even our love. "We love because he *first* loved us," John wrote (1 John 4:19, italics added). And God so loved us.

The heavenly Father's love is indeed vast. And its extent is something God is forever revealing to our hearts. Paul's prayer for the Ephesians was "that according to the riches of his glory he may grant you to be strengthened with power through his Spirit in your inner being, so that Christ may dwell in your hearts through faith—that you, being rooted and grounded in love, may have strength to comprehend with all the saints what is the breadth and length and height and depth, and to know the love of Christ that surpasses knowledge" (Ephesians 3:16–19). How much does God love us? As wide as Christ's outstretched arms on the cross. From heaven to earth and back.

FATHER, I LOVE YOU SO MUCH.
THANK YOU FOR THE REMINDER THAT
YOU LOVE ME MUCH MORE. AMEN.

*Sam McBratney, *Guess How Much I Love You* (Somerville, MA: Candlewick, 2008).

Refining Tools

*"For affliction does not come from the dust,
nor does trouble sprout from the ground, but man
is born to trouble as the sparks fly upward."*

JOB 5:6–7

Some days Job's statement in Job 5:6–7 could be a life verse. Trouble—difficulties and challenges large and small—comes at us in a variety of ways.

The dishwasher stops working. Mine did. It hadn't been cleaning dishes right for a while, but I babied it along, rinsing the dishes after they came out and trying to make sure I kept the apparatus working. Then the computerized system went haywire and it started turning itself on. That was a problem. Finally, it just was unusable.

Another day, I put the wet laundry into the dryer and selected the setting I wanted. An hour later when I pulled them out, they were cool and very damp. The heating element had gone bad.

The bathtub drain clogged. The battery in the garage door opener died. The Keurig sputtered and spit at me. The minivan decided not to run. All of these little inconveniences mark the truth of Job's exasperated proclamation—man is born to trouble.

These kinds of minor calamities come upon us randomly and without warning. That's the way life changes. There is no announcement, no "Get ready for trouble!" No, it just arrives like an undesired guest.

Today you may be facing some small troubles that seem big

at the moment. Remember that God is in the little things too, and He is using every unplanned moment to shape you even closer to His image. And if Job can survive his disasters, so can you. The God he worshipped is there for you when you call.

DEAR LORD, TAKE MY UNWANTED MOMENTS AND MAKE THEM INTO REFINING TOOLS TO SHAPE ME CLOSER TO YOUR IMAGE. THANK YOU FOR BEING THERE IN MY DARK TIMES. AMEN.

Like Sponges

And do not be conformed to this world, but be transformed by the renewing of your mind, so that you may prove what the will of God is, that which is good and acceptable and perfect.

Romans 12:2 nasb

Sponges are curious things. Place one on a wet counter and it slurps the liquid, swelling in size and darkening in color. Whatever it soaks up transforms it. We say children are like sponges because their minds soak up everything around them. Whatever they hear and see transforms them. And the same is true of our grown-up minds. Whatever we fill our heads with transforms us.

A changed mind is at the core of salvation. When we believe in Jesus, God changes who we are, beginning with how we think—our beliefs, our moral compass, and so on. Our former ways no longer characterize us—they belong to minds that have not yet been enlightened by God's truth. Paul told believers, "You must no longer walk as the Gentiles do, in the futility of their minds. They are darkened in their understanding, alienated from the life of God because of the ignorance that is in them, due to their hardness of heart. . . . But that is not the way you learned Christ!—assuming that you have heard about him and were taught in him, as the truth is in Jesus, to put off your old self, which belongs to your former manner of life and is corrupt. . .and to be renewed in the spirit of your minds" (Ephesians 4:17–18, 20–23). New mind intact, a believer starts life as a Christian with a new nature (verse 24), and rather than being "conformed to this world," she is to live out her new nature by being transformed daily.

What fuels this daily transformation? The renewing of the mind. So how do we renew our minds?

First, we need to ask for help. The renewal that the Bible speaks about comes only through the Holy Spirit. On our own, we cannot understand godly things, but with the Spirit abiding in us, we can understand even the thoughts of our Lord (1 Corinthians 2:16).

Then we need to think deeply on God's Word, letting it "dwell" in us "richly" (Colossians 3:16). Philippians 4:8 (NKJV) tells us, "Whatever things are true, whatever things are noble, whatever things are just, whatever things are pure, whatever things are lovely. . .meditate on these things." As we fill our minds with scripture, we're filled with life-changing words. As we soak up His Word, it transforms us.

HOLY SPIRIT, RENEW MY MIND THROUGH THE WORD. I WANT TO BE SO SOAKED IN SCRIPTURE THAT MY EVERY THOUGHT AND ACTION IS TRANSFORMED. AMEN.

Nurturing

She looks well to the ways of her household
and does not eat the bread of idleness.

PROVERBS 31:27

If you've ever seen a mother bird preparing her nest, you have an idea of what nurturing is all about. She flies back and forth, gathering twigs and leaves and bits of fur and brush, trip after trip, adding to the little home where her young will be hatched.

I remember going through the "nesting" days before my first child was born. I had an unexplainable urge to get everything ready. For me, that meant I was out in the grocery store on the day before her birth, waddling down the aisles, putting quick-fix food in my cart. Some women paint rooms or do deep cleaning; others cook and freeze meals. It's part of the instinctual, hormonal response to the motherhood that's about to begin.

Nurturing is both a natural and a learned skill. Most women with normal hormones have maternal feelings and responses. At times these can be damaged through trauma or impaired through chemical imbalance. But the norm is for women to be inclined to nurture. Such is the effect of estrogen and progesterone in our bodies.

The excellent woman of Proverbs leaned into the way God made her and nurtured the people around her. For us, nurturing may be with chocolate chip cookies, or it may be with a counseling session in a daughter's room. There are many ways to nurture, and the wise woman uses them all.

Some of my precious memories of time spent with my own mother took place in my bedroom after I'd finished my homework and she came in to sit and talk and laugh with me. We'd talk over all kinds of things, and that time together created a deep bond that I cherish today. She nurtured me as a daughter, as a woman, as a person. The insight and intuition God gave her allowed her to see the things I needed her to see and say the things I needed her to say. That is the beauty of this calling to nurture.

Today, look around your home and let your mom gut speak to you. You may see someone who needs nurturing before the day is done.

DEAR GOD, YOU DO ALL THINGS WELL, AND YOU CREATED ME WITH THIS ABILITY TO NURTURE OTHERS. SHOW ME HOW I CAN USE IT FOR THE GOOD OF THOSE AROUND ME. AMEN.

Doubtless

Thomas answered him, "My Lord and my God!" Jesus said
to him, "Have you believed because you have seen me?
Blessed are those who have not seen and yet have believed."
JOHN 20:28–29

He's known as doubting Thomas. The resurrected Lord had appeared to the disciples and showed them His nail-scarred hands and side. But Thomas wasn't there, so the disciples had to relay what they'd seen. Upon hearing the incredible news, Thomas was doubtful; he needed proof. Unless he saw and touched the marks on Jesus' hands and side himself, he would not believe.

Thomas wasn't the first believer to have doubts. When God told Moses that He was sending him to free Israel, Moses doubted his own ability. "Who am I," he asked, "that I should go to Pharaoh and bring the children of Israel out of Egypt?" (Exodus 3:11). John the Baptist was imprisoned when he heard reports about "the deeds of the Christ" (Matthew 11:2). In response, he sent a message to Jesus: "Are you the one who is to come, or shall we look for another?" (Matthew 11:3). And Philip—right after Jesus' declaration that He is the way, the truth, and the life and that through Him we know God (John 14:6–7)—requested a bit more evidence: "Lord, show us the Father, and it is enough for us" (John 14:8).

How did God react to the doubters? Out of His love He supplied exactly what each one needed to believe. For Moses, it was reassurance—"I will be with you, and this shall be the sign for you, that I have sent you" (Exodus 3:12). For John, it was confirmation—"Go and tell John what you hear and see: the blind receive their sight and the lame walk, lepers are cleansed and the deaf hear, and the dead are raised up" (Matthew 11:4–5). For Philip, it was the facts—"Have I been with you so long, and you still do not know me, Philip? . . . Believe me. . .or else believe on account of the works themselves" (John 14:9, 11).

And for Thomas, it was physical proof. A week and a day later, Jesus appeared again. To Thomas, in an echo of Thomas's words, He said, "Put your finger here, and see my hands; and put out your hand, and place it in my side. Do not disbelieve, but believe" (John 20:27).

God knows that believing is difficult, especially without sight. "Blessed are those who have not seen and yet have believed," Jesus said (John 20:29). And when we cry out to Him, "I believe; help my unbelief!" (Mark 9:24), He will reach out to us, no doubt about it.

GOD, I BELIEVE IN YOU. HELP ME
SHED MY DOUBTS. AMEN.

Contented

Be content with what you have, for he has said,
"I will never leave you nor forsake you."

HEBREWS 13:5

How much is enough? Considering the overabundance that's out there—from row upon row of vehicles at dealerships to crammed store aisles to the ever-present next-best in devices—it's a question we ought to ask ourselves. There's *so much stuff* our hearts can pine after that the pining can go on and on. No sooner do we get one thing than something else catches our eye, and that something will be enough, surely! But it isn't. Renowned preacher Charles Spurgeon once said, "You say, 'If I had a little more, I should be very satisfied.' You make a mistake. If you are not content with what you have, you would not be satisfied if it were doubled." Solomon too understood the futility of trying to reach a place of satisfaction in the pursuit of more. He shared this piece of wisdom with readers: "It is better to be content with what little you have. Otherwise, you will always be struggling for more, and that is like chasing the wind" (Ecclesiastes 4:6 NCV).

It may or may not be a surprise, but the Bible's definition of enough is radically different from the Western world's definition, where every billboard, commercial, and online ad touts that enough is more. Christians should be able to find satisfaction in the bare necessities. Paul wrote to Timothy, "Now godliness with contentment is great gain. For we brought nothing into this world, and it is certain we can carry nothing out. And having food and clothing, with these we shall be content" (1 Timothy 6:6–8 NKJV). *So a shirt on your back and a meal in your belly is enough? How?*

The kind of contentment Paul wrote about has nothing to do with how much or how little a person owns but everything to do with the one who satisfies. In a passage on God's provision, Paul told believers, "I have learned in whatever state I am, to be content: I know how to be abased, and I know how to abound. Everywhere and in all things I have learned both to be full and to be hungry, both to abound and to suffer need. I can do all things through Christ who strengthens me" (Philippians 4:11–13 NKJV). Paul could be content trusting in God's presence to get him through times of plenty and need. He could be content resting in the God who met his deepest longings. He could be content knowing that what God gave was enough.

GOD, WHERE YOU ARE, NO MATTER WHAT
ELSE FILLS MY LIFE, I WILL BE CONTENT.
AND YOU ARE ALWAYS WITH ME. AMEN.

All Ready?

"Therefore you also must be ready, for the Son of Man is coming at an hour you do not expect."

MATTHEW 24:44

Today could be the day. Christ has promised to return, and He will, any moment now. But somehow in the midst of our day-to-day, the certainty—the immediacy—of Christ's return is sometimes the last thing on our minds.

Knowing us only too well, Jesus cautioned believers to remain alert, to keep the thought of His second coming at the forefront of our minds. He compared the waiting period that would end with His arrival to the time leading up to the flood: "But as the days of Noah were, so also will the coming of the Son of Man be. For as in the days before the flood, they were eating and drinking, marrying and giving in marriage, until the day that Noah entered the ark, and did not know until the flood came and took them all away, so also will the coming of the Son of Man be" (Matthew 24:37–39 NKJV). While the people were caught up in life's daily concerns, the flood came and caught them unawares. This wouldn't be the case for believers who were watching and waiting for Christ to come. Though they could not predict the hour, they could prepare. Jesus said, "Be dressed, ready for service, and have your lamps shining. Be like servants who are waiting for their master to come home from a wedding party. When he comes and knocks, the servants immediately open the door for him. . . . Those servants will be blessed when he comes in and finds them still waiting, even if it is midnight or later" (Luke 12:35–36, 38 NCV).

Peter continued Jesus' themes of watchfulness and readiness at all times, no matter how lengthy the wait. He reminded believers not to be lulled by scoffers into thinking that because the world is humming along as it always has, it always will (2 Peter 3:4). Believers know better. Christ will return, and God will judge: "The day of the Lord will come like a thief. . .and the earth and the works that are done on it will be exposed" (2 Peter 3:10). And since we know what's ahead, "what sort of people ought [we] to be in lives of holiness and godliness, waiting for and hastening the coming of the day of God" (2 Peter 3:11–12)! Let's watch for Him. Let's use this time to get ready, to live every day in anticipation. Today could be the day.

LORD, I'VE BEEN SO PREOCCUPIED WITH
LIVING THAT I HAVEN'T THOUGHT ABOUT YOU
COMING BACK. I'M SORRY. WHEN YOU RETURN,
HELP ME TO BE READY AND WAITING. AMEN.

Really Bad Days

*"For we have been sold, I and my people, to be
destroyed, to be killed, and to be annihilated."*

ESTHER 7:4

We've all had bad days. But probably none of us have found out
that our entire race of people was destined for extinction. That was
what Esther was told. As the new queen, she had busy days and
nights and little time for frivolous concerns. But when her cousin
Mordecai informed her of the plot against the Jewish nation, she
listened. He beseeched her to help from her position of power.
She knew that she might die before she had the chance to tell the
king the problem. But she would die anyway from the edict, so she
decided to take the risk.

Esther hadn't lived a charmed life. Her parents were killed when
she was young, and she was a member of an oppressed people
living captive in a foreign land. She was raised by her cousin and
protected by him up until the day the king commanded that every
eligible young virgin in the city be rounded up as potential queen
material. When we read the story now, we think of the glamour of
the Persian palace and the fascination of the beauty routines. But
for Esther, it was a still more intense form of captivity. She would
never be able to leave the harem once she spent the night with the
king. She would be part of a petted, protected gaggle of women
who lived out their lives in luxury and loneliness.

When she unexpectedly became the queen, Esther was no

doubt happy that her life would have purpose. But then the words of Mordecai made her realize that she was still vulnerable to trouble.

Maybe, like Esther, you have had a difficult life, and just when things seemed about to open up for you, a bigger problem than ever dropped into your path. Take courage from the resolve of a young queen trying to save her people.

"Go, gather all the Jews to be found in Susa, and hold a fast on my behalf, and do not eat or drink for three days, night or day. I and my young women will also fast as you do. Then I will go to the king, though it is against the law, and if I perish, I perish" (Esther 4:16).

Don't be alarmed at the trouble; be resolute in your heart. Bad days are meant to be conquered, and we know the God who can do anything.

FATHER IN HEAVEN, LIKE ESTHER, I TRUST YOU TODAY
TO GIVE ME A PLAN TO DEAL WITH MY TROUBLE.
THIS CHALLENGE OF MINE DID NOT SURPRISE
YOU, AND I NEED YOUR HELP AS I DEAL WITH IT.
THANK YOU FOR YOUR CONSTANT CARE. AMEN.

Holy Pruning

This is my prayer for you. . .that you will be filled
with the good things produced in your life by
Christ to bring glory and praise to God.

PHILIPPIANS 1:9, 11 NCV

God's first recorded order for man was "Be fruitful and multiply" (Genesis 1:28). Christians today are to be fruitful too, but not just in populating the earth. In Romans we're told that when God releases us from the bondage of the law, He does it "so that [we] may belong to another, to him who has been raised from the dead, in order that we may bear fruit for God" (Romans 7:4). And in the book of John, Jesus explained to His disciples and, by extension, to all believers that He handpicked us with plans for us to bear fruit: "You did not choose me, but I chose you and appointed you that you should go and bear fruit and that your fruit should abide" (John 15:16). God's orders? Be fruitful! Yield spiritual fruit—what the New Testament defines as godly attitudes, righteous behavior, praise, and the leading of nonbelievers to faith*—and the more, the better. "By this my Father is glorified," Jesus said, "that you bear *much* fruit" (John 15:8, italics added).

If the prospect of bearing an abundance of fruit is overwhelming, keep this in mind: it is through God that we bear fruit at all, and He is working in us to make us more fruitful. In one of the Bible's beautiful metaphors of Christianity, Jesus becomes the vine, the Father the vinedresser, and believers the branches:

"I am the true vine, and My Father is the vinedresser. Every branch in Me that does not bear fruit He takes away; and every branch that bears fruit He prunes, that it may bear more fruit. You are already clean because of the word which I have spoken to you. Abide in Me, and I in you. As the branch cannot bear fruit of itself, unless it abides in the vine, neither can you, unless you abide in Me.

"I am the vine, you are the branches. He who abides in Me, and I in him, bears much fruit; for without Me you can do nothing." (John 15:1–5 NKJV)

As we abide in the vine, drawing life from Him, God is pruning, cutting away anything in our lives that impedes our growth, lopping off a sin here and trimming back a bad habit there. God's pruning isn't pleasant, but it will make the branches flourish (Hebrews 12:11).

FATHER, I CAN FEEL YOUR PRUNING IN MY LIFE, AND YOUR SHEARS HURT. BUT I'VE SEEN YOU WORK BEFORE, AND IT ALWAYS YIELDS FRUIT. AMEN.

*John MacArthur, *The MacArthur Bible Commentary* (Nashville: Thomas Nelson, 2005), 1407.

Kindness

She opens her mouth with wisdom, and the
teaching of kindness is on her tongue.

PROVERBS 31:26

Professor Higgins in *My Fair Lady* declares that he can recognize a lady by her speech. He then sets out to prove that he can, conversely, make a lady out of a "guttersnipe" by teaching her proper English. The process is amusing and somewhat traumatizing for poor Eliza Doolittle.

Whether Higgins could actually peg a lady by her speech, we're not sure. But we do know that one can tell a godly woman by the kindness of her words.

We live in a very uncivil time. Everyday speech has become crude and crass; words for bodily functions that would never have been condoned in previous generations are now used with barely a blink of the eye. Conversations about intimacy and sexuality are common. Political discussions dissolve into verbal brawls on social media. We are becoming a generation without decorum and kindness.

In such a setting, a godly woman is refreshingly different. She guards her words and uses wisdom in the topics on which she converses. And above all, she is kind in her speech.

Kindness is more than not saying something rude or offensive; it is framing words in such a way that a message doesn't come across as hurtful or demeaning.

The excellent woman knows that the words she says reflect on the Lord she represents. His honor is worth more than her having a cheap parting shot. His agenda is more important than hers. His truth and love must be the standards for her conversations.

In the end, Professor Higgins did successfully transform Eliza into a lady. But it was her falling in love with him that made the most difference; she wanted to be transformed so she could please him and be in his world. And so it is with us. When we love the Lord, we are happy to be transformed into what pleases Him.

FATHER, I WANT TO BE A WOMAN WHO USES
WISDOM AND KINDNESS IN MY CONVERSATIONS.
I WANT TO MAKE YOUR HEART GLAD WITH
THE WAY I SPEAK. I ASK YOU TO HELP WITH
THAT TODAY. IN JESUS' NAME, AMEN.

Making Everything Beautiful

It is not fancy hair, gold jewelry, or fine clothes that should make you beautiful. No, your beauty should come from within you—the beauty of a gentle and quiet spirit that will never be destroyed and is very precious to God.

1 PETER 3:3–4 NCV

Whatever you look like on the outside, odds are there's *something* you would change. Next time you're standing face-to-face with yourself at the mirror, try this: see your appearance not as a result of happenstance, genes mixing with genes, but as the workmanship of the Creator. Of God the psalmist wrote, "You made my whole being; you formed me in my mother's body. I praise you because you made me in an amazing and wonderful way. What you have done is wonderful. I know this very well" (Psalm 139:13–14 NCV). From start to finish, head to toe, God designed you—with care and intention, in an amazing and wonderful way.

Why is it, then, that we so often question our Maker? "Woe to him who strives with him who formed him, a pot among earthen pots!" the Lord said. "Does the clay say to him who forms it, 'What are you making?' or 'Your work has no handles'?" (Isaiah 45:9). Yet we, the creation, look at what the Creator has made and find things we would have done differently. We overlook the truth that when God creates—just as when He plans—He does so with perfection. And He does so with purpose.

That purpose goes deeper than skin and bones. God is most concerned with what's inside. When the Lord sent Samuel to anoint the next king of Israel, the young shepherd David, He told Samuel, "Do not look on his appearance or on the height of his stature. . . . For the LORD sees not as man sees: man looks on the outward appearance, but the LORD looks on the heart" (1 Samuel 16:7). It didn't matter if David was impressive physically; God was peering inside, to his heart. He's still gazing on our hearts, and if our focus is the outer shell, we'll miss it. While we expend a good deal of energy on the surface, trying to make the outer shell more beautiful, God is working within. He is making us beautiful in ways that won't become clear and won't be complete until heaven. Now if only we would begin to see as God sees. If only we would appreciate the beauty God creates in us, standing face-to-face with ourselves at the mirror!

GOD, WHEN I PICK APART WHAT YOU'VE
CREATED, GIVE ME EYES TO SEE AS YOU DO.
I'M BEAUTIFUL TO YOU—OUTSIDE AND IN—AND
I'LL BECOME MORE BEAUTIFUL STILL. AMEN.

Mercy for Guilt

And Jesus said unto her, Neither do I
condemn thee: go, and sin no more.

JOHN 8:11 KJV

A death sentence commuted. You can't get more mercy than that.

Perhaps no biblical story has been cited more often as an example of the mercy and grace of Jesus than the account of the woman caught in adultery, a violation of God's law, clearly sin. Jesus never disputes that fact. He knew she had sinned. And He knew she did it intentionally, for He later told her not to do it again. He knows hearts.

What sins have you committed that Jesus knows about? Does today find you guilty? Maybe, just like her, you have been found out. Maybe today your shame is being made public, to your family, husband, friends, church. Maybe every hiding place is gone, and you feel, like her, thrown down in the sand before the eyes of people who haven't done what you have. Maybe you're shivering like her, with only a blanket thrown around you to hide the naked state in which you were found (or at least it feels that way emotionally).

I have wondered what she felt. What was it like to see the holy, loving eyes of Jesus turn to her? She probably hung her head, averted her eyes. She was guilty and deserved death. And she knew it.

Jesus spoke, not to her, but to the men. "If you haven't ever sinned, throw a stone." Then He stooped and wrote with His finger in the sand. And because they couldn't get Him to do what they wanted, the bad guys drifted off, leaving the problem with Jesus. Let Him deal with it.

Jesus raised up and looked again at her and asked if anyone still accused her. But no one there was without sin—except Him. He was sinless, but He didn't throw a stone; He did something unexpected. Instead of handing down a death sentence, he offered mercy and restoration. And a command: "Go, and sin no more."

What happened then? Did Jesus walk with her back to her home so she wouldn't be a woman alone in a culture where she was suspect? Did He talk to her on the way and encourage her to live a new life?

Maybe. For a man to speak publicly with a woman was socially unacceptable at that time, but Jesus cared more for people than practice. He was the source of everything unexpectedly merciful. And He is still.

LORD GOD, THANK YOU FOR THE DIVINE MERCY YOU SHOWED IN JESUS. TODAY I ASK FOR FORGIVENESS AND ACCEPT YOUR OFFER OF FREEDOM FROM SIN. IN CHRIST'S NAME, AMEN.

Why We Love

We love because he first loved us.

1 JOHN 4:19

Maybe he sat off to the side. Maybe he was hovering around the fringes of the group or standing right in the middle. But after hearing Jesus' expert reply to the Sadducees, the scribe asked his own question. "Which commandment is the most important of all?" (Mark 12:28). Jesus' answer has become the backbone of Christian life: love God with everything in you, and love your neighbor as yourself (Mark 12:29–31). Put simply, love is huge. Paul even wrote that "the whole law is fulfilled in one word: 'You shall love your neighbor as yourself' " (Galatians 5:14; see also Romans 13:9).

Why is love so paramount? Because God Himself is love (1 John 4:8, 16). It is through Him that we know love ourselves. God put an exclamation point on His love at the cross. "In this the love of God was made manifest among us, that God sent his only Son into the world, so that we might live through him. In this is love, not that we have loved God but that he loved us and sent his Son to be the propitiation for our sins" (1 John 4:9–10). God did the loving, and now we respond to His love with love. John continued, "Beloved, if God so loved us, we also ought to love one another" (1 John 4:11).

That's all well and good, but what if your neighbor—whether next door or an ocean away—is someone you don't particularly like? How do you love when your heart isn't in it? Author C. S.

Lewis had this to say: "The rule for all of us is perfectly simple. Do not waste time bothering whether you 'love' your neighbour; act as if you did. As soon as we do this we find one of the great secrets. When you are behaving as if you loved someone, you will presently come to love him."* While this "fake it till you make it" version of love may seem to lack feeling, that is precisely the point according to Lewis, because "Christian Love, either towards God or towards man, is an affair of the will." Once we choose to love, God will work in our hearts. "He will give us feelings of love if He pleases," Lewis concluded.† We are forever directed back to love itself. God loved us, so we love. We love through God in us.

GOD, I TRY SO HARD TO LOVE OTHERS. BUT IT'S BECAUSE OF YOUR LOVE THAT I CHOOSE TO LOVE, AND IT'S BECAUSE OF YOUR PRESENCE THAT I CAN LOVE. HELP ME TO LOVE LIKE YOU DO. AMEN.

*C. S. Lewis, *Mere Christianity* (New York: HarperCollins, 2001), 131.
†Ibid., 132.

"I Don't Get It"

Think over what I say, for the Lord will
give you understanding in everything.

2 TIMOTHY 2:7

The girl sat at the kitchen table—head in her hands, frown on her face. She'd been staring at the numbers scribbled on the notebook paper in front of her for many minutes now. Had she finally solved the problem? Yes, she had! Still locked in her thoughts, she heard the scrape of chair legs beside her. Her father sat down at the kitchen table—head next to hers, love across his face—and scanned the page. Then he tapped his finger on a decimal point. *Click, click* went the gears in her brain. . . Ah! Now she understood.

Each day of our Christian lives, we are maturing, growing spiritually. In the process, sometimes we don't understand; sometimes we don't even realize we're mistaken. What's a girl to do? Rely on God—to point out our failings and flaws and to point us toward understanding.

On one journey during Jesus' earthly ministry, the disciples had not remembered to bring bread. Using the moment to share deeper wisdom, Jesus told them, "Watch and beware of the leaven of the Pharisees and Sadducees" (Matthew 16:6). Now, the disciples were intelligent men, but this time they missed the point. They were so concerned about the physical bread they lacked, they both forgot the ability of the one who stood before them and failed to hear His words. Jesus confronted them with what they really lacked—faith and understanding—and reiterated His lesson: "O you of little faith, why do you reason among yourselves because you have brought no bread? Do you not yet understand, or remember the five loaves of the five thousand and how many baskets you took up? . . . How is it you do not understand that I did not speak to you concerning bread?—but to beware of the leaven of the Pharisees and Sadducees" (Matthew 16:8–9, 11 NKJV). The Bible tells us they *then* understood what Jesus meant (Matthew 16:12). With some help, they got it.

Believers are never without help when we need it. After Jesus' ascension to heaven, the Holy Spirit came to aid us in understanding the things of God. Jesus said, "The Helper. . .will teach you all things" (John 14:26). And again, "When he, the Spirit of truth, is come, he will guide you into all truth" (John 16:13 KJV). Each day we put one foot in front of the other; we do our best to make sense of holy things, knowing that God is beside us, helping us understand.

HOLY SPIRIT, SHOW ME WHERE I'M NOT
GETTING IT. I WANT TO UNDERSTAND. AMEN.

Step 2: Do

*But the one who looks into the perfect law, the law of
liberty, and perseveres, being no hearer who forgets but
a doer who acts, he will be blessed in his doing.*

JAMES 1:25

Take one pill daily. Watch your step. Ferry departs at 10:00 a.m. Read through instructions before beginning. Detour ahead. . . Every day we have a choice—to heed direction or pay no attention to it. Most times, what we're told is for our benefit. Let your medicine gather dust and you won't get any better. Don't look where you're going and you could face-plant. Show up late and you'll miss the boat. Plunge right in and you risk more work. Drive by that detour sign and you might find yourself at a dead end.

God's Word is full of direction too, and it's always beneficial. It tells us how to find life through the Savior and then how to live life in Him. But we shouldn't stop at the first step of hearing. We have to *follow* what the Bible says if we want to reap the benefits. Jesus told the multitudes, "Why do you call me 'Lord, Lord,' and not do what I tell you? Everyone who comes to me and hears my words and does them, I will show you what he is like: he is like a man building a house, who dug deep and laid the foundation on the rock. And when a flood arose, the stream broke against that house and could not shake it, because it had been well built" (Luke 6:46–48). Building our lives on true faith, which leads to obedience, is the only way to gain future security and present peace of mind.

James picked up Jesus' message in a letter to dispersed believers. He wrote, "Do what God's teaching says; when you only listen and do nothing, you are fooling yourselves. Those who hear God's teaching and do nothing are like people who look at themselves in a mirror. They see their faces and then go away and quickly forget what they looked like. But the truly happy people are those who carefully study God's perfect law that makes people free, and they continue to study it. They do not forget what they heard, but they obey what God's teaching says. Those who do this will be made happy" (James 1:22–25 NCV). Did you catch that last part? The hearer who obeys "will be *made* happy." God honors obedience. He blesses those who choose to heed His direction.

So let's read, then do. We will be blessed in the doing.

GOD, THE BIBLE IS NOT MEANT FOR ME
TO GLANCE OVER AND THEN FORGET. ITS
WORDS BRING LIFE. THROUGH YOUR SPIRIT,
HELP ME HEAR AND OBEY. AMEN.

Security

Strength and dignity are her clothing,
and she laughs at the time to come.

PROVERBS 31:25

Every woman I know wants to be confident. We want that inner assurance that we are enough, that we are capable and beautiful, that we have something to offer.

We've talked about strength and how we gain it by embracing the woman God made each of us to be. And when we do that, we also discover the dignity of living in proper balance with the rest of God's world.

Insecurities hound every woman. No matter how accomplished she looks or how successful she is, inside she wonders. We all do. That's why the lie the serpent told Eve is so diabolical. He said that she would be like a god (Genesis 3:5). But what really happened is that she lost her security as well as her innocence. She knew the difference between good and evil after that, and she began to be plagued by fears and doubts and all the other negative emotions that are part of our world because of sin.

The way back to security is found in embracing the truth instead of lies. And we do this by getting close to our Creator and reading His Word.

A woman who knows she was made by the hand of God and created for a special purpose can hold her head up even when things go wrong and even when she doesn't like something about herself. She realizes that God is working out a plan through her and that even her deficiencies somehow are part of that.

Such a woman can laugh at the future, not in a mocking, foolish, irresponsible way but in a trusting, joyful way. She knows that God holds everything in His hands and that He has the final say. She doesn't have to try to figure everything out when she trusts the one who knows all. "He has made everything beautiful in its time. Also, he has put eternity into man's heart, yet so that he cannot find out what God has done from the beginning to the end" (Ecclesiastes 3:11).

FATHER IN HEAVEN, YOU HOLD ALL THINGS IN YOUR HANDS, AND YOU MADE EVERYTHING, INCLUDING ME. TODAY I TRUST YOU FOR MY FUTURE, AND I FIND MY STRENGTH AND DIGNITY IN FOLLOWING YOUR PURPOSE. AMEN.

All-Out Pursuit

"You will seek me and find me,
when you seek me with all your heart."

JEREMIAH 29:13

Number seven of seven, the letter to the church in Laodicea got straight to the point and did not mince words: " 'I [the Amen] know your deeds, that you are neither cold nor hot; I wish that you were cold or hot. So because you are lukewarm, and neither hot nor cold, I will spit you out of My mouth' " (Revelation 3:15–16 NASB). The Laodiceans had not given Christ the cold shoulder, yet neither had they warmly embraced Him. They claimed to believe, yet their actions were still lukewarm and, as such, were repulsive to Christ.

While it was hypocritical faith that defined the Laodicean church and caused Christ's displeasure, even sincere believers can be "lukewarm" in their faith. But nowhere does the Bible praise tepidness. So immense was God's sacrifice, so complete was His mercy, that believers owe Him more than "half-hearted" in return. He deserves total devotion—an all-out pursuit.

The Bible's very language reflects the zeal that should define a life lived for God. Paul considered everything else garbage when compared to knowing Christ and becoming Christlike; his passion was "forgetting what lies behind and *straining forward* to what lies ahead" (Philippians 3:13, italics added). Paul urged Timothy not to let his faithfulness in serving God become an ember; rather, Timothy should "*fan into flame* the gift of God" (2 Timothy 1:6, italics added). Jesus quoted the greatest commandment as "You shall love the Lord your God with *all* your heart and with *all* your soul and with *all* your mind and with *all* your strength" (Mark 12:30, italics added). And David declared, "My soul *followeth hard* after thee" (Psalm 63:8 KJV, italics added).

Believers are to run, not stroll, toward God. We should follow after Him and His ways with a greater intensity than we do anything else.

God is waiting. And "He is a rewarder of those who diligently seek Him" (Hebrews 11:6 NKJV). Are you ready to go all out?

GOD, I HAVEN'T BEEN PURSUING YOU LIKE I SHOULD.
FORGIVE ME. PLEASE SHOW ME WHERE MY FAITH
LIFE IS LUKEWARM, AND INCREASE MY FERVOR.
I SENSE YOU EVEN NOW, CALLING ME, URGING ME
TO PURSUE YOU LIKE NEVER BEFORE. AMEN.

Grace for Our Groans

And He said to me, "My grace is sufficient for you, for My strength is made perfect in weakness." Therefore most gladly I will rather boast in my infirmities, that the power of Christ may rest upon me. Therefore I take pleasure in infirmities, in reproaches, in needs, in persecutions, in distresses, for Christ's sake. For when I am weak, then I am strong.

2 Corinthians 12:9–10 NKJV

Disabilities and afflictions are not usually the image in our minds when we think of power. Rather, they depict weakness. But the apostle Paul, under the inspiration of the Holy Spirit, said that's okay. When we're at our weakest, Christ is showing His strength.

I don't enjoy doctor's office waiting rooms. They're holding tanks for people with miseries. I know. I've been one of them. The cushy chairs and modern art and cheerful fish aquarium can't completely block the thoughts from your mind that there is something wrong with you and you need help. The folks around you are in various states of suffering, depending on which kind of specialist you're seeing. Usually, you can see evidence of their maladies on them or beside them—bandages, casts, canes, patches, oxygen tanks, and the like. And when the next name is called at the door, someone lumbers to his or her feet and shuffles off, hoping for a new miracle drug. Sounds pretty depressing. And, of course, physical ailments aren't the only kind with which we contend. Mental and emotional distress can be "thorns in our flesh" as well.

No one knows for sure what indisposition Paul had, though there have been many guesses. Some say it was his eyesight; others say something else. No matter, because the principle applies to us all in whatever we face.

You can find astounding, unexpected power in your weakest moment. It won't be the kind that lifts you off your bed and makes you want to run a marathon. It won't be the type that makes you feel completely happy in the middle of your battle with the blues. But it will be a power that gives you strength to accept the challenge of the next hour. It will be the grace that helps you make a decision, face the day, receive encouragement from friends.

I don't know what weakness is in your path today—chemotherapy, surgery, bed rest, diagnostic tests, dialysis, physical therapy, organ transplant—but the God of strength does. And He can give the power.

FATHER, I NEED POWER FOR MY WEAKNESS
TODAY. I TRUST YOU FOR IT. AMEN.

Keep Up
the Good Work

And let us not grow weary of doing good, for in
due season we will reap, if we do not give up.

GALATIANS 6:9

With a sigh, she sank into bed. Another day had passed. Another day of trying to do what was right in a world that did so much wrong. Another day of fighting the good fight when she seemed to lose more battles than she won. Another day had passed, and she was weary—muscles and soul.

The longer we're Christians, the likelier we are to know what it means to grow weary. On this earth of ours, cheaters do prosper, and sometimes the good work only makes a dent in the bad. It's not our imagination—Jesus affirmed there would be troubles in this life, while Paul declared that "the days are evil" (Ephesians 5:16)—but doing good is not a lost cause. With His bad tidings, Jesus brought hope. "Take heart; I have overcome the world," He said (John 16:33). And Paul encouraged believers to "[make] the best use of the time" (Ephesians 5:16). For now God's goodwill extends to everyone: the Father "causes His sun to rise on the evil and the good, and sends rain on the righteous and the unrighteous" (Matthew 5:45 NASB). For now God is patiently bearing evil so that His chosen make their way to Him (2 Peter 3:9). But His forbearance won't go on forever.

So for now, believers are not to worry when evil seems to have the advantage; rather, they are to rest in the sovereignty of God, who reigns over the darkness and will make all things right. David wrote of God's saints, "Fret not yourself because of evildoers; be not envious of wrongdoers! For they will soon fade like the grass and wither like the green herb. Trust in the LORD, and do good; dwell in the land and befriend faithfulness. . . . He will bring forth your righteousness as the light, and your justice as the noonday" (Psalm 37:1–3, 6).

And for now, believers are not to grow weary of doing good. Paul told the church in Corinth, "Do not let anything move you. Always give yourselves fully to the work of the Lord, because you know that your work in the Lord is never wasted" (1 Corinthians 15:58 NCV). Whatever we do for God has value. Even at the end of days when the good we do seems to be for naught, we have reason to call on God's strength and keep up the good work.

GOD, ENERGIZE ME TO DO THE GOOD THINGS
YOU'VE PREPARED FOR ME. DOING GOOD
IS NEVER IN VAIN—YOU WILL USE YOUR
PEOPLE'S GOOD WORKS FOR YOUR GLORY
AND REWARD THEM IN HEAVEN. AMEN.

Doing It Differently

*"Moreover, I gave them my Sabbaths, as a sign
between me and them, that they might know
that I am the LORD who sanctifies them."*

EZEKIEL 20:12

Many people treat Sunday like an extra part of the weekend. Actually, it is the first day of the new week. And it is also a sacred day.

Since Jesus rose on Sunday, the New Testament church began meeting for worship then instead of on Saturday. They took the principle of one day in seven as an interlude of rest and worship and applied it to Sunday. If it is the creative plan still at work (as all other aspects of the creation pattern we still affirm), then it is still a day to be set aside as different from the rest.

In our culture, it is a surprise to find those who practice Sabbath rest. Rather than taking the boat to the lake after church or using it as a travel day for the end of vacation, what if we were serious about setting aside Sunday as a time of actual rest and worship? What if we put some boundaries in place that would help us keep it sacred and holy? What if we surprised those around us with an innovative new approach to less stress—Sundays at church and home!

The Quakers, or Society of Friends, objected to the use of traditional names for the days of the week because of the non-Christian Saxon origin. So they called Sunday "First Day." Not a bad reminder to all of us that it should be first in our minds—a day that sets the rhythm for the rest of the week.

God designed the Sabbath as part of His covenant with His people. Keeping the Sabbath was very important in Jewish law and culture. Indeed, God said through Ezekiel that it was even a sign of their sanctification, or "set-apartness." It would surely be the same for us today. Sabbath or Sunday keeping is a practice that marks those who have a reason to make it different. And indeed we do have a reason. We know the creator of the week and the originator of rest.

This week, do something wildly different. Keep Sunday special, sacred, and restful. Plan your activities for other days. You might just bring a little more rest to this world by someone else you influence.

GOD, THANK YOU FOR CREATING THE SABBATH PRINCIPLE FOR US. I WANT TO INCORPORATE MORE REST INTO MY LIFE BECAUSE I KNOW IT HONORS YOU AND IS HEALTHY FOR ME. I'M GLAD I CAN BE PURPOSEFUL ABOUT THIS IMPORTANT PART OF MY WEEK. AMEN.

"I'll Pray for You"

If God be for us, who can be against us? . . . It is Christ
that died, yea rather, that is risen again, who is even at the
right hand of God, who also maketh intercession for us.
ROMANS 8:31, 34 KJV

When we're tossed by life's events and burdened by its demands, is anything so sweet as hearing the words "I'll pray for you"? Intercession for a fellow believer is a precious gift. It's not what's left at the bottom of the barrel but rather is access to an all-loving, all-powerful Father. Prayers are potent things (James 5:16). And if the petitions of our brothers and sisters in Christ have power, how much more so do our Lord's?

Christ's ministry did not end the moment He left this earth. The Bible tells us that He continues to minister to believers from His heavenly throne, interceding to God on our behalf. Hebrews says of the one who is powerful enough to redeem us "to the uttermost," "he always lives to make intercession for [us]" (7:25). Yet Jesus prayed for believers before He returned to heaven. What did He request of His Father? He prayed for God's presence, nature, and love to indwell believers. He prayed that God would be with us now and that we would be with Him in eternity. Spend some time soaking in His words. No prayer is so sweet:

> *"I do not ask for these only, but also for those who will*
> *believe in me through their word, that they may all be*
> *one, just as you, Father, are in me, and I in you, that*

they also may be in us, so that the world may believe that you have sent me. The glory that you have given me I have given to them, that they may be one even as we are one, I in them and you in me, that they may become perfectly one, so that the world may know that you sent me and loved them even as you loved me. Father, I desire that they also, whom you have given me, may be with me where I am, to see my glory that you have given me because you loved me before the foundation of the world. O righteous Father, even though the world does not know you, I know you, and these know that you have sent me. I made known to them your name, and I will continue to make it known, that the love with which you have loved me may be in them, and I in them." (John 17:20–26)

LORD, THANK YOU FOR YOUR PRAYERS. WHAT JOY AND PEACE I FEEL IN KNOWING THAT YOU ARE WITH ME, THAT YOU ARE PRAYING FOR ME! AMEN.

First Things First

Delight yourself in the LORD, and he will
give you the desires of your heart.

PSALM 37:4

She couldn't—shouldn't—complain. Her life was full of blessings. But there was still that one thing. The one missing piece she wanted more than anything. If only it were hers, she would have all her heart desired.

What is it you want? What's the missing piece (or pieces) in your life that you would give anything to grasp? It could be landing your dream job or getting married or starting a family or achieving a long-held goal. Whatever it is, here's some advice rooted in biblical wisdom: don't put the cart before the horse.

To understand, take a couple of steps back. As part of His Sermon on the Mount, Jesus addressed the topic of anxiety. Recognizing that daily cares like food and clothing often consumed the crowd's thoughts, Jesus counseled His audience to think deeper and get their priorities sorted. "Is not life more than food, and the body more than clothing?" He asked them (Matthew 6:25). The Creator of all things knew that being well fed and well dressed would do nothing for a deprived soul. In their minds, then, spiritual concerns needed to take precedence over physical ones: "Therefore do not be anxious, saying, 'What shall we eat?' or 'What shall we drink?' or 'What shall we wear?' For the Gentiles seek after all these things, and your heavenly Father knows that you need them all. But *seek first* the kingdom of God and his righteousness, and all these things will be added to you" (Matthew 6:31–33, italics added). In other words, concern yourself with soul issues first, and God will take care of the rest. A soul relying on God for eternal provision can also rely on Him for earthly care (Romans 8:32).

"Seek first the kingdom of God. . .and all these things will be added to you." We see the same pattern throughout the Bible. "Humble yourselves before the Lord, and he will exalt you" (James 4:10). "Commit your works to the LORD and your plans will be established" (Proverbs 16:3 NASB). "Delight yourself in the LORD, and he will give you the desires of your heart" (Psalm 37:4). Whatever our hopes, dreams, or wishes, the pursuit of them must come second to God in our hearts. And when we put Him first, we discover a miraculous truth: He meets our every need and our every desire.

GOD, YOU KNOW MY HEART'S DESIRE, WHAT
I LONG FOR. EVEN IF IT MATERIALIZED THIS
VERY MOMENT, IT WOULDN'T BE ENOUGH. BUT
WITH YOU FILLING MY HEART TO THE BRIM,
EVERYTHING ELSE FALLS INTO PLACE. AMEN.

His Name in the Night

I remember Your name in the night, O Lord.
PSALM 119:55 NKJV

Night brings many terrors and anxieties. Trees stand taller. Buildings loom larger. Corners descend deeper. Noises echo louder. Fears clutch tighter. Regrets swirl faster. Dread churns harder.

Night is a time when we feel less capable. The absence of light and the coming alive of the nocturnal world give familiar things and places an eeriness that we know we shouldn't care about but do anyway.

In the night, we need power. Power to rest, power to rejuvenate, power to relinquish all things into the Almighty's hands.

Psalm 119 is a passage in which every verse contains some reference to the Word of God. Different names are used, but each of them pertains in some way to the wonderful treasure we have in scripture. In verse 55, the writer recommends an action we can use to fight our overwhelming weakness as the daylight fades and dusk approaches.

We can remember His name:

Jehovah—Provider

Lord—Sovereign

Messiah—Promised One

Jesus—Savior

Almighty God

Everlasting Father

Prince of peace

King of kings

Friend

In every unexpected nighttime moment, His name has the comfort we seek. And His power is revealed if we choose to believe in Him. There is no need to toss and turn alone in the night. Grab hold of His name and believe who He is.

LORD JESUS, YOU ARE LIFE AND PEACE AND ALL I NEED TONIGHT. I TRUST THE POWER IN YOUR NAME FOR THE UNREST IN MY HEART. AMEN.

Foiled?

The Lord of hosts has sworn: "As I have planned,
so shall it be, and as I have purposed, so shall it stand."

ISAIAH 14:24

Do you recognize any of these thoughts? *What if I pick a path that isn't God's will for my life? What if by choosing "this" over "that" I won't be where God wants me? What if I've done something to stop God from working? What if I've missed out on God's best for me?* Whether you're agonizing over a decision you've yet to make or you're worrying over one you've already made, you might wonder if you can mess up the plans God has for you. But the Bible is clear-cut here: we cannot foil God.

Among almighty God's many attributes are His omniscience, omnipotence, and sovereignty. He knows all, controls all, and rules all; therefore, He is fully capable of bringing all His plans to pass. The psalmist declared, "He determines the number of the stars. . . . Great is our Lord, and abundant in power; his understanding is beyond measure" (Psalm 147:4–5), and "The counsel of the Lord stands forever, the plans of His heart from generation to generation" (Psalm 33:11 NASB).

Even in our lowest moments and despite unwise decisions, God's plans remain intact. He is watching over us and has set in motion everything that needs to take place to fulfill them. Remember Hagar? When she fled from Sarai, the Lord sought her in the wilderness and corrected her course (Genesis 16). After running for his life, Elijah asked God to let him die; but God sustained him through forty days of wandering before directing him to his mission (1 Kings 19). And for Jonah, who disobeyed the Lord's command outright, God "appointed a great fish" to bring him to his senses and back to His will (Jonah 1:17).

Through His presence, through circumstances, God guides us. "You have hedged me behind and before, and laid Your hand upon me," we read in Psalm 139:5 (NKJV). So next time you begin to wonder, remember: God has good plans for you (Jeremiah 29:11), and nothing can foil them.

GOD, YOU ARE AWESOME! THANK YOU
FOR THE CERTAINTY THAT YOUR PLANS
FOR ME WILL BE FULFILLED. AMEN.

Beauty

She makes bed coverings for herself;
her clothing is fine linen and purple.

PROVERBS 31:22

It is sometimes thought that women who follow Christ should not care about beauty. But that is wrong. Our womanly beauty is a gift we are to steward well, and the writer of Proverbs 31 had something to say about it.

Appropriate self-care is part of the godly woman's routine. She knows that a sloppy, unkempt woman brings glory to no one, especially not to Christ. She is able to make good fashion choices and appropriate beauty statements because she understands how they fit in with the rest of her life as a follower of Christ.

Men were designed to image strength; women were created to reflect our Creator's beauty. God poured Himself into two human image bearers who, together, would make up an earthly depiction of His attributes. He made them as a pair, as complements. Two men do not make the right image. Neither do two women. Together a man and a woman make the perfect image of Christ and His bride, the church.

Later, we will learn about Lydia, the woman who sold purple goods. She was probably a well-to-do businesswoman, for that kind of merchandise was expensive and sought after. Purple was a fabric of the well dressed.

The words *fine linen* here suggest that this woman had good taste in her choices of fabric for clothing. She had elegant opinions and dressed herself accordingly.

Wherever beauty abounds, Satan will try to destroy it. He hates it because it reminds him of the one who made it. Satan tries to get women today to believe lies about their appearance. Either he suggests they make it their main focus, or he convinces them they aren't worth anything anyway and shouldn't even try. Both lies are destructive. The right attitude toward beauty is a surrender of it to the one who made it and a focus on using it to reflect glory back to Him. This is the attitude of the godly woman, the one who can wear fine linen and purple in the right way.

LORD, I WANT MY WOMANLY BEAUTY TO BE AN OFFERING BACK TO YOU. I WANT IT TO HONOR YOUR IMAGE. TODAY, HELP ME CHOOSE MY ATTITUDE AND MY CLOTHING IN SUCH A WAY THAT EVERYONE WHO SEES ME KNOWS I BELONG TO YOU. AMEN.

Apples to Oranges

Make a careful exploration of who you are and the work
you have been given, and then sink yourself into that.
Don't be impressed with yourself. Don't compare yourself
with others. Each of you must take responsibility for
doing the creative best you can with your own life.
GALATIANS 6:4–5 MSG

If spiritual gifts came with instruction manuals, they might include some words of caution. *Caution?* God's gifts are blessings; He uses them to equip His own. Where is the danger in something so wonderful? But if you've ever become bigheaded over your gift or belittled yourself because of someone else's, you know the importance of handling your gift with care.

Using our gifts carefully is possible only with a right frame of mind. No gift, no matter how big or small, is a result of human effort alone, since God is the one who gifts. We should see our gifts as products of grace, divinely apportioned by God. Paul advised believers, "For I say, through the grace given to me, to everyone who is among you, not to think of himself more highly than he ought to think, but to think soberly, as God has dealt to each one a measure of faith" (Romans 12:3 NKJV). Or, as *The Message* translates Paul's words, "Living then, as every one of you does, in pure grace, it's important that you not misinterpret yourselves as people who are bringing this goodness to God. No, God brings it all to you. The only accurate way to understand ourselves is by what God is and by what he does for us." And what God does—in His wisdom and love—is gift every believer individually. He has assigned each of us a one-of-a-kind part in His kingdom work, complete with a one-of-a-kind gift. Paul went on to say, "Each one of us has a body with many parts, and these parts all have different uses. In the same way, we are many, but in Christ we are all one body. . . . We all have different gifts, each of which came because of the grace God gave us" (Romans 12:4–6 NCV).

One God, many gifts. One God, many ways He works through us (1 Corinthians 12:4–6). How should we handle the gift? Peter wrote, "As each has received a gift, use it to serve one another, as good stewards of God's varied grace" (1 Peter 4:10). We, as the recipients, do our part with the gifts God has given us, no comparing allowed.

GOD, LIKE EVERYTHING IN MY LIFE, MY GIFT IS NOT RANDOM. YOU'VE GIFTED ME PERFECTLY TO FULFILL YOUR PLANS PERFECTLY. PLEASE SHOW ME HOW TO USE MY GIFT FOR YOUR GLORY. AMEN.

Going Home

Jesus answered him, "If anyone loves me, he will keep my word, and my Father will love him, and we will come to him and make our home with him."

JOHN 14:23

There's no place like home. When we're at home, we can breathe deeply, relax. We are secure. We belong. But sometimes even "home" can be uncertain. It may be month after month of struggling to pay the rent or mortgage that makes us question whether we'll have a place to live. It may be a natural disaster that rips our dwelling from us. If our earthly home was all there is, we'd justifiably despair. For the Christian, though, there's more. There's hope. This life is pointing toward the next.

Woven into God's Word is the truth that this earth is impermanent. The world as we know it is passing away (1 Corinthians 7:31; 1 John 2:17), and we are only sojourners on the planet. In fact, far from guaranteeing believers a sheltered existence, Jesus described a nomad's life in response to a scribe's declaration that he would follow Jesus wherever He went: "Foxes have holes, and birds of the air have nests, but the Son of Man has nowhere to lay his head" (Matthew 8:20). Jesus was just passing through, doing the Father's will until joining Him again in heaven. Once adopted into God's family, believers too are to consider this life a temporary residence, a perishable home that God will replace one day. Peter told pilgrim believers, "Friends, this world is not your home, so don't make yourselves cozy in it" (1 Peter 2:11 MSG). And Hebrews 13:14 (NCV) says, "Here on earth we do not have a city that lasts forever, but we are looking for the city that we will have in the future."

Our Lord is in heaven this very minute readying our eternal home. He told the disciples, "Let not your hearts be troubled. Believe in God; believe also in me. In my Father's house are many rooms. If it were not so, would I have told you that I go to prepare a place for you? And if I go and prepare a place for you, I will come again and will take you to myself, that where I am you may be also" (John 14:1–3). One day, we'll be going home. In the meantime, we have another promise—that God will make a home in us, preparing us for that day when we will be forever at home.

LORD, THANK YOU FOR A ROOF OVER MY HEAD.
EVEN IF THAT ROOF BECOMES FRAGILE, I KNOW
YOU ARE WITH ME. AND I KNOW YOU WILL HAVE
A HOME WAITING FOR ME IN HEAVEN. AMEN.

Escape from
the Prowler

No temptation has overtaken you except such as is common to man; but God is faithful, who will not allow you to be tempted beyond what you are able, but with the temptation will also make the way of escape, that you may be able to bear it.

1 CORINTHIANS 10:13 NKJV

Temptation is like a bacteria lurking, a predator stalking, a beast prowling. It is always swirling in the air, always tracking our location, always watching for an opportunity. The words Paul was inspired to write in 1 Corinthians 10:13 seem to indicate that a specific temptation dogs our steps until it catches up to us. We cannot escape the reality of temptation in this life. Even Jesus, the perfect Son of God, was tempted to sin. But He didn't yield. And because He conquered temptation, so can we. "For in that He Himself has suffered, being tempted, He is able to aid those who are tempted" (Hebrews 2:18 NKJV).

Temptation appeals to our weakness. It comes to us when our power is low, when we are tired or hungry or stressed or even relaxed and our guard is down. It comes to us in a moment when the evil offer makes sense in light of our needs. Remember Jesus' temptation by Satan in the wilderness. He was alone and hungry and physically weak, and Satan saw an opportunity. "And when He had fasted forty days and forty nights, afterward He was hungry. Now when the tempter came to Him, he said, 'If You are the Son of God, command that these stones become bread' " (Matthew 4:2–3 NKJV).

Satan does the same to us. He zeroes in on our natural frailties or the strategic vulnerability of an unguarded moment of extremity and makes his play.

But the power of Christ is ours through the Holy Spirit. Jesus used the Word of God to resist. The truth wielded against the enemy will always win. We must put His truth on constant patrol in our hearts and minds so that the blitz of the enemy can be thwarted.

We are promised a way of escape. We are promised His presence. We are promised power.

FATHER GOD, I WANT YOUR POWER OF
CHRIST WHEN I FACE TEMPTATION. GIVE ME
DETERMINATION TO FOCUS ON YOUR WORD
AND OPEN MY EYES TO THE WAY OF ESCAPE YOU
PROVIDE. IN THE NAME OF JESUS, AMEN.

What a Plan!

Oh, the depth of the riches and wisdom and knowledge of God!
How unsearchable are his judgments and how inscrutable his
ways! . . . For from him and through him and to him are all things.
ROMANS 11:33, 36

Centuries before Israel rejected Christ as Messiah, Ezekiel, a prophet
and priest, delivered a promise from the Lord to the nation: "And
I will give you a new heart, and a new spirit I will put within you.
And I will remove the heart of stone from your flesh and give
you a heart of flesh. And I will put my Spirit within you" (Ezekiel
36:26–27). God's people will not continue on with hardened hearts
everlastingly. One day He will replace hearts of stone with hearts
of flesh and fill them with the Holy Spirit. It's part of the plan.

What plan? The plan to extend salvation to every nation. In
one of God's inscrutable ways, He made provision for the Gentiles'
rescue through Israel's rejection of Christ. Paul wrote, "So I ask,
did they stumble in order that they might fall? By no means!
Rather, through their trespass salvation has come to the Gentiles"
(Romans 11:11). The branches broken off allowed others to be
grafted in (Romans 11:17); Israel's unbelief opened the door to
belief for everyone. We had unrepentant hearts before God called
to us and offered renewal. Now God has transformed us through
faith with hearts alive to Him and the indwelling Spirit empowering
and guiding us.

But, as Paul warned, we should never let God's kindness swell us with pride because we accepted what Israel rejected. Israel's spiritual hardness of heart will last only for a time, until God's chosen among the Gentiles find salvation (Romans 11:25). Then God will redeem His chosen nation, His cherished people: "Concerning the gospel they are enemies for your sake, but concerning the election they are beloved for the sake of the fathers. For the gifts and the calling of God are irrevocable. For as you were once disobedient to God, yet have now obtained mercy through their disobedience, even so these also have now been disobedient, that through the mercy shown you they also may obtain mercy. For God has committed them all to disobedience, that He might have mercy on all" (Romans 11:28–32 NKJV).

God's plan is magnificent. "Oh, the depth. . . !" Paul declared. We could spend whole lifetimes contemplating how amazing our God is. "Everything comes from him; everything happens through him; everything ends up in him. Always glory! Always praise!" (Romans 11:36 MSG).

GOD, I'LL NEVER FULLY GRASP THE WHYS AND THE WORKINGS OF YOUR PLANS. THEY ARE TOO WONDERFUL! TO YOU BE THE GLORY. AMEN.

Organization

She is not afraid of snow for her household,
for all her household are clothed in scarlet.

PROVERBS 31:21

Marie Kondo took the world by storm with her new philosophy and techniques for home organization. I know a lot of women were helped with her no-nonsense approach. Most of us have too much stuff anyway but just need a little help deciding what to keep and what not to keep.

In biblical times, most women didn't have that kind of problem. They didn't have the amount of belongings we have today, so storage wasn't an issue. But we do read in Proverbs 31:21 that the woman of the house did have her clothing organized. In fact, she ensured that all in her household were clothed appropriately. Some commentators believe that the word *scarlet* here refers to a specific type of warm clothing that she provided to everyone in her home—family and staff.

Organizing and making sure everyone has what he or she needs is a full-time job. We begin to get a sense for how busy this woman was! Yet most of the women I know are busy like that. My women friends juggle a lot of activities and responsibilities and accomplish a whole lot!

In a spiritual sense, we as mothers should be aware of the "clothing" our children are wearing. We want them to be clothed with Christ, to be wearing the righteousness He gives. As we provide for their earthly needs, let's not forget to monitor their heavenly needs as well. How tragic it would be if they were bountifully prepared for every kind of physical situation but naked and destitute spiritually!

HEAVENLY FATHER, YOUR GRACE IN ME WILL ENABLE ME TO ORGANIZE MY LIFE AND PRIORITIZE THE THINGS THAT ARE MOST IMPORTANT. HELP ME ALWAYS TO BE AWARE OF MY CHILDREN'S SPIRITUAL CONDITION AND NEVER TO FORGET TO PRAY FOR THEM. IN THE NAME OF JESUS, AMEN.

It's a Tie

*" 'Am I not allowed to do what I choose with what
belongs to me? Or do you begrudge my generosity?'
So the last will be first, and the first last."*

MATTHEW 20:15–16

Six o'clock in the morning. The sun was still fresh on the horizon, and a full day's toil awaited, twelve long hours of working hard and bearing the heat of that sun. The vineyard owner had left his house and traveled to the marketplace in search of laborers. He now hired the first batch and promised to pay them a fair wage for their work, which they willingly accepted. Three hours later, the vineyard owner returned to the marketplace and saw others standing around with no work to do. He hired them too but did not specify their wage, just that he would pay what was right. They eagerly agreed and left for the vineyard. Three more times, the vineyard owner went back to the marketplace and hired laborers—at noon, at three, and finally at five, an hour before work stopped for the day. When it was time to pay the laborers, the vineyard owner began with the last he hired—the ones who had worked only a single hour—and paid them exactly what he had promised the first—the ones who had been toiling for those twelve long hours under the sun. These laborers grumbled when they received their wage. Why should they—committed and hardworking as they were—not earn more? But the vineyard owner replied, "Friend, I am doing you no wrong; did you not agree with me for a denarius? Take what is yours and go, but I wish to give to this last man the same as to you. Is it not lawful for me to do what I wish with what is my own? Or is your eye envious because I am generous?" (Matthew 20:13–15 NASB).

The kingdom of heaven is like that, Jesus said. God, the vineyard owner, continually calls us to enter His vineyard and receive eternal life. Like the laborers in the parable, believers do not serve the Master on earth equally. Some come to Christ early and follow Him faithfully for a lifetime; others have only a handful of years or moments. But God does not dispense grace according to what we've "earned." He lavishly offers an undeserved full pardon to everyone who believes. So while the length and labor of our days are unknown to us—whether long or short, filled with toil or ease—eternity is equal. We all cross heaven's threshold in a tie.

GOD, HOWEVER LONG MY LIFE MAY BE AND HOWEVER WELL I SERVE YOU, THANK YOU FOR THE PROMISE OF ETERNAL BLESSING. AMEN.

Unburdened

"Come to Me, all who are weary and heavy-laden, and I will give you rest. Take My yoke upon you and learn from Me, for I am gentle and humble in heart, and YOU WILL FIND REST FOR YOUR SOULS. *For My yoke is easy and My burden is light."*

MATTHEW 11:28–30 NASB

What do you imagine when you hear the word *heavy-laden*? You might picture a mountain climber on her way up a steep slope with a backpack the size of a child. You might see yourself making one trip from car to kitchen with bursting grocery bags in each hand. You might envision a beast of burden lumbering down a road with a pile of goods strapped to its back. But when Jesus spoke of being heavy-laden, He referred to more than the heavy loads physically carried through life. He spoke of being spiritually burdened, of being weighed down and weary from the effort to live a godly life and gain heaven apart from God's grace. He came to offer rest and His yoke—the chance to slough off the old burden once and for all and to find new life through Him.

Jesus' offer was a marked contrast to the legalism popularized by the scribes and Pharisees. Of them Jesus said, "They tie up heavy burdens, hard to bear, and lay them on people's shoulders, but they themselves are not willing to move them with their finger" (Matthew 23:4). Their standards, the burdens they laid on people's shoulders, were impossible. Impossible to live up to and impossible to bear. So impossible that not even the scribes and Pharisees themselves were able to uphold them (Acts 15:10). Jesus, however, released people from the ultimate burden by bearing sin on the cross (1 Peter 2:24).

To receive Christ through faith means a cessation of endlessly, and futilely, working toward righteousness. It means rest in the grace of God. And it means an easy yoke. "Take My yoke upon you and learn from Me," Jesus tells us. When we take Christ's yoke, far from finding a demanding taskmaster, we find a gentle and humble Lord to guide us. We find a God whose commandments are not burdensome (1 John 5:3) and who cares about us so much that we can cast our burdens on Him (1 Peter 5:7). We find His very presence with us day by day, helping us shoulder the blessedly light load. We find rest for our souls.

LORD, I WAS TIRED AND BURDENED BEFORE I MET YOU, BUT YOU BROUGHT RELIEF FROM THE HEAVY LOAD I COULD NOT BEAR. THANK YOU FOR THAT SOUL-DEEP, ABIDING REST THAT COMES ONLY THROUGH YOU. EVERY DAY, I'LL TAKE YOUR YOKE AND WAIT FOR YOUR GENTLE LEADING. AMEN.

Sudden Calm

And he awoke and rebuked the wind and said
to the sea, "Peace! Be still!" And the wind
ceased, and there was a great calm.

MARK 4:39

As I get older, I value "calm" more and more. I enjoy silence more than I used to. My teens loved to keep music going or some other type of action happening. But my mom ears, at times, craved the quiet.

To value a calm, you must contrast it with chaos.

For Jesus' disciples, this happened after a day of being with Him while He taught. They let Him take a nap while they rowed the boat to the other side. But, as is common on the Sea of Galilee, a sudden storm arose, violently slapping the boat around and beginning to fill it with water. Imagine the shrill whistle of the winds and the pitching of the little ship. Think about the darkness on the water with only crude oil lamps for light. Picture them bailing out water with wooden buckets and with their hands, terrified they were going down. And Jesus was sleeping on a cushion. Of course they woke Him. Wouldn't we?

He scolded the wind and waves. He told them to calm down. And they did—just like that. Smooth as glass. A tranquil, beautiful evening with moonlit waters. In an instant.

Storms arise in our lives as suddenly as they do on the Galilee. We can go from smooth seas to vicious waves in a phone call or a text message. Everything begins to pitch and roil, and all we can hear is the moan of the winds as Satan tells us that it's really over this time.

I'm so glad we have the one who brings calm. His voice speaks the frequency that nature recognizes. And it also speaks the code that opens our hearts. When He stands up and addresses our chaos, we know peace is on the way.

What is happening in your life today? What storm has kicked up its heels in your family, in your life, in your health, in your relationships? Turn to Him. Listen to His voice. Expect the calmness He can bring to your heart.

DEAR LORD JESUS, YOU CALMED THE SEAS
WHEN YOU WERE ON EARTH. I NEED YOU
TO CALM MY HEART TODAY. I KNOW THAT
NOTHING IS BEYOND THE POWER OF YOUR
VOICE, AND I TRUST YOUR PEACE. AMEN.

By Your Side

*"It is the L*ORD *who goes before you. He will be with you; he will not leave you or forsake you. Do not fear or be dismayed."*

DEUTERONOMY 31:8

Strength in numbers. If you want support, surround yourself with friendly faces. How much easier it is to stand up for what's right or to stand strong when you're wrongly accused when you have someone to stand by you! But have you ever been in a trying situation and all those friendly faces fell away? What happens when you're left to stand alone?

The Bible chronicles the stories of real people who collectively experienced the scope of real problems. You don't need to search long to find examples of desertion. Even our Lord Jesus Christ knew the sting of having the ones closest to Him shrink back when given the chance to stand by Him. Just after His arrest, His disciple Peter waited outside in the courtyard while He was brought to the high priest, Caiaphas. Once, twice, then thrice, Peter negated claims that he had been among Jesus' followers—"I do not know him"; "I am not"; "I do not know what you are talking about" (Luke 22:57, 58, 60). Seeing into Peter's heart, Jesus would later forgive his denial; He would, in fact, ask His Father to forgive the ones who crucified Him (Luke 23:34). But that day, Jesus faced His accusers alone.

Paul also stood accused and alone. Near the end of his ministry, Paul was imprisoned in Rome, likely a result of Nero's persecution of Christians. When he was brought before the court, nobody defended him. "At my first defense no one came to stand by me, but all deserted me. May it not be charged against them!" Paul wrote to Timothy (2 Timothy 4:16). Despite outward abandonment, though, Paul had faith that he was never truly alone: "But the Lord stood by me and strengthened me, so that through me the message might be fully proclaimed and all the Gentiles might hear it. So I was rescued from the lion's mouth. The Lord will rescue me from every evil deed and bring me safely into his heavenly kingdom" (2 Timothy 4:17–18). God was still with Paul, strengthening him and working through him to preach good news in bad circumstances. And because of God's present presence, Paul could count on Him tomorrow and always.

God will *never* leave you or forsake you. Whatever you're going through, even if it appears that you stand alone, God is standing by.

GOD, I REJOICE IN YOU. I THANK YOU, FOR YOU ARE A CONSTANT PRESENCE IN MY LIFE. THOUGH EVERYONE MIGHT DESERT ME—EVEN THOSE DEAREST TO ME—YOU WILL DRAW ME CLOSE (PSALM 27:10). AMEN.

Compassion

She opens her hand to the poor and
reaches out her hands to the needy.

PROVERBS 31:20

- Florence Nightingale was called the "lady with the lamp" because of her care of soldiers.

- Catherine Booth was an integral part of founding the Salvation Army with her husband.

- Corrie ten Boom was the leader of a resistance group who rescued Jews in Holland.

Women have long been leaders in compassionate ministry to others. Perhaps the female hormone that makes us nurture babies and children also softens our hearts toward those in need. Men are often involved in caring for others too, and they have certain gifts in these areas that we do not. But there is no substitute for women reaching out their hands to the needy.

Jesus told us that helping others is the same as helping Him.

"For I was hungry and you gave me food, I was thirsty
and you gave me drink, I was a stranger and you
welcomed me, I was naked and you clothed me, I was
sick and you visited me, I was in prison and you came to
me." Then the righteous will answer him, saying, "Lord,
when did we see you hungry and feed you, or thirsty and

give you drink? And when did we see you a stranger
and welcome you, or naked and clothe you? And when
did we see you sick or in prison and visit you?" And the
King will answer them, "Truly, I say to you, as you did
it to one of the least of these my brothers, you did it to
me." (Matthew 25:35–40)

The woman in the Proverbs 31 tribute didn't spend her days feathering her own nest, so to speak. She had eyes to see and a heart that cared, and she did what she could.

There are things and people in our world for which we need open eyes: sex trafficking, abortive and postabortive women, battered women, substance abuse addicts, single moms.

All of these women need the love of Jesus and the heart of a friend. Some of us don't have opportunities to be involved in actual outreach. But we can pray and give and care. Part of the unexpected loveliness of a woman of God is her compassion for others. Let's model it today.

HEAVENLY FATHER, THERE ARE SO MANY
HURTING WOMEN IN YOUR WORLD. SHOW
ME HOW TO BE A CONDUIT OF LOVE AND
GRACE IN SOME WAY TODAY. AMEN.

A Mother's Miracle

So she went from him and shut the door behind herself
and her sons. And as she poured they brought the vessels
to her. When the vessels were full, she said to her son,
"Bring me another vessel." And he said to her, "There
is not another." Then the oil stopped flowing.

2 KINGS 4:5–6

Times are tough for single moms today, but I think they're a little better than they were in ancient times. Take this woman's story.

Her husband, a prophet, died. And the family had some debts that were due. Children were one of a family's most valuable assets, and a creditor could put them into indentured service to pay off the money owed. This woman knew this was going to happen, so she went to the man of God for advice.

Do you remember the story? He asked what she had of value in her home, and all she had was a jar of oil. But it was a valuable commodity that could be sold. There just wasn't much of it. Now here's where the miracle began. Acting on his advice, she borrowed containers from everyone she knew and then filled them from her jar. Wait a minute! Yes, that's right. The jar became a warehouse supply of oil. She could sell the oil in the containers to pay the debt. (Maybe she also paid her neighbors for the containers—I've always wondered about that!) At any rate, her sons were spared, and her debts were paid. Talk about relief and gratefulness!

God cares about your mothering situation today. He sees the

miracle you need. The Bible tells us that He is especially near to the widow and the fatherless. "Father of the fatherless and protector of widows is God in his holy habitation" (Psalm 68:5).

There is no situation that faces you or your children where He is not sovereign. When friends can't help, He can. When social programs fall short, He is there. When you are alone, He is nearby.

I have a friend who has found herself tragically alone as a single mom. The care of her three small children has fallen solidly on her shoulders. She has had to grieve the heartache of her aloneness as well as try to be mother and father to little ones who don't understand all the reasons. She has suffered much. At times I wonder how a person can endure such heartrending circumstances. But I know she has seen the truth of Psalm 68:5. God has been their support and tower, and He has used His people to show that in a tangible way.

You may feel alone with your mom needs, but you aren't. Take them to the one who uses jars of oil to pay debts. He'll make a way for you.

FATHER IN HEAVEN, I BRING YOU MY NEED TODAY. YOU SEE MY CHILDREN AND THEIR VULNERABILITY. YOU UNDERSTAND MY HELPLESSNESS RIGHT NOW. PLEASE DO THE WORK THAT ONLY YOU CAN DO. AMEN.

At Peace

Put into practice what you learned from me, what you heard and saw and realized. Do that, and God, who makes everything work together, will work you into his most excellent harmonies.

PHILIPPIANS 4:9 MSG

A few moments away, that's what she needed. A few moments to pause her restless thoughts. Lately her life was a jumble of discordant parts, a muddle of experiences and circumstances that had not yet blended into a melodious whole. Yes, just a few moments away. . . She turned on some music and closed her eyes. As the soothing notes filled her head, she remembered her God, thinking of all the ways He had been, was, and would be at work in her life. Jumble of parts notwithstanding, she sensed a deep harmony.

God's Word doesn't promise us that we'll know precisely what God is up to or how He will work things out in our lives. But it does promise us that in times of confidence and times of concern, we can have peace—peace that He is working all things together for good (Romans 8:28). How is that peace possible? Because it comes from God. Like the night Jesus said to the storm at sea, "Peace! Be still!" (Mark 4:39), only God can bring peace into our lives despite what's raging around us. Jesus told the disciples, "I have said these things to you, that *in me* you may have peace. In the world you will have tribulation. But take heart; I have overcome the world" (John 16:33, italics added). And the prophet Isaiah wrote of God, "*You keep* him in perfect peace whose mind is stayed on you, because he trusts in you" (Isaiah 26:3, italics added). When we mentally place ourselves in God's hand and wait and rely on Him for the order and purpose we crave, He gives us peace.

At the close of one of his epistles, Paul said, "Rejoice in the Lord always; again I will say, rejoice! . . . The Lord is near. Be anxious for nothing, but in everything by prayer and supplication with thanksgiving let your requests be made known to God. And the peace of God, which surpasses all comprehension, will guard your hearts and your minds in Christ Jesus" (Philippians 4:4–7 NASB). God is near, so tell Him, with gratitude for all He does, what's worrying you. His peace will empty you of doubt and fear while filling you with the knowledge that God is working everything together in perfect harmony.

GOD, SO MUCH IS UNSETTLED IN MY LIFE THAT I FEEL UNSETTLED. I'M UNEASY AND UNCERTAIN. PLEASE TAKE THE WORRY AND REPLACE IT WITH CALM. YOU ARE AT WORK, SO I AM AT PEACE. AMEN.

Blessed

Every good gift and every perfect gift is from above,
and comes down from the Father of lights, with whom
there is no variation or shadow of turning.

JAMES 1:17 NKJV

Look around and you'll see them. Look up and down, right and left, behind and before, without and within, and you'll recognize God's gifts to us. His many blessings have His name written on them. The sun that warms, the rain that waters—*From: God.* The fruit and vegetables that nourish—*From: God.* The beauty of nature that delights—*From: God.* The companionship of others that heartens—*From: God.* The love and mercy that restore—*From: God.* And those are only a start. The psalmist said, "For the LORD God is a sun and shield; the LORD will give grace and glory; no good thing will He withhold from those who walk uprightly" (Psalm 84:11 NKJV). And John 1:16 (MSG) tells us, "We all live off his generous abundance, gift after gift after gift."

Why is God so good to us? Because He is goodness itself. The scriptures declare His goodness, verse to verse. "Oh give thanks to the LORD, for he is good; for his steadfast love endures forever!" (1 Chronicles 16:34). "I say to the LORD, 'You are my Lord; I have no good apart from you' " (Psalm 16:2). "Oh, taste and see that the LORD is good!" (Psalm 34:8). "Your flock found a dwelling in it; in your goodness, O God, you provided for the needy" (Psalm 68:10). "Truly God is good to Israel, to those who are pure in heart"

(Psalm 73:1). "Praise the LORD, for the LORD is good; sing to his name, for it is pleasant!" (Psalm 135:3). "The LORD is good to all, and his mercy is over all that he has made" (Psalm 145:9). Our God is good, and as James pointed out, He will always be so. He does not shift like the sun, moon, and stars He created. Throughout the ages He has blessed us through His goodness, and He will go on sending blessings from above. Just look around and see.

FATHER, YOU ARE SO GOOD; YOU ARE SO GOOD
TO ME. THANK YOU FOR THE BLESSINGS I SEE
EVERY DAY AND EVERYWHERE. AMEN.

superfood

How sweet are thy words unto my taste!
yea, sweeter than honey to my mouth!
PSALM 119:103 KJV

Did you eat any superfoods today? Unfortunately, that *superb* mac and cheese does not count. No, superfoods are an exalted group of nutrient-packed, occasionally expensive, mostly tasty edibles that some believe boost health. It's the açai in your smoothie, the kale in your salad, and the salmon on your plate. They swoop in and fight the bad while nourishing the good. Yet whatever the superfood du jour may be, there is nourishment of another kind that has been around for ages: God's Word.

Moses had led Israel through the wilderness for forty years by the time he spoke the words recorded in the book of Deuteronomy. Along with the particulars of the law, Moses reminded the people how God had provided food. God's decree—His Word—that manna appear like dew each morning satiated Israel's physical hunger and directed His children to the source of spiritual fullness. Moses said, "[The LORD your God] took away your pride when he let you get hungry, and then he fed you with manna, which neither you nor your ancestors had ever seen. This was to teach you that a person does not live on bread alone, but by everything the LORD says" (Deuteronomy 8:3 NCV).

We see similar images of God's Word as spiritual "food" else-where in scripture. Jeremiah wrote, "Your words were found, and

I ate them, and your words became to me a joy and the delight of my heart, for I am called by your name, O Lord, God of hosts" (Jeremiah 15:16). And Ezekiel described his encounter with the Lord like this: "And he said to me, 'Son of man, eat whatever you find here. Eat this scroll, and go, speak to the house of Israel.' So I opened my mouth, and he gave me this scroll to eat. And he said to me, 'Son of man, feed your belly with this scroll that I give you and fill your stomach with it.' Then I ate it, and it was in my mouth as sweet as honey" (Ezekiel 3:1–3). The prophets did not actually eat the parchment and ink that displayed God's words; their ingesting was symbolic of taking in the Word and allowing it to work in them. When we study the Bible, chewing on its words and internalizing them, we experience lasting benefits. God's Word sustains us and grows us. It nourishes us. Even when the words are hard to digest, they are as sweet as honey.

GOD, KEEP REMINDING ME HOW IMPORTANT
THE BIBLE IS. I WILL EAT YOUR WORDS DAILY
SO THAT I AM NOURISHED. AMEN.

Light

She perceives that her merchandise is profitable.
Her lamp does not go out at night.

PROVERBS 31:18

Women are often associated with light. Light is both illuminating and warming.

In the days when the American West was being settled, men often went ahead of women and children to choose sites for cabins or to lay railroad lines. They created rough, raw settlements in wilderness places. But when the women came, so did refinement. They illuminated the need for things that men would have done without. They brought the warmth of lamplight and fireside to lonely outposts.

The writer of this proverb about the virtuous woman said that her lamp doesn't go out at night. His meaning may be that she works late, but it could also be that she makes sure everything in her home is well supplied.

Remember the parable Jesus told about the wise and foolish maidens? Those who were wise had brought extra oil so they could refill their lamps as they waited for the wedding ceremony to begin. God always commends us for being prepared in both earthly and heavenly ways.

As women, we need to be prepared for the darkness around us, culturally and spiritually. Satan will try to distract us so that we will ignore the light of the Holy Spirit within us. Thus we must stay on our guard.

In his letter to the Philippian church, Paul wrote that we should be "blameless and innocent, children of God without blemish in the midst of a crooked and twisted generation, among whom you shine as lights in the world" (Philippians 2:15).

Men are light-bearers too. All of us have the responsibility to shine the light of truth and grace onto those around us. In doing so, we reflect our Lord, who said, "I am the light of the world. Whoever follows me will not walk in darkness, but will have the light of life" (John 8:12).

DEAR JESUS, I WANT TO REFLECT YOU TO THOSE AROUND ME. AS I LIVE MY LIFE TODAY AS A CHRISTIAN WOMAN, SHOW ME THE WAYS I CAN SHINE SO THAT OTHERS MAY COME TO YOU. AMEN.

Sweet Sorrow

You have kept count of my tossings; put my tears in your bottle. Are they not in your book?

PSALM 56:8

A coin has two sides, and so does this life. There is joy and there is sorrow. We pray for more of the one and much less of the other because sorrow hurts intensely. We feel it through and through, like the sobs that convulse our whole body. We question why us and what for. While a cure-all answer doesn't exist, the Bible does assure us: God knows our sorrow, and He promises everlasting joy.

The prophet Isaiah used these words to describe the Lord: "He is. . .a man of sorrows, and acquainted with grief" (Isaiah 53:3 KJV). Jesus Christ did not experience just one side of the coin while He dwelled among us. Jesus felt deep sorrow and, ultimately, the anguish of the cross; He shed tears. Luke recorded Him weeping over Jerusalem's future (Luke 19:41), but it is John's short verse that most of us remember: "Jesus wept" (John 11:35). What's the story behind the verse? Jesus and His disciples were on the road, preaching and healing, when Jesus heard that His beloved friend Lazarus was sick. By the time He made His way to Bethany, Lazarus had been entombed four days. At the sight of Lazarus's sisters and the group that had gathered to mourn with them weeping, Jesus "groaned in the spirit and was troubled" (John 11:33 NKJV). And then He wept. Over their pain. Over the suffering that had its origin in the Fall. Praise be to God—Jesus saves us from our fallen state! "Surely he has borne our griefs and carried our sorrows" (Isaiah 53:4).

Psalm 30:5 (KJV) says, "Weeping may endure for a night, but joy cometh in the morning." Sadly, sorrow comes to us all, but we have hope if we keep our hearts trained on the joy that is to come. We find a glimpse of that future in the book of Revelation. John wrote, "And I heard a loud voice from the throne saying, 'Behold, the dwelling place of God is with man. . . . He will wipe away every tear from their eyes, and death shall be no more, neither shall there be mourning, nor crying, nor pain anymore, for the former things have passed away.' And he who was seated on the throne said, 'Behold, I am making all things new' " (21:3–5). In view of eternity, this brief life is only a night. God is hastening the morning.

GOD, I AM SORROWFUL RIGHT NOW. BUT YOU ARE CATCHING MY EVERY TEAR, AND ONE DAY YOU WILL WIPE THEM AWAY FOR GOOD. UNTIL THEN, BE WITH ME THROUGH THE SUFFERING; PLEASE BRING ME JOY AGAIN. AMEN.

Debtors Who Forgive

Be kind to one another, tenderhearted, forgiving one another, even as God in Christ forgave you.

Ephesians 4:32 NKJV

Forgiveness is a theme about which there are varying opinions. Many of them are based on the ideas that make sense to us as humans. But they are all flawed in some way. That's because forgiveness is a divine concept and must be understood through the words of the one who instituted it.

Prevalent ideas about forgiveness focus on feeling charitable toward the perpetrator of the wrong. The belief is that I must feel forgiving in order to be forgiving. This is not so. Forgiveness is an act of the will; it is based on my decision to seek the other's good instead of harm.

Forgiveness is our responsibility as receivers of God's forgiveness to us. We cannot hoard for ourselves this mercy we've been given and then turn on others with retribution. No, we are debtors to grace to pass on the gift of forgiveness.

The power of forgiveness comes when we need it, when we make the choice to obey God's command to forgive. I do not need the grace to forgive unless I have been sinned against. In the moment when my realization of the wrong done collides with my awareness that I cannot hold this memory in my heart, I can turn to Christ and expect that He will help me. He has promised to do so.

DEAR FATHER, THANK YOU FOR FORGIVING ME.
I KNOW THAT YOUR POWER WILL BE THERE IN
THOSE MOMENTS WHEN I NEED TO FORGIVE
OTHERS. I REST IN THIS TODAY. AMEN.

Royal Wedding

I promised to give you to Christ, as your only husband. I want to give you as his pure bride.

2 Corinthians 11:2 ncv

From the dress to the flowers, a bride spends countless moments preparing for the wedding. She's getting ready for her groom. Likewise, the church is getting ready for its bridegroom: Jesus Christ. How does God demonstrate this relationship between Christ and His bride? Through the earthly example of marriage. Read these verses with that in mind:

Husbands, love your wives as Christ loved the church and gave himself for it to make it belong to God. Christ used the word to make the church clean by washing it with water. He died so that he could give the church to himself like a bride in all her beauty. He died so that the church could be pure and without fault, with no evil or sin or any other wrong thing in it. In the same way, husbands should love their wives as they love their own bodies. . . . No one ever hates his own body, but feeds and takes care of it. And that is what Christ does for the church, because we are parts of his body. The Scripture says, "So a man will leave his father and mother and be united with his wife, and the two will become one body." That secret is very important—I am talking about Christ and the church. (Ephesians 5:25–32 ncv)

Christ paid dearly (a bride-price, if you will) to bestow righteousness on us. Through faith, we are united to Him. He transforms us into a bride without spot, wrinkle, or blemish; He cherishes us. Theologian Martin Luther wrote, "Who then can value highly enough these royal nuptials? Who can comprehend the riches of the glory of this grace? Christ, that rich and pious husband, takes as a wife a needy and impious harlot, redeeming her from all her evils, and supplying her with all His good things."*

One day a glorious marriage supper will take place. On that day the betrothed will appear before the bridegroom. On that day we will hear the shout, " 'Hallelujah! For the Lord our God the Almighty reigns. Let us rejoice and exult and give him the glory, for the marriage of the Lamb has come, and his Bride has made herself ready' " (Revelation 19:6–7). Let the preparations begin.

LORD, I'M THRILLED THAT YOU'VE ASKED ME TO
BE PART OF YOUR BRIDE. I'M GETTING READY:
STAYING TRUE TO THE WORD AND READYING
MY HEART FOR HEAVEN, CLOTHING MYSELF IN
RIGHTEOUS ACTS—FINE LINEN, CLEAN AND BRIGHT
(REVELATION 19:8). I LOVE YOU SO MUCH. AMEN.

*Martin Luther, *Christian Liberty* (Philadelphia: Lutheran Publication Society, 1903), 18–19, https://books.google.com/books?id=jv9EAAAAYAAJ.

It's Personal

The amazing grace of the Master, Jesus Christ, the
extravagant love of God, the intimate friendship
of the Holy Spirit, be with all of you.

2 CORINTHIANS 13:14 MSG

If you've watched some rendition of Richard Rodgers and Oscar Hammerstein's musical *The King and I*, you may remember the lyrics to a song the character Anna sings: "Getting to know you, getting to know all about you. Getting to like you, getting to hope you like me." When we get to know people, it's personal. We learn and respond to who they are. In Christianity, the Trinity—Father, Son, and Spirit—is made up of three *persons*. Now, it might be easy to think of the Father as a person, and even easier to think of the Son as a person (He was flesh and bone while on earth, after all). But what about the Spirit? Although it's difficult to wrap our mind around the Spirit, He is a person too.

And we can get to know Him. The Bible tells us about the personality of the Holy Spirit. Here's just a sampling of His traits: He aids believers (John 15:26). He thinks deeply (1 Corinthians 2:10–11). He comforts (Acts 9:31). He convicts (John 16:8). He guides (John 16:13). He feels and intercedes (Romans 8:26–27). He has power (Romans 15:13). He empowers (1 Corinthians 12:11). He dwells with us (John 14:17).

As we begin to think of the Holy Spirit as a person, He becomes more than a hazy doctrinal truth; He becomes a companion. Keep in mind, though, that the deep fellowship that Paul included in his benediction at the end of 2 Corinthians is a two-way street. Believers have a responsibility not to grieve (Ephesians 4:30) or to quench (1 Thessalonians 5:19) the Spirit—we grieve Him when we stubbornly cling to leftovers from our old nature; we quench His fire when we allow sin to kindle. But when we open our whole selves to Him, He will help us get to know all about Himself.

HOLY SPIRIT, YOU ARE NOT UNKNOWABLE—YOU ARE A PERSON! MAY YOU ALWAYS BE REAL TO ME, AND MAY I NEVER PUT DISTANCE BETWEEN US. AMEN.

Strength

She dresses herself with strength and makes her arms strong.

PROVERBS 31:17

A lot is said today about a woman being strong and brave. But God originated that idea in millennia past.

Around the turn of the twentieth century, women began to revolt in cultural ways. They marched for the right to vote. They demanded the right to wear trousers and cut their hair short. They insisted on freedom from sexual restraints; "petting parties" became popular, and contraception came about as a way to liberate women from the consequence of pregnancy. They took up smoking, which traditionally had been a male pursuit. They were known as "flappers." They began to look for ways to prove that they were independent and, in their eyes, strong.

God's idea of strong womanhood is a bit different from what the flappers promoted. He didn't design women to be in competition with men but rather to find their strength in something entirely different—their femininity.

Woman is inherently strong because God made her. Eve became weak when she listened to the serpent and doubted her Creator. And that's what weakens women today.

- We are told to exploit our sexuality.

- We are told to downplay our femininity.

- We are told to be anything *we* want.

- We are told that women are better than men.

- We are told that chivalry is offensive.

- We are told that girls rule.

Listening to the lies of the culture won't make us stronger, but weaker.

We dress ourselves with strength by embracing our God-given femininity. That is a place only we can fill. We don't need to try to imitate the place men have to fill. God created us differently and wonderfully. The strength of both males and females lies in their creative design. And only the God who made us has the right to tell us how that works.

Every day, you and the women around you are being attacked by the same enemy who confronted Eve. God wants you to refuse the lies and be a reflection of the truth by embracing His image in a strong, feminine way. Mentor the young women around you. Celebrate the beauty and womanly ways you see in them. Gather with women in your church and school groups who can affirm you in your desire to bless the world through the distinct modality into which you were placed—a woman who knows her purpose and how to fill it.

CREATOR GOD, I ACCEPT THE ASSIGNMENT OF FEMININITY YOU HAVE GIVEN ME. TEACH ME HOW TO EMBRACE IT AND REFLECT YOU WELL WITH IT. HELP ME TO HONOR THE PLACE OF MEN AND NEVER BELIEVE I NEED TO COMPETE WITH THEM TO BE STRONG. IN JESUS' NAME, AMEN.

Partners in Pursuit

Keep on working to complete your salvation with fear and trembling, because God is working in you to help you want to do and be able to do what pleases him.

PHILIPPIANS 2:12–13 NCV

Sanctification: a fancy name for God making believers holy. Once He adopts us into His family, God initiates the process of transforming us to be like Christ, a process that continues throughout our lives and accumulates with each successive day. While the work of sanctifying—the power behind it—belongs to God, we as believers are to pursue holiness in our lives with a healthy dose of respect (Paul called it "fear and trembling"). We are to keep at it.

The "keep on" of Philippians 2:12 (NCV) implies more than occasionally dipping a toe in the water. Our pursuit of holiness should be intently focused, methodical, dogged. Paul said of himself, "I do not run aimlessly; I do not box as one beating the air" (1 Corinthians 9:26), and "I press toward the goal for the prize of the upward call of God in Christ Jesus" (Philippians 3:14 NKJV). Peter too, when he reminded believers of God's calling, used language that emphasized the immediate nature of seeking after holiness:

> "So don't lose a minute in building on what you've been given, complementing your basic faith with good character, spiritual understanding, alert discipline, passionate patience, reverent wonder, warm friendliness, and generous love, each dimension fitting into and developing the

others. With these qualities active and growing in your lives, no grass will grow under your feet, no day will pass without its reward as you mature in your experience of our Master Jesus. . . . So, friends, confirm God's invitation to you, his choice of you. Don't put it off; do it now" (2 Peter 1:5–8, 10 MSG). While such a way of life takes effort, the benefits are twofold. Believers will have confidence in their salvation when they see the virtues they are pursuing manifest in their lives, and they will have an unimaginable reward awaiting them in heaven. Peter concluded, "Do this, and you'll have your life on a firm footing, the streets paved and the way wide open into the eternal kingdom of our Master and Savior, Jesus Christ" (2 Peter 1:11 MSG).

If the way you would describe your life right now doesn't sound like Paul's and Peter's descriptions, but you wish it did, don't despair. Never underestimate God's power to work in you. He is already shaping your desires, and He will give you the ability to do what pleases Him.

GOD, FOR ME, PURSUING HOLINESS HAS BEEN WILLY-NILLY. PLEASE HELP ME TO LIVE WITH MORE PASSION AND PURPOSE THAN I EVER HAVE BEFORE. AMEN.

No Peeking!

God has given them a desire to know the future.
He does everything just right and on time, but people
can never completely understand what he is doing.

ECCLESIASTES 3:11 NCV

It was time! Her favorite part of the day was about to start. Teeth brushed, pajamas on, the little girl bounced into bed and snuggled under the blanket. "I'm ready!" she called. Minutes later, her father took his customary seat beside the bed, book in hand. "Now where were we?" he said, grinning, as he flipped the pages to the bookmarked spot then began to read. So lost in the fictional world was the girl that the sound of the closing book covers jolted her back to Kansas. "One more chapter, pleeease! I want to know what happens next," she begged. "No more tonight," her father answered. With a kiss on her forehead, he said, "You'll just have to wait and see."

Our stories are unfolding each day. Don't you sometimes want to know what happens next—the specifics of God's story line for you? But in life, there's no staying up late to read a few more pages or skipping a few chapters ahead. We live sentence by sentence, even word by word.

This was the message Jesus delivered just before His ascension. By that point, the disciples had a rough idea of God's earthly kingdom, yet they didn't know *when*. So they asked Jesus. "Lord," they said, "will you at this time restore the kingdom to Israel?" (Acts 1:6). Naturally, they wanted to know what was about to happen—"Lord, is it now, because we're itching to find out!"—but Jesus reminded them that some details of God's plan were not their prerogative: "It is not for you to know times or seasons that the Father has fixed by his own authority" (Acts 1:7).

We humans are often curious about the next page; God has purposely made us with eternity in our hearts (Ecclesiastes 3:11). God, though, is still sovereign over the *when* and *what*. Solomon in his wisdom came to understand this truth well: "I've also concluded that whatever God does, that's the way it's going to be, always. No addition, no subtraction. . . . That's so we'll quit asking questions and simply worship in holy fear" (Ecclesiastes 3:14 MSG). What God does goes. But remember: God is full of goodness and faithfulness. We can trust Him to do all things "just right and on time." We can worship Him in wonder of His mastery of all that is—as we wait for the story to unfold, without knowing what's going to happen next.

GOD, I'M EAGER TO SEE WHAT'S NEXT
IN MY LIFE. HELP ME TO REST IN YOU,
CONTENT THAT YOU KNOW AND CONTROL
EVERY PAGE AND THE ENDING. AMEN.

Sudden Healing

Now a woman, having a flow of blood for twelve years,
who had spent all her livelihood on physicians and could not
be healed by any, came from behind and touched the border
of His garment. And immediately her flow of blood stopped.

LUKE 8:43–44 NKJV

Having a menstrual disorder is inconvenient and life altering in any culture, but for a Jewish woman, few things were worse. Because of the ceremonial purity laws, a woman with an ongoing menstrual flow was unclean and could not mingle in public, attend religious ceremonies, or even be close to her family. They would all be considered unclean from touching her or anything she touched. She was, for all intents and purposes, isolated.

Behind the purity laws, of course, was a good God who cared about His people. For the protection of women during their bodily processes and for the control of disease in a culture that didn't understand bacteria and sanitation, He had instituted strict laws to govern His people's lifestyles. This was to keep them from having many of the problems other nations had. But in cases like hers, the laws prevented her from living a normal life.

She'd heard about Jesus. And she believed He might be her answer, her healing.

Think about what it took for her to get to Him. She was probably weak. Blood loss for twelve years depletes the body and leads to anemia and extreme fatigue during any kind of exertion. Maybe she was actually on her hands and knees from weakness and that was how she happened to be near the hem of His garment. We don't know. But we do know she had faith. Jesus proclaimed that her faith had made her whole.

Immediately, the blood loss stopped. She was healed instantly. Something she had longed for and had spent all her money on did happen in a moment.

What condition have you fought for years? What spiritual anemia has made you weak? Come to Jesus in faith. We cannot see Him with our physical eyes, but we can see Him with the eyes of faith.

"Blessed are those who have not seen and yet have believed" (John 20:29 NKJV).

DEAR LORD, THANK YOU FOR THE HEALING
YOU BRING TO BODIES AND TO SOULS. TODAY
I REACH OUT BY FAITH AND BELIEVE YOU CAN
HEAL THE SPIRITUAL NEED I HAVE. AMEN.

Resourcefulness

She considers a field and buys it; with the
fruit of her hands she plants a vineyard.

PROVERBS 31:16

One of the things I recall about living near Ohio's Amish country was the skill of the women in tending their flower beds. Our family enjoyed spending a summer evening driving through the countryside, up the little lanes and down through homey villages. We would see Amish men at work in their fields with teams of horses, Amish teen girls on bicycles running errands in town, Amish children in their miniature garb, and Amish women busy in their flowers.

While men took care of growing things in the fields, the flowers around the house and in the yard were the pride and joy of the women. I've not seen many hanging baskets that compare with the gorgeous blooms they had. And beside their porches and by their trees and wherever else they could grow them were neat rows of beautiful flowers. These women who lived a Plain life in many respects had great appreciation for beauty, and it showed.

Contrast this with the story in the Bible about Jezebel, who confiscated the vineyard of a man named Naboth and had him killed so she could give the place to her whining husband. That's the exact opposite of the trait God's Word commends.

It seems as though this woman described in Proverbs 31 had an understanding of real estate and property values. She had the knowledge and the skill to buy a field and then to plant her own vineyard. She had learned how to be resourceful, and everyone around her reaped the benefit of it.

God has given you the opportunity to be resourceful. It may not be in the area of property, but there are ways you can bless your home and family that you may not have considered yet. If you are married, your husband shouldn't be left wondering about your activities, but you should let him know your skills and discuss how they could benefit everyone.

This woman in Proverbs embodied impressive skills, but so do you. You just may need to uncover them and polish them up a bit. You never know what may happen when you do!

DEAR GOD, HELP ME DISCOVER HOW MY GIFTS AND SKILLS CAN BENEFIT MY FAMILY. I KNOW THAT I ENJOY _____. SHOW ME IF THIS IS SOMETHING I CAN USE IN A WAY I HADN'T ALREADY CONSIDERED. AMEN.

With All Boldness

For God has not given us a spirit of fear, but of power and of love and of a sound mind.

2 TIMOTHY 1:7 NKJV

Let's paint a scene. It's ancient Galilee, and Jesus, newly risen from the dead, has gathered His followers on a mountain. The rocky, treeless terrain stretches out in all directions with patches of vegetation here and there. The wind whips the edges of their robes around their ankles. The sea is a gray expanse below. At the sight of Jesus, some break into shouts of worship for their Lord; others hold back, uncertain, wary. Then Jesus begins to speak. "All authority in heaven and on earth has been given to me," He says (Matthew 28:18). Right away, Jesus declares His sovereignty. "Listen up!" He was saying. "This is God speaking." Now comes the assignment: "Go therefore and make disciples of all nations, baptizing them in the name of the Father and of the Son and of the Holy Spirit, teaching them to observe all that I have commanded you. And behold, I am with you always, to the end of the age" (Matthew 28:19–20). From then on, Christ followers had an extraordinary commission.

Believers today still share in the holy task of spreading the gospel. It's still our assignment. Yet how often do we relegate the job to someone else? How often is the greatest thing the least on our list of to-dos? How often do we let timidity stop us? Instead, we should follow the example of those first-century believers who took God's words seriously. In the book of Acts, the biblical account of the immediate aftermath of what we call the Great Commission, one of the first recorded prayers is a prayer for guts. Fresh from a round of the Sanhedrin's bullying, Peter and John met with friends and relayed the council's order to say no more about Jesus. The group responded as one: "Now, Lord, look upon their threats and grant to your servants to continue to speak your word with all boldness" (Acts 4:29). *Nothing* would stop these Christians from completing their assigned task. God's work was simply too great to keep silent.

Truly, God does a miraculous work in us when He gives us life through His Son. And never forget that along with this marvelous new life, He gives us a spirit to match—one of power and love and a sound mind. He uses us to spread the good news.

Shout it from the rooftops!

LORD, I KNOW MY MISSION—TO TELL OTHERS
WHAT YOU HAVE DONE AND ARE DOING IN ME.
GIVE ME BOLDNESS TO TAKE YOUR MESSAGE
WHEREVER I GO. REMIND ME THAT YOU ARE
WITH ME EVERY STEP OF THE WAY. AMEN.

100 Percent Pure

How can a young person live a pure life? By obeying your word.
Psalm 119:9 NCV

Sex is everywhere. Television parades it. Magazines advertise it. Movies flaunt it. Music puts it to catchy tunes. Books indulge in it. Even our clothing choice can shout about it. For the Christian woman striving for holiness in a sex-saturated culture, purity is an issue that must be addressed.

God created sex just as surely as He created man and woman. Within His design, sex is a blessing. But sin alters that design. Sin takes sex out of context; it takes a God-given desire and blows it out of proportion.

God's Word does not downplay the seriousness of impurity. When Paul wrote to the church in Corinth (a city that was filled with immorality much like our own culture), he emphasized both the danger of sexual sins and the weightier spiritual consequence: "Run away from sexual sin. Every other sin people do is outside their bodies, but those who sin sexually sin against their own bodies. You should know that your body is a temple for the Holy Spirit who is in you. You have received the Holy Spirit from God. So you do not belong to yourselves, because you were bought by God for a price. So honor God with your bodies" (1 Corinthians 6:18–20 NCV). God redeemed us. He sacrificed dearly to unite us with Christ. He paid a high price to make us His living temples on earth, rescued from hell to glorify Him in heaven. We owe Him our all, including our bodies, and sexual sin damages us from every angle, bringing with it physical risks, an emotional toll, and spiritual harm. That's why God—in His holiness and love—sets the standard so high.

What is that standard? "But among you there must not be even a hint of sexual immorality, or of any kind of impurity" (Ephesians 5:3 NIV). Not even a hint. Nada. Nothing. And if we think the extent of purity is being chaste before marriage and faithful after we say "I do," we have another thing coming. Purity reaches all the way to the heart. What we watch, read, listen to, and think about affects us deeply and matters too. So how can we *possibly* stay pure surrounded by impurity? We must be on our knees and in the Word. We must ask God every day to saturate us so completely with His purity that there's no room for a hint of anything else.

GOD, ONLY WITH YOUR HELP CAN I BE TOTALLY PURE—MIND, BODY, AND SOUL. SHIELD MY EYES AND EARS; GUARD MY HEART. I WILL BE HOLY BECAUSE YOU ARE HOLY (1 PETER 1:16). AMEN.

Squeaky Clean

Create in me a clean heart, O God;
and renew a right spirit within me.

PSALM 51:10 KJV

Winter, long and dark, had made its exit, and spring, promising and bright, had taken its place. Weak but warming sunshine cheered the landscape. Color flooded the world. Birdsong once again welcomed the morning. The woman opened the windows in her home, letting the fresh breeze spill in and fill every corner with sweetness. Then she got to work. Floor to ceiling, wall to wall, she began to clean: scrubbing the residue of the past, swiping dust that had been hidden by the shadows, bringing order to clutter, tossing the worn out, introducing newness. When she was finished, she surveyed the job well done and smiled. She hardly recognized the space before her, now as promising and bright as the spring.

Spring cleaning, the yearly rite of passage for homes, might not be as popular now as it was in our grandmothers' or great-grandmothers' day. When was the last time you hauled carpets out-of-doors or washed down every surface in your home come spring? But we still know how good it feels to have a fresh start—in our homes and in life.

God is an expert at giving fresh starts, an expert "spring cleaner." "Come, let us talk about these things," the Lord says. "Though your sins are like scarlet, they can be as white as snow. Though your sins are deep red, they can be white like wool" (Isaiah

1:18 NCV). Before God begins to work in our lives, we are in need of a deep clean, but He takes those grody, sinful lives of ours and transforms them. He purges the old life and makes us brand-new (2 Corinthians 5:17). John the Baptist anticipated the life-altering effect that God's Son would have as He cleaned out lives. *The Message* translates John's words, "I'm baptizing you here in the river, turning your old life in for a kingdom life. The real action comes next: The main character in this drama—compared to him I'm a mere stagehand—will ignite the kingdom life within you, a fire within you, the Holy Spirit within you, changing you from the inside out. He's going to clean house—make a clean sweep of your lives" (Matthew 3:11–12).

This cleaning house doesn't end at salvation. When God takes up residence in believers, He continues to remove gunk and replace it with holiness. Day to day He cleanses us from sin (1 John 1:9), day to day He cleans hearts and renews spirits—until that day when we'll hardly recognize ourselves in heaven.

GOD, YOU'VE WASHED AWAY MY GUILT
FOR GOOD, AND NOW YOU'RE CLEANING
UP MY LIFE. THANK YOU! AMEN.

Inspiration

She is like the ships of the merchant;
she brings her food from afar.

PROVERBS 31:14

In ancient times, merchants brought the glories of trade to other lands. There were no supermarkets or chain stores. There was no online retail. Everything was brought by ship, carefully packed and preserved. Cargo on merchant ships was precious. If it was lost, both the shipping company and the merchant suffered loss. This is why it was such a big deal that the mariners tossed the goods on their ship into the sea when God sent a storm after Jonah (see Jonah 1:5).

When the biblical author wrote Proverbs 31 about womanhood, he knew about merchant trade. He was very well acquainted with what items were imported from faraway places. There were spices from the Orient and citrus from the islands, silk from Persia and cotton from Egypt. And he envisioned this woman as an adventurer, bringing delight to the senses of her family with the wonderful way she prepared their meals and kept their home.

The closest I ever got to exotic trade was in the marketplace in Juarez, Mexico. I enjoyed the banter and the colorful sights and the bustle of many people, but I was a very inexperienced shopper in that kind of setting. The merchants likely got more of my money than they should have. But this Proverbs woman knew how to gather resources for her home that inspired the people she loved.

What about you?

Sometimes we forget to lay out the meat to thaw or realize we don't have the right ingredients for the special dessert. We may even have to substitute a quick carryout pizza for dinner. Life happens like that sometimes. The heart of the matter is that we can be more than a galley cook to those in our homes. We can provide inspiration for their days by the way we nourish their senses through normal, everyday things like food.

DEAR GOD, THIS IS A CHALLENGING PART OF THE DESCRIPTION OF A GODLY WOMAN. HELP ME APPLY THIS TO MY LIFE IN A POSITIVE WAY SO I CAN INSPIRE THOSE IN MY HOME. AMEN.

Glory to God

But we have this treasure in earthen vessels, that the excellency of the power may be of God, and not of us.

2 CORINTHIANS 4:7 KJV

A group of art students walked into a museum. They passed from room to room, pointing at one painting then another, nothing catching their eye for more than a moment or two. But toward the end of their visit, they saw a painting that was like none other. Its brushstrokes awed them; its beauty enthralled them. "This painting is a master!" they exclaimed in unison. . . . Yes, those students had it wrong. The painting was a master*piece*, the work of an artist. Its brushstrokes, its beauty pointed to the painter.

Our lives as Christians should point to the one through whom we gain life—to Christ. His disciples knew this and were quick to redirect any misplaced glory during their ministry. Once, as Peter and John headed to the temple, they saw a lame beggar at the gate asking for alms. When he called to the two, they turned to him, but instead of offering money, Peter extended his hand, then healed the man in Jesus' name. This man who had never walked before literally leaped for joy. Crowds hurriedly gathered around Peter and John after witnessing the miracle and must have been gushing over them, because Peter said, "Why do you gaze at us, as if by our own power or piety we had made him walk? . . . It is the name of Jesus which has strengthened this man whom you see and know; and the faith which comes through Him has given him this perfect health" (Acts 3:12, 16 NASB). "We're only the instruments!" Peter could have said. It was God's power at work in a man who had no power of himself, not even the power to walk, that shouted "To God be the glory!"

God's Word compares our earthly lives to earthen vessels. In biblical times, clay pots were common; people used them every day and they were easily broken. We may wonder why our lives are like these plain, breakable pots. If God wants to declare His glory, why not make us shining golden vases? But God's glory shines brightest when He does miraculous things through jars of clay. Paul wrote, "We have this treasure from God, but we are like clay jars that hold the treasure. This shows that the great power is from God, not from us" (2 Corinthians 4:7 NCV). The pot that is nothing alone highlights the treasure.

These unfinished, fragile vessels point directly to the Master working through us.

GOD, USE THIS LIFE OF MINE—THIS JAR
OF CLAY—TO DISPLAY YOUR GLORY. AMEN.

The Practice
of Silence

To everything there is a season, a time for every purpose under heaven. . . . A time to keep silence, and a time to speak.

ECCLESIASTES 3:1, 7 NKJV

Realizing that there is a time for silence is not welcome. Once we learn to express ourselves in words, we like to give opinions, not listen to them. But God's Word tells us that silence helps us grow and learn. And there are times when we must practice it.

Silence makes me think of two religious practices in particular. One is the vow of silence practiced by some monastic orders as a tool in drawing near to God. Those who undertake this vow have varying guidelines to follow, but all involve some restriction on the spoken word for a specified period of time.

The other example is that of the Quakers, or Society of Friends, whose tradition it was—and still is in some places—to sit in silence in the meetinghouse and wait for the Spirit to move upon a brother or sister with a word from God for all.

Both of these illustrations, whether we agree with them or not, indicate that silence can be a means of quieting ourselves and listening for the voice of God. Oftentimes the clamor of my own thoughts is as loud as the other noise in my setting. It follows, then, that silence must be learned in the heart as well as by the mouth.

Psalm 46:10 (NKJV) admonishes us to "be still, and know" in our hearts that the Lord is God. The silence we need to embrace must fill our beings and usher our souls into His presence so we can hear His voice.

The power of silence in difficult moments is especially challenging, but the Holy Spirit is faithful to check us in those moments so that we can turn to Him for strength. Silence can be healing, restorative, merciful, and loving. This is the power that He wants to show through us.

DEAR LORD, I NEED TO LEARN THE GRACE OF SILENCE. I ASK YOU TO GIVE ME THE POWER TO HOLD MY TONGUE AT THE APPROPRIATE TIMES AS I LISTEN TO YOUR SPIRIT'S CAUTION. IN JESUS' NAME, AMEN.

He's Calling

And those whom he predestined he also called,
and those whom he called he also justified, and
those whom he justified he also glorified.

ROMANS 8:30

The lazy summer day was winding down. The heat of the after-
noon and the buzzing of cicadas were giving way to the cool of
evening and a chorus of tree frogs and crickets. The young girl
had been playing in her backyard kingdom for hours. Wrapped
up in an imaginary world, she was oblivious of the passing time,
of the cicadas and crickets and tree frogs, of the scorching heat
or the kiss of cool as the day wore on. But then a sound caught
her attention. She'd recognize it anywhere: the sound of her
mother calling her name. Time to go in for the night.

God calls to us too. First Samuel 3, part of the Old Testament
account of Samuel's life, is one memorable example. Samuel's
mother, Hannah, had kept her promise and dedicated to God the
son she had prayed for. Samuel, now an adolescent, had been assist-
ing Eli the priest for years when he heard God's call. It was nearly
dawn, and Samuel was lying down in the temple. Suddenly a voice
broke the silence as the Lord called to him. Samuel, thinking Eli
needed him, replied, "I'm here!" and ran over to the priest. Eli told
Samuel, "It wasn't me; go back to sleep," and Samuel obeyed. The
Lord would call twice more—"Samuel!"—and Samuel would rush
to Eli's side twice more. On the second of these trips, Eli realized

who was calling. He advised Samuel to lie down again and, if he heard God call, to answer, "Lord, I'm listening." God did call again, and Samuel heard the voice he as God's prophet would come to know well. So began a lifetime of Samuel listening and God guiding. The Bible tells us, "And Samuel grew, and the Lord was with him and let none of his words fall to the ground" (1 Samuel 3:19).

God's calling is a wondrous thing, if you think about it. God determined, before the foundation of the world, the ones He would call; the ones He calls He makes right with Himself, and those He makes right He will one day glorify in heaven. Until that day, the Lord calls to our hearts like a shepherd to sheep: "He calls his own sheep by name and leads them out. When he has brought out all his own, he goes before them, and the sheep follow him, for they know his voice" (John 10:3–4). Truly, we'd recognize it anywhere.

LORD, YOU CALLED ME TO YOUR FOLD,
AND YOU CALL TO ME EACH DAY. PLEASE KEEP
MY HEART OPEN TO HEAR YOUR VOICE. AMEN.

Trust

The heart of her husband trusts in her, and he
will have no lack of gain. She does him good,
and not harm, all the days of her life.

PROVERBS 31:11–12

Trust is one of those basic building blocks of relationship. It's almost impossible to have a meaningful relationship without it. A woman who cultivates the trust of her husband is a wise woman.

The Bible has a lot to say about women who are destructive. Some translations call her the "strange woman." Others refer to her as the "immoral woman." Here are some of her attributes:

- Flatters with her words (Proverbs 2:16).

- Practices deceit (Proverbs 5:3).

- Forsakes the husband of her youth (Proverbs 2:17).

- Forgets the covenant of her God (Proverbs 2:17).

- Keeps those who go to her from returning (Proverbs 2:19).

- Seduces with her eyes (Proverbs 6:25).

- Reduces men to a crust of bread (Proverbs 6:26).

- Preys on precious life (Proverbs 6:26).

- Destroys strong men (Proverbs 7:26).

- Makes her house the way to hell (Proverbs 7:27).

This is the kind of woman who cannot be trusted. She uses deceit, flattery, seduction, and manipulation. She is a black widow kind of woman, who uses a man for her purposes and then destroys him.

But the woman God celebrates is one who invites her husband's trust in her. She is good for him and does good to him. She will not bring harm to him. He can trust her every day of his life.

Since the Garden of Eden, Satan has appealed to women's pride to get them to use their power over their husbands. And in our culture today, that approach is still prevalent. The growing disdain for distinct masculinity is distorting our view of the relationship between good men and good women.

We must cling to this ancient text inspired by God. The godly woman invites trust and lives up to it. That's a power that is rare and wonderful.

FATHER, I WANT TO BE A WOMAN WHO CAN BE TRUSTED BY THE GOOD MEN IN MY LIFE. EMPOWER ME TO LIVE IN TRUTH AND BE A SAFE PLACE FOR MY HUSBAND. IN JESUS' NAME, AMEN.

No Sole Souls

Lift up a song for Him who rides through the deserts,
whose name is the LORD, and exult before Him. A father
of the fatherless and a judge for the widows, is God in His
holy habitation. God makes a home for the lonely.
PSALM 68:4–6 NASB

Has your heart ever sung a country ballad about being lonely? Sometimes loneliness is more serious than a breakup, it's true. You don't have to be alone either to be lonely. You can be lonely in a relationship, lonely in the midst of friends, lonely in a crowd. But the Bible gives hope in loneliness. God's Word testifies of His concern for those without family (Psalm 10:14; James 1:27) and His care for those who are hurting (Psalm 34:18). And He doesn't leave any of us in our lonely state. He "makes a home for the lonely."

How?

He adopts us into His family. Once while Jesus spoke to a group of people, His mother and brothers arrived outside and sent a message to Him. Jesus' response probably surprised those who heard: "He answered, 'Who is my mother? Who are my brothers?' Then he pointed to his followers and said, 'Here are my mother and my brothers. My true brother and sister and mother are those who do what my Father in heaven wants' " (Matthew 12:48–50 NCV). As a Christian, you belong to a worldwide family of believers. You are part of a family tree that extends from earth all the way to heaven. Paul wrote, "So then you are no longer strangers and aliens, but you are fellow citizens with the saints and members of the household of God" (Ephesians 2:19). Reach out to your church family in your loneliness; God is making a home for you there.

He assures us of His presence. Moses' words to Israel just before they passed over the Jordan into the Promised Land remind believers of God's abiding presence through thick and thin: "The LORD your God will go with you. He will not leave you or forget you" (Deuteronomy 31:6 NCV). Wherever you go, whatever condition you're in, God promises never to leave, never to forsake. His presence is powerful enough to banish loneliness from even the loneliest heart. As you commune with Him every day and become aware of Him with you every moment, the truth is tangible—God has made a home in you (John 14:23).

That's cause for song, a song of praise.

GOD, MY LONELINESS LIES TO ME, BUT I WILL BELIEVE YOU—I AM NEVER ALONE! YOUR PEOPLE AND PRESENCE SURROUND ME. AMEN.

Please Who?

The fear of human opinion disables;
trusting in GOD protects you from that.
PROVERBS 29:25 MSG

Have you ever heard the term *PK*? It stands for preacher's kid, which is interesting but not what this devotion is about. Today you'll want to ask yourself if you are a *PP*, as in people pleaser. On the surface, being a people pleaser doesn't seem bad. What's wrong with tailoring your actions in consideration of someone else? Even Paul advised believers to please and not offend (1 Corinthians 10:32–33). But Paul also wrote, "Do you think I am trying to make people accept me? No, God is the One I am trying to please. . . . If I still wanted to please people, I would not be a servant of Christ" (Galatians 1:10 NCV).

Paul's allegiance was a choice, and it wasn't to people but to Christ—a one-eighty from his previous devotion. Before Paul became a Christian, he persecuted Christians zealously. Acts 8:3 says he was "ravaging the church." Then the Lord called and he followed. He left behind a life of pursuing the praise of his Jewish peers for a lifetime of serving his Lord and Master. He gave up earthly credit for eternal reward. He was imprisoned and stoned and mocked for Christ's sake without budging an inch. No one would ever say of Paul that he "loved the glory that comes from man more than the glory that comes from God" (John 12:43).

While on the surface people pleasing may seem harmless,

underneath we have our priorities reversed. Our first thought should not be whether people will applaud what we do, but whether God will applaud. Paul was all about being a God pleaser, and his passion revealed a heart aligned with God's. To the Thessalonians he wrote, "Just as we have been approved by God to be entrusted with the gospel, so we speak, not to please man, but to please God who tests our hearts. For we never came with words of flattery, as you know, nor with a pretext for greed—God is witness. Nor did we seek glory from people" (1 Thessalonians 2:4–6). Paul's motive wasn't self-seeking, as the motive behind people pleasing so often is. It wasn't to save face or promote himself; it was to do *God's* will. When he did "please people," it was with God and His salvation in mind: "I, also, try to please everybody in every way. I am not trying to do what is good for me but what is good for most people so they can be saved" (1 Corinthians 10:33 NCV).

As He did in Paul, God still works powerfully through lives focused on pleasing Him.

GOD, SHOW ME WHERE I'M PLEASING PEOPLE
INSTEAD OF PLEASING YOU. AMEN.

Power of a Voice

She, supposing Him to be the gardener, said to Him, "Sir, if You have carried Him away, tell me where You have laid Him, and I will take Him away." Jesus said to her, "Mary!" She turned and said to Him, "Rabboni!" (which is to say, Teacher).

JOHN 20:15–16 NKJV

Mary couldn't stop crying. The weekend had been the worst of her life. The Rabbi, the Lord, who had cast demons from her and changed her life from misery to joy, had been crucified like a criminal. Earthquakes had wracked the city. The believers were in hiding, afraid of reprisals. And now when Mary and her friends had come to anoint His body, they'd discovered that it apparently had been taken to another location.

She was crushed. She could not fulfill a last service to the one who had given her back her life. The two men in white in the tomb asked her why she was weeping, and she tried to explain. Then she turned and saw Jesus, but she didn't know it was Him. Through her tears, He looked like one of the workmen there. She asked, "Where have you taken my Lord?"

And then He spoke her name: "Mary." And she knew that voice. It was the voice that had called to her when her mind was imprisoned in hell on earth. It was the voice she had heard from a distance as the darkness left her soul and light came flooding in. It was His voice, the voice of life.

Mary Magdalene had twice received unexpected joy. The first

was when Jesus cast seven spirits from her (see Luke 8:2), and the second was when He cast away her despair on Easter morning.

Perhaps you too need to hear the power of Jesus' voice. Today voices everywhere are creating fear and anxiety and dread. But His voice brings freedom and joy.

HEAVENLY FATHER, THANK YOU FOR SENDING YOUR SON TO SPEAK PEACE TO OUR WORLD. THANK YOU FOR THE POWER OF HIS VOICE AND THE POWER OF HIS RESURRECTION THAT TRIUMPHS OVER EVERYTHING. LIKE MARY, I WORSHIP YOU TODAY. AMEN.

A Certain Disciple

Now there was in Joppa a disciple named Tabitha.
ACTS 9:36

In Greek, her name was Dorcas, which may sound funny to our ears but has a beautiful meaning: "gazelle." Tabitha was a Christ follower who is introduced in the book of Acts. We don't learn much about her; in fact, the biblical account of Tabitha takes up less than ten verses. But we can learn so much *from* her. Here's her story:

> *Now there was at Joppa a certain disciple named Tabitha,*
> *which by interpretation is called Dorcas: this woman was*
> *full of good works and almsdeeds which she did. And it*
> *came to pass in those days, that she was sick, and died:*
> *whom when they had washed, they laid her in an upper*
> *chamber. And forasmuch as Lydda was nigh to Joppa,*
> *and the disciples had heard that Peter was there, they*
> *sent unto him two men, desiring him that he would not*
> *delay to come to them. Then Peter arose and went with*
> *them. When he was come, they brought him into the*
> *upper chamber: and all the widows stood by him weeping,*
> *and shewing the coats and garments which Dorcas made,*
> *while she was with them. But Peter put them all forth,*
> *and kneeled down, and prayed; and turning him to the*
> *body said, Tabitha, arise. And she opened her eyes: and*
> *when she saw Peter, she sat up. And he gave her his hand,*
> *and lifted her up, and when he had called the saints*

and widows, presented her alive. And it was known
throughout all Joppa; and many believed in the Lord.
(Acts 9:36–42 KJV)

God worked through Tabitha's life in a big way, starting with small acts of kindness. She gave to the poor. She sewed garments. Tabitha wasn't curing diseases or preaching to crowds, but she *was* blessing others. And God would eventually use her to bring healing and tell of Himself. God raised His faithful disciple back to life, and the news spread—no doubt told first by those closest to her (some of the recipients of her good works) and then repeated throughout the whole town. The result? Many believed.

Our efforts may seem insignificant to us, only small ripples in the pond; but there's no telling what God will do through our lives. Would Tabitha ever have guessed how God would use her? God is able to take our everyday efforts and multiply them in eternal ways, ways we could never guess and may never know. He can take our faithful lives and make waves.

GOD, YOU MAY NEVER PERFORM A MIRACLE IN ME,
AS YOU DID IN TABITHA, BUT YOU CAN ALWAYS USE
EVERYTHING I DO IN MIRACULOUS WAYS. AMEN.

Rewards of Tears

*Those who sow in tears shall reap in joy. He who continually
goes forth weeping, bearing seed for sowing, shall doubtless
come again with rejoicing, bringing his sheaves with him.*

Psalm 126:5–6 NKJV

Tears are an investment.

As a farmer sows seeds in the ground, investing for a harvest
of grain, so a Christian sows tears of determination, investing for
a harvest of souls.

Gardening is the oldest job—the first job—on earth. Adam
and Eve, the first couple, were assigned to tend the Garden of
Eden even before sin entered the world. Work preceded sin. God
created us to be purposeful and useful. It is intriguing to me that
the job He gave them was working with the botanical life He had
created. He knew it was good for them. And I think gardening is
good for us today. Working with the soil and seeing things grow,
tending to the beauty of flowers and vegetables and herbs, harvest-
ing the bounty He produces—these are activities that cause us to
be more balanced and content. In fact, according to some study I
read about, farmers are the happiest people on earth. I believe it.
Working God's earth has that effect.

Sowing tears for the spiritual well-being of others is like gardening. We see the barren ground of their souls, and we tenderly
work the ground and pray over it and share the precious seed of
the Word of God whenever we can. Then we hover over it and

watch as God uses other people and events to water the seed in their lives. We stand by with joy as little signs of spiritual life begin to appear. We are thrilled to see blossoms and growth. And finally, one day, we rejoice in the full harvest of a life committed to Christ. And that person goes on to repeat the cycle.

We don't hear a lot about soul winning, but it is still very close to God's heart. Proverbs 11:30 tells us that whoever wins souls "is wise." God wants all the people of the earth to know about His love for them and His plan to redeem them. You and I need to be open to being "tear sowers." There is no greater joy than seeing a new life in Christ begin.

DEAR GOD, YOU ARE NOT WILLING THAT ANYONE PERISH IN ETERNITY WITHOUT YOU. TODAY, SHOW ME HOW I CAN SOW IN TEARS AND REAP IN THE JOY OF A SOUL HARVEST FOR YOU. AMEN.

What It Takes

And he gave the apostles, the prophets, the evangelists,
the shepherds and teachers, to equip the saints for the
work of ministry, for building up the body of Christ.

Ephesians 4:11–12

Fill in the blank: It takes a _____ to raise a child. If you answered *village*, you got it. The African proverb has become popular over the last couple of decades; it highlights the community involved in child-rearing—the family and friends and neighbors and professionals who surround a child and guide her as she grows. Now fill in this blank: It takes a _____ to raise a Christian. The answer? *Church*. It takes a church—more accurately, it takes *the* church—to raise a Christian. God designed it that way.

Ephesians 4:11 tells us that the Lord gave apostles, prophets, evangelists, and pastors. Why? To help His body—all believers—grow.

> *Christ gave those gifts to prepare God's holy people for*
> *the work of serving, to make the body of Christ stronger.*
> *This work must continue until we are all joined together*
> *in the same faith and in the same knowledge of the Son*
> *of God. We must become like a mature person, growing*
> *until we become like Christ and have his perfection.*
>
> *Then we will no longer be babies. We will not be*
> *tossed about like a ship that the waves carry one way*
> *and then another. . . . No! Speaking the truth with love,*

we will grow up in every way into Christ, who is the head. (Ephesians 4:12–15 NCV)

God surrounds His children with a community of leaders—the apostles and prophets of yesterday and the evangelists and pastors of today—who equip us for service and guide us as we mature. God works through others to build us up and, sometimes, to correct us. One account of Paul and Peter found in Galatians 2 exemplifies this. When Peter stopped fellowshipping with Gentiles because he didn't want to look bad to the Judaizers, Paul opposed him. "Think about what you're doing, Peter!" he basically said (Galatians 2:14). Peter's conduct was damaging their message and leading others astray, but with some shepherding, the whole body was strengthened.

Who's your "village"? Through whom is God working to help raise you, His child? Think about the individual people—from pastors to teachers to fellow church members—whom God has placed in your life to speak His truth. Pray for them. Thank God for them.

GOD, YOU HAVE BLESSED MY LIFE WITH GODLY MEN AND WOMEN TO GUIDE ME. THEIR WORDS AND ACTIONS HELP ME GROW, AND THEIR PRESENCE REMINDS ME OF HOW YOU ARE PRESENT IN MY LIFE IN SO MANY WAYS. THANK YOU, GOD. PLEASE BE WITH THEM AS THEY DO YOUR GOOD WORK. AMEN.

Women of Our Word

But as for me, I shall walk in my integrity;
redeem me, and be gracious to me.

PSALM 26:11

We've all met her before—the woman who says a lot of good-sounding words but hardly ever makes good on them. She makes promises but doesn't keep them. She tells you one thing and then does another. She paints a pretty picture of herself that doesn't always match what you see. But while we can recognize her easily when she's somebody else, can we spot her in ourselves?

God doesn't take what comes out of our mouths lightly. Here's why. For such a little organ, the tongue has great power. James wrote, "If we put bits into the mouths of horses so that they obey us, we guide their whole bodies as well. Look at the ships also: though they are so large and are driven by strong winds, they are guided by a very small rudder wherever the will of the pilot directs. So also the tongue is a small member, yet it boasts of great things. How great a forest is set ablaze by such a small fire! And the tongue is a fire" (James 3:3–6). The tiny tongue has a huge influence. Our words influence our whole being. We should be careful in how we speak, especially when it involves others. We need to speak with integrity. Jesus told the crowds, "And don't say anything you don't mean. This counsel is embedded deep in our traditions. You only make things worse when you lay down a smoke screen of pious talk, saying, 'I'll pray for you,' and never doing it, or saying, 'God be with you,' and not meaning it. You don't make your words true by embellishing them. . . . Just say 'yes' and 'no.' When you manipulate words to get your own way, you go wrong" (Matthew 5:33–37 MSG).

There's another reason why God takes our words seriously. Ultimately, we are to reflect Him. We are to model His holiness (1 Peter 1:16), and He never twists His speech or lies or goes back on His Word. He speaks with integrity: "God is not man, that he should lie, or a son of man, that he should change his mind. Has he said, and will he not do it? Or has he spoken, and will he not fulfill it?" (Numbers 23:19).

How's your verbal integrity? Do you mean what you say? "Those who deal truthfully are His delight," Proverbs 12:22 (NKJV) says. God is pleased when we speak truly. We have His Word on it.

GOD, HELP ME NOT TO BE CARELESS
WITH MY WORDS. EACH ONE HAS WEIGHT;
MAY THEY ALL REFLECT YOU IN ME. AMEN.

Mentoring Power

Older women likewise are to be reverent in behavior,
not slanderers or slaves to much wine. They are to
teach what is good, and so train the young women.

Titus 2:3–4

Coffee chats. They're a social media thing. But they're also a Bible thing.

You've heard of mentoring, right? It's when a more mature Christ follower takes a less mature Christ follower under her wing by meeting regularly to talk about life and how the Bible applies to it. Mentoring is a life-enriching resource that is gaining momentum in our culture.

I don't know if they had the same kind of system in the New Testament days, but the idea that Titus is going for here applies. We are to teach others so they can in turn pass what they learn on to someone else. That's the heart of mentoring. And we need the Spirit's power to do it.

Younger women want to be mentored in the faith. Older women wish they could help the younger women. But both are afraid to make the first move. We need to break through our barriers and inhibitions and make it happen.

Mentoring works best when there is trust. Mentees and mentors must feel safe and have confidence that what is shared is privileged information. And because trust takes time, mentoring relationships progress slowly and become richer the longer we are in them.

Our local coffee shop is often the scene of meetings for conversation about the Bible. My husband and I see them—a couple of women or a meeting of two guys—with Bibles and notebooks open and a serious conversation taking place. It makes us happy every time we see it. It means that God's people are taking His Word seriously and that the Christian community wants to continue to be shaped in biblical ways.

Maybe you need this means of grace in your life. Maybe you need to give instruction to someone else. Why not open your heart and ask the Lord for direction and power to accomplish it?

DEAR FATHER, YOU HAVE GIVEN OTHERS WISDOM
THAT I NEED. AND I HAVE WISDOM TO SHARE WITH
OTHERS. EMPOWER ME TO FIND THE CHANNELS
THROUGH WHICH I CAN SHARE YOUR WISDOM
WITH OTHERS. IN CHRIST'S NAME, AMEN.

Bona Fide

In this you greatly rejoice, though now for a little while, if need be, you have been grieved by various trials, that the genuineness of your faith, being much more precious than gold that perishes, though it is tested by fire, may be found to praise, honor, and glory at the revelation of Jesus Christ.

1 PETER 1:6–7 NKJV

His friends hardly knew him. His wife told him to curse God and die. Job had hit rock bottom, and the descent was swift. Just moments ago, or so it must have seemed, his life looked much different. Job had been rich—rich in family, wealth, and health. He had seven sons and three daughters. He owned thousands of head of livestock. His household boasted a large number of servants. He was the envy of his neighbors, "the greatest of all the people of the east" (Job 1:3). But in a bizarre sequence of events, Job lost everything: first the Sabeans stole the oxen and donkeys and killed some servants; next a fire burned the sheep and killed more servants; after that the Chaldeans raided the camels and killed yet more servants; then a strong wind leveled the house where Job's children were gathered together and they died. The final blow? Painful sores covered Job from head to foot.

What landed Job at the bottom? Nothing Job had done. He was "blameless and upright, one who feared God and turned away from evil" (Job 1:1). No, Satan—sure that Job's faith hinged on God's blessings—put Job to the test, and God—sure that Job's faith would withstand Satan's barrage—allowed it. Of course, God knew best. Job may have had low moments in the depths, but he came out with his faith intact because his faith was genuine; it was the real deal straight from God.

God's presence and working are behind the "In this" of Peter's words too. Here's how the New Century Version translates 1 Peter 1:5–7: "God's power protects you through your faith until salvation is shown to you at the end of time. This makes you very happy, even though now for a short time different kinds of troubles may make you sad. These troubles come to prove that your faith is pure."

When we reach the other side of trials still believing, still trusting God, we have proof of genuine faith. More than that, God refines our hearts through trials, removing the impurities like dross from gold. Unlike gold, though, true faith can never be destroyed, but only made purer.

LORD, EVEN WHEN TRIALS BRING ME TO MY
KNEES, YOU BRING ME THROUGH, FAITH
AND ALL. WHATEVER HAPPENS IN MY LIFE,
BLESSED BE YOUR NAME (JOB 1:21). AMEN.

Just Be Patient

May the Lord lead your hearts into
God's love and Christ's patience.

2 THESSALONIANS 3:5 NCV

She tapped her fingers as she waited for her coffee to brew, then tapped her foot as she waited for her roommate to surrender the bathroom. She tapped the steering wheel as she crawled behind a slower driver on the way to work. She tapped her pencil as she waited for a colleague to return her call. More finger tapping as she waited for IT to fix her email, more foot tapping as she watched the cashier take *forever* to ring up groceries, and more steering-wheel tapping as she hit every red light on the way home. By the end of the day, she was tapped out!

If patience is a virtue, we could all stand a dose sometimes. Modern life just doesn't foster patience; we're used to high-speed everything. But before we decry modernity too much, we should remember that patience was an issue even in biblical times.

Paul frequently urged believers to be patient: "Therefore I, the prisoner of the Lord, implore you to walk in a manner worthy of the calling with which you have been called, with all humility and gentleness, with patience, showing tolerance for one another in love" (Ephesians 4:1–2 NASB). "Put on then, as God's chosen ones, holy and beloved, compassionate hearts, kindness, humility, meekness, and patience, bearing with one another" (Colossians 3:12–13). "Live in peace with each other. . . . Encourage the people who are afraid. Help those who are weak. Be patient with everyone" (1 Thessalonians 5:13–14 NCV).

Why did Paul push patience? Because he was well aware of the patience of his Lord. "The saying is trustworthy and deserving of full acceptance, that Christ Jesus came into the world to save sinners, of whom I am the foremost," he wrote. "But I received mercy for this reason, that in me, as the foremost, Jesus Christ might display his *perfect patience* as an example to those who were to believe in him for eternal life" (1 Timothy 1:15–16, italics added). The Lord did not tap His foot and say, "Forget you, Paul!" He was patient, perfectly so, and He is patient with us too. How often do we linger, yet He waits for us? How often do we sin, yet He bears with us? Truly, "the riches of his kindness and forbearance and patience" are meant to draw us to Him (Romans 2:4).

So what do we do? Let's turn impatience into prayer. Let's ask God to use each would-be impatient moment as a chance to display His patient heart.

LORD, YOU HAVE BEEN SO PATIENT WITH ME.
HOW CAN I SAY THANK YOU ENOUGH?
PLEASE HELP MY HEART MATCH YOURS. AMEN.

Daily Dependence

*Our Father which art in heaven, Hallowed be thy
name. . . . Give us day by day our daily bread.*

LUKE 11:2–3 KJV

Are you a squirrel or a sparrow? Squirrels are the stockpilers,
gathering enough nuts to last the winter, while sparrows are the
scavengers, feasting each day on nature's provisions. In human
equivalents, squirrels are the bulk-food buyers and sparrows are the
daily marketers. If we're thinking of our stomachs, either approach
has its perks. But what about our spirits?

Second Corinthians 9:8 says, "God is able to make all grace
abound to you, so that having all sufficiency in all things at all times,
you may abound in every good work." It stands to reason that if
God will richly provide material resources, He will richly meet spiritual needs as well. He is able to give us every last needed drop of
power, joy, peace, faith. . . But we cannot come to Him and expect
a week's, month's, or year's worth of power, joy, peace, or faith at
a time. D. L. Moody compared the Christian's need to manna: "I
cannot but believe that the reason for the standard of Christian life
being so low, is that we are living on stale manna. . . . The Israelites
used to gather the manna fresh every day: they were not allowed
to store it up."* How do we apply manna gathering to our lives?
"If we would be strong and vigorous, we must go to God daily. A
man can no more take in a supply of grace for the future than he
can eat enough to-day to last him for the next six months, or take

sufficient air into his lungs at once to sustain life for a week to come. We must draw upon God's boundless stores of grace from day to day, as we need it."[†]

It was this daily dependence on the Father that Jesus included in what we call the Lord's Prayer. He taught the crowds to come to God day by day for their needs.

And we can learn from the sparrow too. Jesus said, "Look at the birds of the air: they neither sow nor reap nor gather into barns, and yet your heavenly Father feeds them. Are you not of more value than they?" (Matthew 6:26). God promises to care for us. Why *not* go to Him every day for every need?

GOD, HOW OFTEN DO I FILL UP ON YOU THEN GO
FOR DAYS ON MY OWN, ONLY TO FIND I'M RUNNING
ON FUMES? I NEED YOU EVERY SINGLE DAY! AMEN.

[*]D. L. Moody, *The D. L. Moody Year Book: A Living Daily Message from the Words of D. L. Moody*, comp. Emma Moody Fitt (New York: Fleming H. Revell Company, 1900), 170–71, https://books.google.com/books?id=RQ6K3B8okAIC&dq.
[†]Ibid., 171.

Relationship

"Many women have done excellently, but you surpass
them all." Charm is deceitful, and beauty is vain,
but a woman who fears the LORD is to be praised.

PROVERBS 31:29–30

Overall, the most important thing about the excellent woman is her relationship with God.

The entirety of Proverbs 31 on the excellent woman points to verse 30. All of these attributes that set her apart and make her a wonderful person are there because she is in touch with her Creator and has a relationship with Him.

What does it mean to fear the Lord?

- The fear of the Lord is the beginning of wisdom (Psalm 111:10).

- The fear of the Lord is the beginning of knowledge (Proverbs 1:7).

- The fear of the Lord is to hate evil (Proverbs 8:13).

- The fear of the Lord prolongs life (Proverbs 10:27).

- The fear of the Lord gives strong confidence (Proverbs 14:26).

- The fear of the Lord is a fountain of life (Proverbs 14:27).

To fear the Lord is to acknowledge His sovereignty and live with reverence for His authority over us. A woman who does this understands much about her purpose in this world. She is listening for the voice of her God and trying to reflect Him in everything she does. That is why she does things excellently. That is why her relationship with Him is more vital than earthly beauty or charm. The outer beauty perishes, but the inner beauty is unfading (see 1 Peter 3:4).

HEAVENLY FATHER, MY UNDERSTANDING OF
YOU AND MY RELATIONSHIP WITH YOU SHAPE
THE WOMAN I AM. GIVE ME GRACE THIS DAY
TO LIVE IN YOUR LIGHT AND LOVE. AMEN.

Power of Life

Now when the Sabbath was past, Mary Magdalene, Mary the mother of James, and Salome bought spices, that they might come and anoint Him. Very early in the morning, on the first day of the week, they came to the tomb when the sun had risen. And they said among themselves, "Who will roll away the stone from the door of the tomb for us?" But when they looked up, they saw that the stone had been rolled away—for it was very large. And entering the tomb, they saw a young man clothed in a long white robe sitting on the right side; and they were alarmed. But he said to them, "Do not be alarmed. You seek Jesus of Nazareth, who was crucified. He is risen! He is not here. See the place where they laid Him. But go, tell His disciples—and Peter—that He is going before you into Galilee; there you will see Him, as He said to you."

MARK 16:1–7 NKJV

Few things are more startling than an open grave, especially when you expect it to be closed. The women had been wondering who would roll away the massive stone, but they didn't expect it to be done for them already. They didn't realize it, but the power of the Almighty had moved that stone.

It was early morning and misty, and they were confused. No one had risen from the dead before. They hadn't been able to comprehend that Jesus meant that He would actually come out of the tomb after three days. They went inside to see if perhaps the body would still be there. It wasn't, but a young man in a white robe was. And he had an amazing message.

We've heard the Easter story so often that we miss the awe in the details. These were women just like you and me, going to perform a last burial rite for a beloved Friend. They knew the disciples were in hiding and that their future looked bleak. They knew that the Rabbi they'd all followed was dead. But somebody still had to take care of the things of life, and preparing the body was one of them. These women, like so many of us after a tragedy occurs, pushed back their tears and carried on with the mundane tasks of life. But today would be anything but mundane. Can you imagine what they thought when they heard the angel's words?

The news that Jesus had risen was just the beginning of a new chapter in the women's lives. Very soon they would be gathered with the other believers in a room above the city, waiting for the promise of His life in them through the power of the Holy Spirit. Very soon the world would know that things would never be the same. Very soon these women would be part of a movement that would march from Jerusalem into Judea and Samaria and the uttermost parts of the earth to proclaim the most unexpected message the world has ever heard—Jesus is risen and coming again!

DEAR FATHER IN HEAVEN, THANK YOU FOR RAISING JESUS FROM THE DEAD AND FOR GIVING HIS RESURRECTION LIFE TO ME THROUGH THE POWER OF THE HOLY SPIRIT. PLEASE MAKE MY LIFE A TESTAMENT TO THE CHANGE HE BRINGS. IN JESUS' NAME, AMEN.

Rewards of Submission

Then Mary said, "Behold the maidservant of the Lord! Let it be to me according to your word."

LUKE 1:38 NKJV

Perhaps no woman in history has been talked about more than Mary, the mother of Jesus. By her own words, she acknowledged that people of every generation would call her blessed. What a privilege to give birth to the Messiah! And it came as a reward for her attitude of submission.

We know the story very well. Mary was a small-town girl, a virgin betrothed to a carpenter. One day an angel appeared to her, and everything in her world changed. Much has been written and sung about her and Joseph and their journey to Bethlehem. Some have even talked about the shame she endured and the stigma under which she probably lived her life. But we need to highlight her submission.

Did Mary have a choice? Yes. Every human being, even the chosen mother of Christ, has free will. It seems she could have refused this assignment from heaven. She could have used her confusion as an excuse or declined because of the awkwardness of explaining it to family members. She could have said no to the privilege of feeling His life inside her and being the first person on earth to know He was coming. She could have declined to go through the embarrassment of being pregnant before her wedding.

She could have rejected all the joy and all the pain. But she didn't. Mary said yes. She said, "Let it be." She submitted her desires and her plans to one greater. And she didn't even know how it would all turn out! We can read the rest of the story; she couldn't.

Submission to God is a sign of true faith, of trust. It shows our heart of obedience toward Him. Many today are afraid to submit. Perhaps they have been taken advantage of by someone in power; maybe they have been brought up with the lie that you shouldn't bow to anyone or anything—do life your way. Either of these attitudes can damage our understanding.

But the God who asked Mary to give birth to Jesus is in charge of our lives as well. And He asks us to submit to His plan for us, not to harm us, but to love us through it.

DEAR FATHER, THANK YOU FOR SENDING YOUR SON TO THIS EARTH. THANK YOU FOR MARY'S SUBMISSION. I WANT TO FOLLOW HER EXAMPLE AND SEE THE WONDERFUL REWARDS IN MY OWN LIFE AS I SURRENDER MY WILL TO YOU. AMEN.

Looking and Listening

I do not cease to give thanks for you, remembering you in my prayers, that the God of our Lord Jesus Christ, the Father of glory, may give you the Spirit of wisdom and of revelation in the knowledge of him, having the eyes of your hearts enlightened, that you may know. . .what is the immeasurable greatness of his power toward us who believe.

EPHESIANS 1:16–19

Jesus was a master storyteller. The Gospels are dotted with His parables—from the parable of the prodigal son to the parable of the wedding feast; from the parable of the fig tree to the parable of the good Samaritan, and many in between. Why all the parables? There's more to it than an effective oratory style. Jesus tells us so.

The disciples wondered about Jesus' parables too. After Jesus told the first parable of His ministry, the disciples asked Him why—"Why do you speak to [the people] in parables?" (Matthew 13:10). Here was His answer: "To you it has been given to know the secrets of the kingdom of heaven, but to them it has not been given. For to the one who has, more will be given, and he will have an abundance, but from the one who has not, even what he has will be taken away. This is why I speak to them in parables, because seeing they do not see, and hearing they do not hear, nor do they understand" (Matthew 13:11–13). Rather than making spiritual truth clearer to those who do not believe, parables conceal it. Those with hearts hardened to God will find their eyes and ears closed to His truth. But to those who do believe? God opens eyes and ears and reveals His mysteries. Jesus concluded, "Blessed are your eyes, for they see, and your ears, for they hear" (Matthew 13:16).

God's gift to His own is understanding, and that not just adequate but abundant. "Those who have understanding will be given more, and they will have all they need," Jesus said (Matthew 13:12 NCV). To those to whom God gives, He keeps giving. As we read His Word, God uses His Spirit to bring sight and hearing to our hearts; He is helping us understand more and more of His truth according to His immeasurable power—"the utter extravagance of his work in us who trust him" (Ephesians 1:19 MSG). May Christ's command be our desire: "Whoever has ears, let them hear" (Matthew 11:15 NIV).

GOD, THANK YOU FOR GIVING ME EYES TO SEE AND
EARS TO HEAR; THANK YOU FOR SHEDDING LIGHT
ON YOUR WORD AND IMPARTING UNDERSTANDING
TO MY HEART. PLEASE BE WITH ME AND WORK
IN ME EACH TIME I READ THE BIBLE. AMEN.

By Name

He telleth the number of the stars;
he calleth them all by their names.

PSALM 147:4 KJV

It's one of the first things you're given. It's one of the first things you're asked. It's your name. Names are personal. They identify who we are: "I'm Liz." "I'm Ellie." "I'm Zoey." "I'm. . ." Someone knowing your name can make you feel special, set apart. You're no longer a nameless face among other nameless faces. You're. . .

Psalm 147, a celebration of God's power and knowledge, tells us that our mighty God takes time to name His creation. "He telleth the number of the stars; he calleth them all by their names. Great is our Lord, and of great power: his understanding is infinite. . . . Sing unto the LORD with thanksgiving; sing praise upon the harp unto our God: who covereth the heaven with clouds, who prepareth rain for the earth, who maketh grass to grow upon the mountains" (Psalm 147:4–5, 7–8 KJV). Just think: the one who presides over the universe knows the stars by name!

And He knows our names too. In fact, often when God wanted to reassure His children of His care, He would remind them that He knew their names. The Lord told Moses, "This very thing that you have spoken I will do, for you have found favor in my sight, and I know you by name" (Exodus 33:17). He said to Israel, "Fear not, for I have redeemed you; I have called you by name, you are mine" (Isaiah 43:1). Describing Himself—the Good Shepherd—Jesus said,

"The sheep hear his voice, and he calls his own sheep by name and leads them out" (John 10:3). And again the Lord said, "Can a woman forget the baby she nurses? Can she feel no kindness for the child to which she gave birth? Even if she could forget her children, I will not forget you. See, I have written your name on my hand" (Isaiah 49:15–16 NCV).

Our names are dear to God, forever in His sight and always in His mind. Possibly the least-favored parts of the Bible to read are those filled with lists of names. But even if our eyes cross and our brains lose track of all those names, God knows each one and the face behind it. He has compiled an even longer list of names too. If you are a believer, God calls your name, and He has written it in the Lamb's book of life (Revelation 21:27).

GOD, YOU SPOKE THE WORLD INTO EXISTENCE AND YET YOU SPEAK MY NAME. THANK YOU FOR KNOWING ME PERSONALLY, FOR CALLING ME TO YOU. I PRAISE YOUR NAME, EL HAYYAY, GOD OF MY LIFE! AMEN.

Increasing Luminosity

But the path of the righteous is like the light of dawn,
which shines brighter and brighter until full day.

They reached the overlook before dawn, inky darkness all around, and there they waited. First came just a shimmer along the horizon, a glow of color like a slash across the dark morning. But the brightness spread out and up, growing stronger. Silhouettes of clouds appeared as the sky became a wash of yellow to blue above the deep brown earth. Soon the sun peeked over the edge of the land, rising higher with streaks of light catching the mist. The landscape—once invisible under night's cloak—took shape as the sun rose, illuminated inch by inch from farthest coast to the grass beneath their feet. By noon, not a hint of darkness would remain.

Proverbs 4:18 compares the path of the righteous—believers—to a sunrise, which is faint at first but keeps getting brighter and brighter until it can be no brighter at noon.

What is the source of the light? God! The scriptures frequently tell of God's light. Notably, John wrote, "This is the message we have heard from him and declare to you: God is light; in him there is no darkness at all" (1 John 1:5 NIV). And David said of God, "For with you is the fountain of life; in your light do we see light" (Psalm 36:9).

Only because of God's light do we ourselves have light. Jesus said, "I am the light of the world. Whoever follows me will not walk in darkness, but will have the light of life" (John 8:12). Before Christ, we are shrouded in darkness so much so that we cannot see our way clearly to God. But Christ came to earth and shed light. He illuminates God's truth and takes us from the darkness of sin to the brightness of life in Him. "In the past you were full of darkness," Paul wrote to believers, "but now you are full of light in the Lord. So live like children who belong to the light. Light brings every kind of goodness, right living, and truth" (Ephesians 5:8–9 NCV). With light to guide our way, we can "learn what pleases the Lord" (Ephesians 5:10 NCV). And so our paths become brighter and brighter as we glow with increasing righteousness, as our hearts shine brighter and brighter with God's truth, until we can be no brighter one day in glory.

GOD, YOU BROUGHT ME OUT OF DARKNESS
INTO LIGHT. THANK YOU FOR THE PROMISE THAT
EVEN WHEN DARKNESS FLOODS THIS WORLD,
MY PATH WILL ONLY GET BRIGHTER. USE YOUR
LIGHT IN ME TO LIGHT THE WAY TO YOU. AMEN.

Sweet Dreams

If you lie down, you will not be afraid;
when you lie down, your sleep will be sweet.

PROVERBS 3:24

All was quiet outside her four walls. All was still inside too, except for her. She was tossing and turning. Left to right, back to stomach, she sought a comfortable position only to find a cramped arm or stiff neck. Hour after hour, she waited for sleep, only to watch each hour tick by.

Sleepless nights can befall even the best of sleepers. Who hasn't experienced, at least once, the frustration of trying to drift off to sleep and not being able to? And if sleeplessness is more often than not? Well, you've likely exhausted the entire repertoire of tricks to avoid spending yet another night staring at a dark ceiling.

Christians aren't immune to sleepless nights, but we haven't begun to tap, let alone exhaust, our resources until we turn to God. He isn't just hovering over the universe. He cares about us personally—noticing "every toss and turn through the sleepless nights" (Psalm 56:8 MSG)—and He is behind a good night's sleep. Psalm (127:2) says, "He gives to his beloved sleep." Instead of tossing and turning, we can turn to the one who gives sleep. Instead of counting sheep, we can meditate on His Word. Instead of feeling restless, we can rest in Him.

Next time you're lying awake in the wee hours, think of the psalmist's words: "He who watches over you will not slumber;

indeed, he who watches over Israel will neither slumber nor sleep. The LORD watches over you. . .the sun will not harm you by day, nor the moon by night" (Psalm 121:3–6 NIV). Call on God in your sleeplessness. He's with you day *and* night.

LORD, HERE I AM AGAIN, WIDE AWAKE WHEN
I SHOULD BE FAST ASLEEP. PLEASE CALM MY
MIND AND RELAX MY BODY; USE THIS TIME
TO BRING ME TRUE REST IN YOU. AMEN.

Startled by Scars

He heals the brokenhearted and binds up their wounds.

PSALM 147:3

Lord, take away this pain, please. Heal me.

Have you ever prayed a prayer like that?

Most of us have. The Bible tells us that Jesus healed people's bodies and spirits when He walked on this earth, and we know that God can heal our physical and emotional pain as well. Many prayer requests in church focus on healing. Lists of prayer requests are printed in bulletins. Stories of tragedies and requests for prayer are posted on social media.

God wants us to ask Him to intervene in our lives. But He also wants us to understand that healing comes in many ways. And we might be surprised at the way it comes to us.

God can heal instantly. And He does sometimes. We've heard the testimonies of those miraculously healed of cancer or some other terminal illness.

God can heal gradually. In these cases, He uses doctors and medications and therapies and time.

God can heal eternally. This is the answer we usually don't want, because it means the person has to leave this earth to receive healing.

But all three of these are healings. And what is sometimes just as surprising is the amazing beauty of the scars left behind.

Most of us don't think of scars as beauty marks. But God does.

He sees in them the workings of His will in our lives. Our scars are ministry points, even if they are not outwardly visible. Emotional scars that have beautifully healed over become permanent memory moments that we can pull out and use to comfort someone else experiencing something similar.

And perhaps most importantly, Jesus has scars. His scars tell the story of His love for us. They are eternal marks of love.

Today if you're praying for healing, remember that it comes in different ways and that a scar is just the reminder of the love that bound up your wound.

DEAR LORD, I HAVE BEEN WOUNDED IN LIFE, AND I BRING MY PAIN TO YOU. PLEASE BIND UP THE BATTERED PLACES AND HEAL ME AS YOU SEE BEST. THANK YOU FOR THE BEAUTY OF SCARS. AMEN.

Rewards of Willingness

One who heard us was a woman named Lydia, from the city of Thyatira, a seller of purple goods, who was a worshiper of God. The Lord opened her heart to pay attention to what was said by Paul. And after she was baptized, and her household as well, she urged us, saying, "If you have judged me to be faithful to the Lord, come to my house and stay."

Acts 16:14–15

Lydia was probably a wealthy businesswoman. No doubt she had a spacious, well-appointed house. And she was willing to share it.

In their travels, Paul and Silas met believers on the Sabbath by the river in the town of Philippi. The Christians in those days often had no buildings to use and may even have chosen to meet in a place where they wouldn't attract attention since the practice of Christianity was often squelched and the cause of persecution. Paul and Silas would meet with the local members of the body and encourage them and stay as long as they could to help establish them.

In this particular town, there was a group of women who met for prayer. The missionaries met with them, and afterward this woman named Lydia approached them with a request. She asked them to stay with her while they were in the area. She opened her home as a base of operations and probably as a source of spiritual enrichment to her household, since the Bible tells us that all of them had just been baptized as proof of their faith in Christ.

The story that follows is the account of the slave girl whose demons were exorcised and whose master then had Paul and Silas thrown into prison, with their feet fastened in stocks. After their midnight praise service and the earthquake God sent, there was a revival in the jail and the jailer and his family came to faith in Jesus.

Would this have happened had Lydia not allowed the missionaries to use her home? We don't know.

We do know that a willingness to share what we have results in rewards. At times I have been reluctant to share my home or my resources or my time. You have probably had those times as well—for a variety of reasons, not all of them selfish. But when we make the sacrifice and open up our palms in good ways, God can take the blessings we have and bring others to Him.

DEAR LORD, I DON'T HAVE THE RESOURCES LYDIA HAD, BUT I DO HAVE SOMETHING. HELP ME TO RECOGNIZE WHEN I NEED TO OFFER HELP AND GIVE ME A WILLING HEART. IN THE NAME OF JESUS, AMEN.

Unexpected Joy

Remember those days in the past when you first learned
the truth. You had a hard struggle with many sufferings,
but you continued strong. Sometimes you were hurt and
attacked before crowds of people, and sometimes you shared
with those who were being treated that way. . . . You even
had joy when all that you owned was taken from you.

HEBREWS 10:32–34 NCV

What on earth?! Imagine yourself as one of these Hebrews. You've struggled through one episode of suffering after another, faced ridicule and linked arms with those who faced it. Your property is seized, and how do you take it? Joyfully. As in, "I'm joyful, even though everything I possess has been plundered!" Not the reaction you might expect, but neither is it an isolated incident. Take, for instance, the time the apostles were arrested and beaten but "left the presence of the council, rejoicing" (Acts 5:41). How could the apostles and the Hebrews accept persecution with joy? The rest of the verses tell how: the apostles rejoiced "that they were counted worthy to suffer dishonor for [Jesus'] name (verse 41), and the Hebrews "knew [they] had something better and more lasting" to call their own (Hebrews 10:34 NCV).

How can we look on trials as "pure joy" (James 1:2 NIV)? By seeing beyond the temporal to the eternal. By focusing on the ways tribulation prepares us for that better and lasting something. "We also glory in tribulations," Paul said, "knowing that tribulation produces perseverance; and perseverance, character; and character, hope. Now hope does not disappoint, because the love of God has been poured out in our hearts" (Romans 5:3–5 NKJV). As we are being built through trials, we always and with complete confidence have hope because of God's work in us. Hope of what? Our inheritance in eternity—what Peter described as "an inheritance incorruptible and undefiled and that does not fade away, reserved in heaven for you" (1 Peter 1:4 NKJV).

Jesus once compared the kingdom of heaven to treasure hidden in a field. A man who found the treasure buried it and, joyful, went and sold all that was his to make the field his own (Matthew 13:44). With such joy do we anticipate heaven, so that everything on earth pales by comparison.

GOD, WHEN TRIBULATION AND PERSECUTION
COME MY WAY, HELP ME TO MEET THEM WITH
JOY. YOU ARE WORKING GOOD THROUGH
THEM NOW AND INTO ETERNITY. AMEN.

Low Boiling Point

*Always be willing to listen and slow to speak. Do not
become angry easily, because anger will not help you live
the right kind of life God wants. So put out of your life
every evil thing and every kind of wrong. Then in gentleness
accept God's teaching that is planted in your hearts.*

JAMES 1:19–21 NCV

"It makes my blood boil!" Ever said or thought that or something
like it? Truth is, lots of things can make our blood boil in life. Friends
and family—though most of the time we want to wrap them in
hugs—can make us want to fling up our arms in exasperation.
Injustice and violence from Hometown, USA, to the other side of
the globe can make us clench our fists against evil. And those are
just cursory examples.

Since the causes of anger are so prevalent, we may be tempted
to justify anger. Even Jesus got mad! One year at Passover, He
went up to Jerusalem and, upon entering the temple, witnessed a
scene that made His blood boil. Those who traveled to the city to
celebrate Passover couldn't always bring sacrificial animals with
them; they didn't always have the correct currency to offer either.
So some merchants and money changers decided to profit from the
worshippers' lack, selling oxen, sheep, and pigeons in the courts
and charging fees to exchange money. Upset by the way these
people were filling God's holy place with unholiness, Jesus drove
them out, overturned the tables, and demanded they change their
ways (John 2:13–16).

Anger itself is not sin. But unlike God's perfect Son, who knew how to be angry without sinning, we need to be cautious about anger. Ephesians 4:26–27 says, "Be angry and do not sin; do not let the sun go down on your anger, and give no opportunity to the devil." And Psalm 37:8 tells us, "Refrain from anger, and forsake wrath! Fret not yourself; it tends only to evil." As anger permeates our hearts, it pushes out goodness. Our anger leads to hate; it leads to vengeance, which is not ours. "Do not take revenge, my dear friends," Paul wrote, "but leave room for God's wrath, for it is written: 'It is mine to avenge; I will repay,' says the Lord. . . . Do not be overcome by evil, but overcome evil with good" (Romans 12:19, 21 NIV). Our God will repay—justly, perfectly. So take a deep breath! We can release anger from our hearts, freeing space for goodness instead.

GOD, I'M SO ANGRY I COULD SCREAM!
CALM ME DOWN, PLEASE. I WANT TO LET
GO OF THIS ANGER AND GRAB HOLD OF ALL
THE GOOD THAT COMES FROM YOU. AMEN.

Heart Healthy

*Dear friend, I pray that you may enjoy good health and that all
may go well with you, even as your soul is getting along well.*

3 JOHN 2 NIV

"Work to live; don't live to work" is the mantra of many who strike
a balance between work and life outside of work, between laboring
and enjoying the fruits of that labor. Work takes up a great deal of
our time, and if we aren't careful, it can consume *us*.

Now shift gears to a different kind of work—working out. Do
you exercise to live, or do you live to exercise? Keeping our bodies
fit and healthy is important; with nine-to-five desk jobs, commuter
lifestyles, and sedentary pastimes to cope with, we need all the
moving around we can get! But "moving around" these days isn't a
walk in the park. There are gym memberships, training regimens,
fitness crazes. Working out can take up a great deal of our time,
and if we aren't careful. . .

So what does the Bible say about exercising? Not too much. You
might have heard one of the few verses, if not the only, depending
on your criteria: "For bodily exercise profiteth little" (1 Timothy 4:8
KJV). To see Paul's point, let's look at the verse in context:

> *By telling these things to the brothers and sisters, you
> will be a good servant of Christ Jesus. You will be made
> strong by the words of the faith and the good teaching
> which you have been following. But do not follow foolish
> stories that disagree with God's truth, but train yourself*

to serve God. Training your body helps you in some ways, but serving God helps you in every way by bringing you blessings in this life and in the future life, too. What I say is true, and you should fully accept it. This is why we work and struggle: We hope in the living God who is the Savior of all people, especially of those who believe. (1 Timothy 4:6–10 ncv)

When ordering our lives, God trumps self—and spirit trumps body. Strengthening ourselves through God's Word and training ourselves for godliness yields health and blessings that last forever, while exercising our bodies only touches the temporary shell. Take care of God's living temple on earth—your body. Stay fit to serve Him. But remember to monitor your heart when you work out, and not just beats per minute.

LORD, MY LIFE IS ONLY A MIST, HERE AND THEN GONE (JAMES 4:14). I WANT TO BE HEALTHY, BODY AND SOUL, BUT MAY I ALWAYS PUT MORE EFFORT INTO WORKING OUT MY HEART OF FAITH THAN MY HEART OF FLESH. AMEN.

Soar!

*But they that wait upon the L*ORD *shall renew their strength; they shall mount up with wings as eagles.*

ISAIAH 40:31 KJV

She mentally calculated her next steps, envisioned the days and weeks ahead, and sighed. The point in her mind flagged "You are here" seemed impossibly far from where she needed to wind up. How would she ever go on?

We've all heard the advice, right? "Take it one day at a time." "Put one foot in front of the other." But sometimes even that good advice falls flat. When the days stretch endlessly and we're too bone-tired to lift our limbs, we wonder where we'll find stamina to keep going. For you, maybe it's a project at work. Maybe it's health issues. Maybe it's difficulties with your child. Maybe it's paying off your debt. Maybe it's a rocky marriage. Maybe it's unemployment. Whatever it is you're facing, hear some biblical advice: don't go it alone.

Paul knew what it was like to be brought to the end of himself. In Asia, he faced such extreme circumstances that he *could not* continue on in his own effort. Paul, though, recognized God's hand even in those most desperate moments: "We were so utterly burdened beyond our strength that we despaired of life itself. Indeed, we felt that we had received the sentence of death. But that was to make us rely not on ourselves but on God who raises the dead. He delivered us from such a deadly peril, and he will deliver us. On him we have set our hope" (2 Corinthians 1:8–10). Paul couldn't do a little himself and then depend on God for the rest; no, he had to depend on God wholly. He had to fall back on his God, trusting God to uphold him.

Where is God when another day or another step seems unbearable? Where He always is. With us. Waiting to support our weight as we fall back on Him. "Do you not know? Have you not heard?" Isaiah wrote. "The LORD is the everlasting God, the Creator of the ends of the earth. He will not grow tired or weary, and his understanding no one can fathom. He gives strength to the weary and increases the power of the weak. Even youths grow tired and weary, and young men stumble and fall; but those who hope in the LORD will renew their strength. They will soar on wings like eagles; they will run and not grow weary, they will walk and not be faint" (Isaiah 40:28–31 NIV).

LORD, YOU CAN WORK MIGHTILY THROUGH ME.
YOU CAN LIFT ME UP LIKE AIR UNDER AN
EAGLE'S WINGS. BE MY STRENGTH, BE MY
POWER SO THAT I CAN GO ON. AMEN.

I Can't Stand
My Relatives

Miriam and Aaron spoke against Moses because of
the Cushite woman whom he had married.

NUMBERS 12:1

All of us have prayed about an irritating person in our lives. But God puts them in contact with us for a reason. His purpose in giving us family is not so that we may be coddled and comforted but so that we will continue to grow in His likeness. Everything He allows in our lives is for that reason. In fact, when one is considering marriage, it is good to contemplate the idea that God is going to use this person not only to love me but to refine me. It might change our perspective on the conflicts we go through in marriage if we had that mindset.

Moses' siblings had a problem with their sister-in-law. The Bible doesn't tell us just what it was, only that they spoke against him because of her. Perhaps they didn't like the fact that he had married a woman of another ethnicity. Perhaps they thought that her background as the daughter of a nomadic priest was unsuitable for the wife of the deliverer (see Exodus 2:16, 21). Maybe they just didn't get along with her personality; maybe they didn't like the way she cooked. We don't know. But it was something that they weren't letting fade away.

God dealt with them severely because of their mistreatment of Moses. In Bible times, judgment was usually swift and severe.

Today, in the dispensation of grace, God doesn't strike us with leprosy like He did Miriam (Numbers 12:10). But He does want us to get along with the people around us and those in our families.

A surprising thing might happen when we pray about our familial relationships, though. God probably won't remove our family members from our lives, but He will give us the power we need to get along with them and even to discover things we can like about them.

You see, most often it's our selfishness that gets in the way. We like people to conform to our ideas and opinions. Growing close to someone who doesn't like what we like is difficult. But that's where grace comes in, and it's available to us now!

DEAR LORD, I'VE BEEN PRAYING ABOUT THE
DIFFICULT PERSON IN MY FAMILY, BUT I'VE JUST
BEEN ASKING YOU TO FIX HER [HIM] AND NOT
ACKNOWLEDGING THAT I NEED TO CHANGE TOO.
DO YOUR WORK IN ME AND HELP ME TO LOVE
HER [HIM]. IN THE NAME OF JESUS, AMEN.

Chew Over This

But Mary treasured up all these things,
pondering them in her heart.

LUKE 2:19

The day was an ordinary one until Mary received an extraordinary visitor. What had she been doing before the angel appeared? Was she absorbed in household chores? Was she thinking about her upcoming marriage to Joseph? Was she settling down for the night? Whatever it had been, suddenly in her ordinary day there was Gabriel saying, "Greetings, O favored one, the Lord is with you!" (Luke 1:28). Her confusion must have shown, because Gabriel told her not to fear. He had been sent from God to deliver an extraordinary message: Mary would give birth to God's Son. Now, Mary marveled at this news. She was a virgin—how could she have a baby? But Gabriel assured her that God could do anything through His Holy Spirit. And Mary? She said "Okay!" and offered herself as a willing servant of God.

From that ordinary-turned-extraordinary day on, Mary's life wasn't typical, and it couldn't have been easy. Even though Joseph followed the Lord's command and married her, Mary likely found herself on the other end of some sidelong glances and gossip. Fast-forward about nine months, and Mary delivered Jesus, following an arduous journey to Bethlehem. Depleted yet brimming with love for the newborn babe, Mary heard the "good tidings of great joy" (Luke 2:10 KJV) from the shepherds and "treasured up all these things, pondering them in her heart." God was working in her, and He was working in the world in miraculous ways. It was a lot to contemplate, a lot to cause her to wonder what God was doing.

Fast-forward about thirty years to when Mary watched Jesus die on the cross. She must have wondered what God was doing then, but the faith that had prompted her to say "Okay!" to God all those years ago would keep her trusting Him in the darkest hour. The first verses of Mary's song—known as the *Magnificat*—reveal her heart of trust: "My soul praises the Lord; my heart rejoices in God my Savior, because he has shown his concern for his humble servant girl. . . . The Powerful One has done great things for me. His name is holy. God will show his mercy forever and ever to those who worship and serve him" (Luke 1:46–50 NCV).

God is still doing great things. Let's join the psalmist—and Mary—in pondering: "I will meditate on all Your work and muse on Your deeds. Your way, O God, is holy. . . . You are the God who works wonders" (Psalm 77:12–14 NASB).

GOD, I WORSHIP YOU! TODAY AND COUNTLESS
DAYS AHEAD, I WILL THINK ON ALL THE WAYS YOU
ARE WORKING IN AND AROUND ME. AMEN.

Rewards of Ministry

Now there was in Joppa a disciple named
Tabitha, which, translated, means Dorcas.
She was full of good works and acts of charity.

ACTS 9:36

Have you ever known a woman whose whole life was devoted to cheerfully serving others? If you have, you've been blessed just to be around her.

I'm thinking of some women I've known who have the gift of blessing others with their cooking, their sewing machines, their cleaning abilities, their helpfulness. Sometimes they're very quiet about it, and you don't really realize how large a contribution they make until they're gone.

That was the case with Dorcas. She lived in the city of Joppa and was an important part of the church there. In fact, she had a closet ministry. She helped fill the closets of widows in need of clothing. The Bible tells us that she was full of charitable works. When she suddenly took ill and died, her church family was stunned, shocked, bereaved. And did they ever miss her smiling face and helpful hands!

God allowed the apostle Peter to raise her back to life in the name of Jesus, and no doubt her ministry continued without a hitch. When you're called, you're called. She could not stop doing what was in her heart to do.

You may be involved in some type of ministry that feels like a dead end. It can be that way sometimes. We don't always see the widows' gratefulness. Sometimes the hours are long. It feels like we're in a tiny corner of the world by ourselves. We're not seeing the results we'd imagined.

Don't give up. Like Dorcas, you may be contributing far more than you know. The little acts of kindness you do every day matter to the ones who receive them. And the ministry in which you're involved would do less if you weren't part of it.

When Dorcas died, the church sent two men right away to get the apostle. They weren't content to be without her. They knew they needed her gifts and presence. And your church needs you too!

Refuse the lies of Satan that your contributions don't matter. Go sew a tunic today! (Or the twenty-first-century equivalent!)

FATHER, I KNOW I HAVE AN IMPORTANT
PART TO PLAY IN THE MINISTRY OF MY CHURCH.
HELP ME FILL MY SPOT TODAY WITH ENTHUSIASM
AND EXCELLENCE LIKE DORCAS DID. AMEN.

"My Pleasure!"

"The LORD your God is in your midst, a mighty one who will save; he will rejoice over you with gladness; he will quiet you by his love; he will exult over you with loud singing."

ZEPHANIAH 3:17

A father cradles his newborn baby, a delicate bundle wrapped in strong arms. With eyes of joy, he gazes at her face. For weeks (years!) after, he thrills at the chance to tell others of his child. A groom stands in place at the front of the church, shoulders back, back straight; but there's no hiding his eagerness. He radiates the elation he feels inside, the pure joy at seeing his bride.

Think about God, and your first thoughts might be of an almighty, majestic, supreme, sovereign being. Rightfully so. He is all of that and more besides. He is the overjoyed Father—holding us in His arms, beaming ear to ear, brimming with love—and He is the jubilant bridegroom—breaking into song over His beloved. He is a God who delights in us. His Word declares it over and over, as in these examples from Psalms:

- "He brought me out into a broad place; he rescued me, because he delighted in me" (Psalm 18:19).

- "The LORD delights in those who fear him, who put their hope in his unfailing love" (Psalm 147:11 NIV).

- "For the LORD takes delight in his people; he crowns the humble with victory" (Psalm 149:4 NIV).

It was with joy in mind and not sadness, willingly and not begrudgingly, that our Lord died and rose again to give us life through faith in Him: "Looking unto Jesus, the author and finisher of our faith, who for the joy that was set before Him endured the cross, despising the shame, and has sat down at the right hand of the throne of God" (Hebrews 12:2 NKJV). And it is with joy and not cheerlessness, wholeheartedly and not half-heartedly, that He works in us today and will one day bring us into His presence: "Now unto him that is able to keep you from falling, and to present you faultless before the presence of his glory with exceeding joy, to the only wise God our Saviour, be glory and majesty, dominion and power, both now and ever" (Jude 24–25 KJV).

Whether you are soaring high or feeling down, praise God for who He is—the Mighty One who saves *and* delights in you. He is at work, and it is His pleasure.

GOD, I CAN'T BELIEVE IT! YOU REIGN OVER THE UNIVERSE, YET YOU DELIGHT IN ME. WHAT AN AWESOME TRUTH! HOW AWESOME YOU ARE! MAY YOU BE MY DELIGHT TOO. AMEN.

Put into Practice

*As for me, You uphold me in my integrity, and set me
before Your face forever. Blessed be the LORD God of Israel
from everlasting to everlasting! Amen and Amen.*

Nicholas Herman of Lorraine was a soldier until he saw a leafless tree in the lifeless cold of midwinter. He thought of how, come spring, the leaves and flowers and fruit would return, and he was suddenly aware of God's caring, powerful presence in the world as he had never been aware of it before. He converted and became a Carmelite monk, best known as Brother Lawrence and for a posthumous collection of his letters aptly titled *The Practice of the Presence of God*.

For the rest of his life, Brother Lawrence *practiced* being with God—he made a habit of turning his thoughts to God, of remaining in His presence. His heart likely joined the psalmists who reveled in God's company and called for others to join them: "Oh give thanks to the LORD; call upon his name. . . . Glory in his holy name; let the hearts of those who seek the LORD rejoice! Seek the LORD and his strength; seek his presence continually!" (Psalm 105:1, 3–4); "Make a joyful noise to the LORD, all the earth! Serve the LORD with gladness! Come into his presence with singing! Know that the LORD, he is God! It is he who made us, and we are his" (Psalm 100:1–3). Don't miss a key point in that last verse: we come into God's presence, but God is the one behind us. As David wrote,

"You [the LORD]. . .set me in your presence forever" (Psalm 41:12). Brother Lawrence also acknowledged the aide behind his practice, saying that when a believer "is a little too much absent" from God, "GOD presently makes Himself to be felt in his soul to recall him."*

How would a seventeenth-century monk counsel us today? No doubt to do as he did: "Think often on GOD, by day, by night, in your business, and even in your diversions. He is always near you and with you: leave Him not alone. . . . Do not then forget Him, but think on Him often, adore Him continually, live and die with Him; this is the glorious employment of a Christian. In a word, this is our profession; if we do not know it, we must learn it."† Let's begin putting his words into practice.

GOD, WHETHER I'M AT WORK OR PLAY, I CAN BE
WITH YOU IN MY THOUGHTS. NUDGE MY HEART
WHEN MY MIND DRIFTS TOO LONG FROM YOU
SO THAT I RETURN TO YOUR PRESENCE. AMEN.

*Brother Lawrence, *The Practice of the Presence of God* (Mansfield Centre, CT: Martino Publishing, 2016), 24.
†Ibid., 33.

Startling Deliverance

By faith Moses, when he was born, was hidden for three months by his parents, because they saw that the child was beautiful, and they were not afraid of the king's edict.

HEBREWS 11:23

It was a terrible time to have a new baby. The life of a slave laborer was hard and gave little time for mothering. Moreover, the pharaoh had ordered all infant boys to be killed. Nevertheless, Jochebed gave birth to a beautiful baby boy. The midwives were on her side and refused to toss him into the Nile. And so the family hid him for as long as they could, until one day they had to make other arrangements.

Whose idea it was to float him in a basket in the river, we don't know. But surely no weaver ever worked more carefully than Jochebed as she made his floating bed and waterproofed it with pitch. Maybe she had to work on it at night when her other labors were over. Maybe she huddled in a corner, trying to hide the light as she kept at her task. But she was resolute in her decision and calm in her attitude. She and her husband were not afraid of the king who held their lives at his disposal. They trusted in Jehovah, whose care reached further than any earthly monarch.

Did Jochebed know that the princess went to the river to bathe? Did she intend for Moses to be found? It's very possible. She stationed her daughter there as a sentinel, to keep tabs on what happened. Miriam had probably been instructed in what to say, but who could have guessed that it would turn out so beautifully? The new life that endangered them all became the source of their deliverance.

What new thing has God brought into your life that seems negative and dangerous? What is He telling you to do to help His plan go forward? Weave a basket? Stand guard?

Step out in faith and do it. Deliverance comes in unexpected ways.

DEAR FATHER, THANK YOU FOR THE SURPRISING
WAYS YOU BRING DELIVERANCE TO OUR WORLD.
HELP ME FOLLOW WHAT YOU HAVE FOR ME
TO DO TODAY. IN JESUS' NAME, AMEN.

Dig Deeper

As newborn babies want milk, you should want the pure and simple teaching. By it you can mature in your salvation, because you have already examined and seen how good the Lord is.

1 PETER 2:2–3 NCV

She lovingly called it "the tome." She had first discovered the tome as a little girl at her grandfather's house. Back then the large book was almost too cumbersome for her child's arms to carry. Undaunted, she would heft it off the shelf each visit and admire the marbled endpapers and leather spine. At first she only studied the pictures inside, but over the years, she began to read the captions, then the text. Layer by layer she read, until she practically knew the tome by heart.

Peter, when describing God's Word, compared it to milk. Like infants hunger after milk, believers should have a desire for God's Word. Reading the Bible is one way we mature as Christians. As we drink the Word, God uses it to form us like milk fueling a baby's development.

The writer of Hebrews employed a similar image to warn believers who were languid and even falling away: "About this we have much to say, and it is hard to explain, since you have become dull of hearing. For though by this time you ought to be teachers, you need someone to teach you again the basic principles of the oracles of God. You need milk, not solid food, for everyone who lives on milk is unskilled in the word of righteousness, since he is a child.

But solid food is for the mature" (Hebrews 5:11–14). Christians are "born again," meaning God gives us eternal life and we are born into His family. From our new birth on, we grow, and as we grow, we learn through God's Word. We aren't supposed to live on the basics but to advance in spiritual knowledge—to eat solid food.

God's Word is rich and living. We can study it for a lifetime and never exhaust all it has to say. But how often do we stop at a sip when we should gulp? How often are we content with an appetizer when we should dig in to the meat course? If you aren't digging in, do so! Every sip and bite of the Word has the potential to work in us; just think of what deep Bible study can do. Not sure where or how to begin? Pick a book, pick a chapter. Read, then repeat. Read until the words fill your head, remembering that the one who wrote the words also whispers to your heart.

GOD, BE WITH ME AS I DELVE INTO YOUR WORD.
USE IT TO GROW ME AND DEVELOP ME. AMEN.

Unchanging

"For I the Lord do not change."

MALACHI 3:6

Flux is one funny word. It means fluctuation or change. Things and people can be "in a state of flux," and certainly this is true for Christians, who begin to change from the first moment of belief on. Before Christ, we are trapped in our sin; we are defined by it. "And such were some of you," Paul wrote following a list of unrighteous titles (like idolater and thief). "*But* you were washed, you were sanctified, you were justified in the name of the Lord Jesus Christ and by the Spirit of our God" (1 Corinthians 6:11, italics added). Once called sinners, now we are saints. God liberated us from our sin and defines us by Christ. He is making us ever more Christlike, transforming us "into the same image from one degree of glory to another" (2 Corinthians 3:18).

Unlike us, though, God remains sure and steady. With all the changing going on—through growth spurts and seeming dormancy, good days and bad—we can fix our hearts on the one who does not change. A. W. Tozer wrote about this immutability of God: "The concept of a growing or developing God is not found in the Scriptures. . . . For a moral being to change it would be necessary that the change be in one of three directions. He must go from better to worse or from worse to better; or, granted that the moral quality remain stable, he must change within himself, as from immature to mature or from one order of being to another. It should be clear that God can move in none of these directions. His perfections forever rule out any such possibility."* So while God is perfecting us, finishing us (Hebrews 12:2), He Himself is perfection. Perfect holiness, perfect wisdom, perfect love, perfect grace, perfect glory. . .

Perfect presence. "I AM WHO I AM," God told Moses (Exodus 3:14). The New American Standard Bible notes that the "I AM" of Exodus 3:14 is "related to the name of God, *YHWH*. . .which is derived from the verb *HAYAH, to be*." God is. Stretch your mind as far as it can go backward or forward in time, and even beyond that point, God is. He says, "I am the Alpha and the Omega. . .who is and who was and who is to come, the Almighty" (Revelation 1:8). What does that mean for us? In our yesterdays, todays, and tomorrows, and into eternity, we are never without the unchanging one who is.

GOD, YOU ALWAYS WERE, ALWAYS ARE, AND ALWAYS WILL BE. I BOW TO YOU, AND I THANK YOU FOR ALWAYS WORKING IN ME. AMEN.

*A. W. Tozer, *The Knowledge of the Holy* (New York: HarperSanFrancisco, 1961), 49.

Every Little Detail

If riches increase, set not your heart upon them.

PSALM 62:10 KJV

We've all heard the saying "Don't count your chickens before they hatch."

Turns out, that old wise saying is one we should take to heart. If there is anything that can happen unexpectedly, it's money trouble. Everything can be fine, and then *wham*, the bottom drops out. Black Tuesday in 1929 was just such a day—the stock market completely collapsed. The economic effects of the attacks on September 11, 2001, followed that unexpected, blue-skied Tuesday morning. Individual family financial trouble often arrives without notice—the car breaks down, the washing machine stops, a medical crisis occurs, a husband or wife loses a job. Without warning, we are in emergency mode.

When you think about it, money is just a symbol of something to which we give value. The metal and fabric of our coins isn't worth anything except the symbolic worth attached to it by our government. Natives of undeveloped areas would have no knowledge that a hundred-dollar bill would be fought over if found on a street in New York City. Currency from other time periods has value because of its historicity, not because it's worth an actual amount today. It's all related to what the symbol represents.

Our money today represents the worth of the gold in our treasury. Other nations have similar systems. Because the treasury holds something in its possession that has recognized value, it can assign a degree of worth to pieces of paper. But what if the gold disappears? The paper is worthless.

Sudden financial distress reminds us that earthly riches are unstable. The writer of this psalm said we should not set our hearts on them. Jesus said in His Sermon on the Mount, "Do not lay up for yourselves treasures on earth, where moth and rust destroy and where thieves break in and steal; but lay up for yourselves treasures in heaven, where neither moth nor rust destroys and where thieves do not break in and steal. For where your treasure is, there your heart will be also" (Matthew 6:19–21 NKJV).

When trouble comes and money gets low and the bank accounts look skinny, we have to remember that our security is not in that, but in Christ. Whether our nation or our families flourish or lag economically, He is the source of our stability. He is able, out of His great riches, to supply what we need today and every day. After all, that's what He'll be doing for eternity for those who love Him—taking care of every little detail. We can trust Him to do that for us today too.

LORD, I PROCLAIM THAT YOU ARE MASTER
OF MY LIFE AND MY MONEY. TODAY I HAVE
UNEXPECTED FINANCIAL NEEDS. I BRING THEM
TO YOU AND TRUST THAT YOU CAN TAKE CARE
OF EVERY DETAIL. IN JESUS' NAME, AMEN.

Reward

Give her of the fruit of her hands, and let
her works praise her in the gates.
PROVERBS 31:31

Better than fireworks or applause or trophies, the words "Well done" are an eternal reward.

The gates of a city were where important announcements were made. Business transactions were conducted there in ancient times. They were the town hall, the hub of events and activities. When the writer of Proverbs 31 said that the excellent woman would be praised in the gates, it was an acknowledgment that the whole city would hear the praise this woman received. And how would that happen? People would be talking about her because of the "fruit of her hands." In the Bible, "fruit" often refers to the works we do. So this woman would be known for her excellent character and remarkable works, and even those conducting business at the city gates would mention her name. That was pretty amazing in a day when women weren't especially valued or discussed. It was a great reward.

But even better than that is a reward every godly woman can look forward to. A great day is coming when we will all stand before the throne of God. Our works will be examined, and rewards will be given. "For we must all appear before the judgment seat of Christ, so that each one may receive what is due for what he has done in the body, whether good or evil" (2 Corinthians 5:10).

The godly woman will have no greater joy than to hear words of commendation from her Lord. Maybe they will be something like these words from Jesus' parable: "Well done, good and faithful servant. You have been faithful over a little; I will set you over much. Enter into the joy of your master" (Matthew 25:21).

DEAR HEAVENLY FATHER, SOMEDAY I WILL STAND BEFORE YOU, AND I WANT YOU TO BE PLEASED WITH HOW I REFLECTED YOU ON EARTH. HELP ME TO LIVE MY LIFE WITH ETERNITY IN VIEW. IN JESUS' NAME, AMEN.

MORE INSPIRATION FOR YOUR BEAUTIFUL SOUL

GOD CALLS YOU FORGIVEN

ISBN 978-1-64352-637-9

GOD CALLS YOU WORTHY

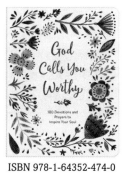

ISBN 978-1-64352-474-0

These delightful devotionals—created just for you—will encourage and inspire your soul with deeply rooted truths from God's Word. Each devotional reading will assure you that God's Word is unchanging and will help you to grow in your faith as you become the beautifully courageous woman the heavenly Creator intended you to be!

Flexible Casebound